FORGIVE US OUR PRESS PASSES

𝔉𝔒ℜ𝔊𝔍𝔙𝔈 𝔘𝔖 𝔒𝔘ℜ PRESS 𝔓𝔄𝔖𝔖𝔈𝔖

Incorporating

FORGIVE US MORE PRESS PASSES

IAN SKIDMORE

Revel Barker
Publishing

Forgive Us Our Press Passes was first published by
Gomer Press in 1983.
This revised and extended edition published by Revel Barker in
February 2008.
Second impression: March 2008

A catalogue record for this book is available from the British Library
ISBN 978-0-9558238-0-0

Published by Revel Barker
revelbarker@gmail.com
A division of
Buchan Publishing Limited
66 Florence Road
BRIGHTON
BN1 6DJ
United Kingdom

Printed in the UK by Lightning Source, Milton Keynes

Professional wit and best-selling author Ian Skidmore devised and presented one of BBC Radio Wales' most popular programmes, Radio Brynsiencyn, with a branch on Radio 4 UK.

In 40 years he wrote twenty six books and, until he was sponsored by the Marquess of Anglesey for a generous pension from the Royal Literary Fund for services to Welsh culture, earned almost as much as he would have done if he had spent the decades on social security. His books include biographies, histories, war stories and two comic novels set in a mythical Welsh island with an uncanny resemblance to Anglesey, for many years his home until he was forced by frenzied nationalists into exile in the Fens,. He no longer writes satire, for the very good reason that every time he dreams up an improbable situation, say, an American invasion of a Commonwealth island; the siting of missile bases in the face of local opposition; British armed landings in support of a political party – it happens within the year.

Forgive Us Our Press Passes should be safe. It's an account of the author's past; the years he spent as a freelance reporter based in Chester and working in North Wales and a decade on the *Daily Mirror* where he became an unwilling night news editor.

It is unreliable autobiography and shouldn't be taken too seriously. All the stories in the book are based on fact, but the details may be blurred and the characters are mostly composites. This is because of libel laws and because the author doesn't remember too good. Like the late Earl of Rochester he spent the years under advisement in a mist of perpetual revelry and hopes his readers will approach his book in the same happy way. It has one claim to literary fame. It took two months to write and nine years to find a publisher. But then so did Jane Austen's first book.

DEDICATION

For Nicky and Lynne
Who were not warned
By the awful example of their parent
And for Gay, who was,
And Laura, who ought to be
And Sally and Sam

PART ONE

Take One

I stopped the car outside the Windy Ridge Transport Cafe. Procul Harum was, as always, on the radio and the vast, flat plain of the county in which I had chosen to operate as a freelance reporter stretched before me.

In the foreground the meadows were wide, bounded by hawthorn and occasional oaks, but so far did the prospect stretch that in the distance the hawthorn borders were narrow, like railway lines with thin, green ribbons of grass where the sleepers should have been. It was a great place to be a cow in, but there was no sign of the pulsating life I needed for the crop of stories I was going to have to harvest – or starve.

The worst thing about being a freelance reporter, I had been told, was that every Monday morning you woke up out of work and by Friday you had to have found either a week's wages or rich friends.

All my friends were broke, my car was rented, I had a month's pay in the bank, two suits, five shirts and a gleaming gold watch that had been presented to me at my farewell party.

The newspaper I had worked for, and looked forward to retiring from at the age of sixty-five, had been bought out and closed down, all in a day, and there had been no room for me on the editorial staff of the national newspaper that had gobbled it up. I had been offered other jobs. I might have stayed doing casual shifts and holiday reliefs but that prospect was not attractive. I could not rid myself of the sense of bereavement I had felt when my own paper closed down. Newspapers are living things for most of the people who work on them. To work day shifts in our offices, for the newspaper that had taken us over and was now produced there, would have been like working in the coffin of a dead friend.

A fortnight earlier I had no idea of becoming a freelance. My old newspaper had folded the day before, and I was sitting at the news desk, playing with the lead cylinder that Don, the news editor, used as a paperweight.

I rolled it slowly over the map of that part of Britain in which my paper had circulated.

'I'm helluva sorry,' said Don. 'I tried, but they only want five reporters and your name was not on the list they sent me.'

'It's OK,' I said, 'I'll do something else; I'll be a brain surgeon.'

Don grinned.

'I'll give you your first job,' he said. 'You can put a brain in the new editor.'

We were both grinning now.

'Seriously,' continued Don, 'what are you going to do?'

It was not me who said it. It was some imp of destruction that had taken lodgings in the back of my head and I was as surprised as Don when it came out.

'I'll freelance,' I said.

'Where?'

I had no idea. I looked at the paperweight trundling slowly along the map. I saw it had passed the industrial area that surrounded the city in which we sat.

'Wherever this paper-weight stops,' I told him.

We both watched the paper-weight now, and suddenly the rumbling noise that it made seemed deafening.

'It's getting bloody near the sea,' said Don. 'We'll need to buy you an underwater typewriter for your farewell if it doesn't stop soon.'

Fortunately, just short of the coastline, the paper-weight came to a rolling halt on the Welsh border. For a moment it rocked to and fro and then it settled in the largest patch of green on that part of the map.

'I'll get you the number of the *Farmer's Journal*,' said Don discouragingly. 'Give it another wee push. You could make a fortune in Ireland.'

I shook my head and reached for the gazetteer. 'Never nudge your luck,' I told no-one in particular, as I thumbed through the pages looking for the county town nearest to the place the paper-weight had picked. I felt suddenly relieved now that the decision had been made for me and the entry in the gazetteer, when I found it, was heartening. 'Chester. Pop. 75,000,' I read. 'Industries: brewing, farming and net fishing. Garrison town, seat of County Authority and extensive Roman remains. One theatre, three cinemas, produce and livestock markets. Cathedral.'

'I like the bit about brewing,' I said.

Don had been more practical. As I read the gazetteer he was searching the card index that was the register of correspondents. He found the card for Chester and read it.

'Could be worse,' he told me. 'There's no full-time freelance, just a couple of linage pools on the local weeklies. They'll have the sport tied up so your bread and butter linage is gone but you won't have any union trouble.'

Nothing like a linage pool exists in any industry but ours. The reporters who comprise the pool sell the stories they have already written for their own newspaper – and the ones their own paper wouldn't touch with a barge pole for fear of upsetting the local establishment – to other newspapers outside their circulation area. If you can imagine the shop assistants of Woolworth's selling their firm's goods to British Home Stores you can get the idea. But it did mean that the weekly papers could pay low wages, and the editor usually got a cut of the profits, so nobody complained.

Despite these minor flaws, freelancing had seemed a marvellous idea in the warm office reading the gazetteer entry. Standing in the car park on Windy Ridge, looking down at the endless miles of wall-to-wall meadowland, I began to have doubts.

In theory there was nothing simpler than setting up as a freelance. As a friend of mine said, 'All you need is a pencil, the back of your cheque book to write on, the price of a phone call... and thirty years' experience.' I'd worked on national newspapers for twelve years which I reckoned was the equivalent to thirty years of normal life. Now I'd been accredited to every national newspaper as their Chester and North Wales correspondent. As a staff man I'd built up contacts in the city and I knew I could reckon on finding at least one story a week in the local papers that I could develop for the dailies. Adverts in newsagents' windows, parish magazines and the advertisements columns of almost every newspaper produce surprisingly rich harvests in saleable copy. I could transfer all phone charges to the newspaper when I dictated copy or sold my ideas; any phone box would serve as an office. If a story was not of the highest quality, I could submit it, which meant that I would only be paid if it was used. If it was a decent yarn, I could tell the news desk about it, they would order it and I would get paid whether they used it or not. In the years that followed most of my stories were ordered. I knew about the ten o'clock panic.

At around 10.30am all the executives stream into the editor's office on a newspaper for the morning conference. The news and picture gathering executives take their schedules, which should carry at least fifteen items each, with them. Only around five of these ideas for news stories need to stand up as contenders for space in the paper. The other ten are for throwing around and creating an impression of activity. And at ten o'clock in the morning when the news editor arrives at his desk, only beaten by a short head by his deputy, there is not a lot of time before the conference to harvest a crop of schedule lines. When I was considering a possible story the presence of a schedule line was the most important thing in its favour. It had to be short so that it would look crisp on the schedule and it helped if it was amusing. News editors are almost always witty men and appreciated a laugh early in the morning. I gave them a one man cabaret. The technique took years to perfect, but my little act earned me more in order fees than I would have got taking it round the Working Men's Clubs. And it taught me the technique of broadcasting, which at the age of fifty, would give me a new career.

In those days there were six morning newspapers and on a good day you could get an order from every one of them. An order fee in the early sixties was around three guineas, and starting the day on the equivalent of a week's salary for a staff man at that time always had a great soothing effect on the mind.

It was like driving through Toy Town. At first I could only see the square tower of the cathedral but presently I reached tree-lined suburbs of detached houses and, when I had crossed a canal bridge, I was confronted by the City Gate. A wall, twenty feet high, built of immense blocks of sandstone, surrounded the city and the late afternoon sun had washed it a pale pink. I thought of Samarkand and then, through the arch of the gate, I saw a straight road of timbered shops and Gothic buildings that all looked like banks. There were galleries over the shops in the main streets, straight and wide, that quartered the city. They followed the plan of a long-dead Roman architect but it was the most English of cities. From the Eastgate, as I drove through it, I could see a further gate and, beyond that, the glass surface of the Dee estuary.

The place had a good feel about it and my spirits had lifted considerably by the time I had parked my car and, in a small, panelled bar crammed with curios, ordered the first drops in the ocean of ale I was to swallow there over the next twenty years. The more I explored the city the better I liked it. At night the galleries were like mysterious tunnels and I thought that when I began to write my television play, the newspaperman's version of the pools win, it would be a thriller and I would set the chase scene in these sinister galleries. Unfortunately, before I began counting my royalties, I had to do something about the immediate needs of my bank manager whose plaintive whimpers could be heard in every post.

I had taken a room at a city centre pub, handy for the Town Hall, the magistrates' courts and the police station, the frontiers of my new world.

The door to the police station was always locked to prevent evil-doers from running off with the whistles and truncheons but there was a small sliding hatch at the side of the door with a bell marked 'ring for attention'. I rang it, the hatch slid open and a policeman's head, vaguely indecent without the helmet, appeared in the opening. Framed in the hatch, he looked like a picture on the wall, an impression he enhanced by total immobility. I broke a silence that might otherwise have continued indefinitely.

'Good morning,' I said. 'Press. I've come for the morning conference.'

The silence continued for a moment as thought made its way through uncharted areas of his mind.

'Dunno about that,' he said at length, dubiously. 'I'll have to see the sergeant.'

The frame emptied, to be refilled moments later by the portrait of a sergeant. It was like hanging day at the Royal Academy and I found myself mentally awarding marks for composition and colour.

'Yes?' asked the portrait.

I repeated my request and the portrait head wiggled unnervingly. The idea that I was being treated to a private view of a series of life-like paintings was so strong that when the head in the frame moved I jumped, nervously.

'I'm afraid it's beyond my province to issue such an authority,' the painting said pompously. 'I shall have to seek advice.'

I did not think much of the portrait of the inspector that presently appeared. Impressionist, I told myself. It seemed comprised of dots, after the manner of Pissarro, which I identified as skin eruptions of vivid purple and red. The chief inspector was pure stucco and not to my taste either but the final portrait, that of the superintendent, was a dazzler. The silver buttons and the pips on his shoulder were gleaming highlights against the black background of his uniform.

'Acrylic,' I told myself. 'But not a very good likeness.'

'Can I help you?' the superintendent asked suavely. Something in the

5

way he said it told me that it was unlikely but I ploughed on with my familiar request. They were great on head shaking in this force, I discovered. I presumed that the lower orders had learnt from the superintendent whose style was masterly. The slow and stately movements of his head combined in one movement, right to left, authority, regret and a thwarted desire to please.

'All our press work is handled by Mr Armitage of the *Gazette,*' he said at last, and looked at me as one would look at an unfamiliar commercial traveller who was trying to oust a tried and trusted supplier. I argued as hotly as I could but the sensation that I was talking to a picture on the wall was strong and I was uneasy.

'Just a moment,' he broke in at last, slamming the hatch closed at the same moment. I stared at the empty plywood shutter and, then, with a great metal yawn, the police station door opened. It was the constable again.

'Super-says-to-come-in-fourth-door-on-the-left,' the constable said all in one breath, and vanished.

I stepped into the Looking Glass and searched for the Queen of Hearts. The fourth door on the left opened, I went in and found myself in a minute office that was crowded with four other reporters, all from the same paper I learned later, and all members of the linage pool. I sat down amid a welcoming murmur of hostility, ostentatiously took out my new reporter's note book, the first real note book I had used for years, and waited for the arrival of the superintendent. He looked surprised when he saw me, a clever move, which silently arrayed him with the tweed-suited Borgias around me who were mentally stirring into the cup of tea a policeman now handed me a stiff two fingers of cyanide.

The superintendent looked grave as he seated himself behind his desk. He did not speak as he arranged a bulky file precisely at right angles to his in-tray. His eyes swept the military ranks of pen, pencil, ruler and paper-knife which were drawn up, in review order, on his desk. Most people put things down unthinkingly, but this man, if you had asked him, would have been able to tell you precisely why he laid his pencil down on the spot on which he had lain it.

From his look as he surveyed each one of us in turn I knew that any moment I was going to get the story of the decade and the hairs on my neck crackled in expectation. His glance was heavy with 'Can I trust them?' nuances and there were hints of 'Am I doing the right thing?' in the way his fingers drummed on the desk.

6

'Gentlemen,' he said, 'have you all got note books and pencils?' And I'm ashamed to say that I joined in the chorus of assent.

'Right,' he said. 'Let's proceed, shall we?' and he cleared his throat. 'I regret to tell you that a bicycle has been stolen from the front of the public library.'

In a life that has been a long drawn out sigh of anti-climax I remember that sentence as the high point. As I looked wonderingly about me I noticed that the four men from the weekly paper were scribbling industriously as the superintendent read what must have been the most detailed description of a bicycle, setting aside the manufacturer's specification, in the history of that machine. Hysterically I began to make up intros... 'An international gang of bicycle thieves terrorised a city last night (Mon).'

I left the police station needing a drink more badly than I can remember. Fortunately I had been given an introduction. When he had learnt the name of the city in which I planned to freelance, Toby, our Dublin stringer, had rung me to tell me about two friends of his who had opened a dining club there. 'Couple of Trinity men,' he said. 'Sure, you'll love 'em. They're a gas. They had Dublin by the ears when they were here,' he said and, remembering my own visits to the International Capital of Eccentricity, I knew that I had to meet them. Anyone who made his name among that collection of the world's improbables had to work at the business of living twenty-four hours a day. On the Day Of The Bicycle they were just the sort of company I needed as a guard against taking the world too seriously and I made my way to the address that Toby had given me.

The dining club was called The Symposium, a pleasing Platonic allusion that gave the lie to Toby's belief that neither partner had attended a single lecture during the three years they spent in dalliance in Dublin.

Afterwards they told me they had chosen the name as a hint that good conversation was as welcome as pound notes, indeed more so; but when I went in and met Walter Payne for the first time I thought there was another, vainer purpose behind the choice of name. Walter was the image of Socrates. He was standing behind the bar opening a bottle of champagne when I went through the impressive frosted-glass doors and, for a moment, I thought the little statue in the British Museum had sprung to life, changed into a neat business suit, a brocaded waistcoat and a fine gold watch-chain and hastened north.

'Good morning, my dear boy,' he said affably. I looked round me and a sensation of *déjà-vu* began tickling at my ears. As I took in the decor I knew with absolute certainty that I had been in the club before. Everything was so familiar. I recognised, without knowing how or why, the row of banquettes covered in plum, plush velvet, the huge brass and cast-iron charcoal grill, the eighteenth century cartoons that covered the wall, the scuffed wood-block floor that looked as though it had been down for centuries; even the wine racks, crates turned on their side and built one on top of the other at the back of the bar, were old acquaintances. And, yet, it was impossible. I had never been in this club in my life.

Walter, who had a fine collection of looks quizzical, threw a sample in my direction, the champagne halted in mid-pour. 'Sorry,' I said. 'I feel like Mole when he barked his shin on the door-stop.'

He smiled happily. 'A literary gentleman! How nice!' He beamed. 'May I give you a glass of champagne? I was about to take one myself. So much quieter than Alka Seltzer, I find.'

It is a happy augury to be given a free glass of champagne the first time you walk into a new watering hole and I accepted it with thanks, all thought of the bicycle theft banished.

'I cannot get rid of the idea that I've been here before,' I said. 'And yet it's impossible.'

'A little conceit of the management,' said Walter and introduced himself. 'My partner and I hate going into new places and we thought to bring little memories of earlier haunts with us, when we opened here.'

He waved a narrow, flawlessly-manicured hand at the charcoal grill and I liked the way he talked with the commas in place.

'The Dolphin, Dublin?' He introduced it with the little query at the end of the sentence that was his own private hallmark. I was with him at once and pointed to the wine rack.

'El Vino?'

He clapped his hands happily. 'Exactly!'

'The cartoons. The Pen and Ink?" – "Just so!' He was skipping on the spot and his Socratic beard was waving like a pennant. 'And the banquettes and tables?'

'Jamay's?'

The beard lashed from wall to wall. 'Precisely,' he boomed, his arms raised in delight. 'Let me give you another glass of champagne.'

Several glasses later I spoke again. 'I can't quite identify the floor,' I said, 'and yet...' I thought for a moment that he was going to jump over the counter but he seemed to change course in mid-air and ran up and down the bar in little trills of movement. His eyes scrambled half out of their sockets and, apparently to calm himself, he took an exquisite enamelled watch out of his waistcoat pocket and looked at the time. Reassured that the world had not stopped in that ecstatic moment, he replaced the watch and transferred his look of approval to the floor.

'*The piece de resistance,*' he confessed with a trace of shyness.

'My partner and I,' he began – I noticed that he always used his Jorkinsian mode, never the name of his partner. I began to wonder if he existed – 'were distressed to discover, when we opened our establishment six months ago, that the floors gleamed in a regrettably pristine fashion. We therefore employed the services of four urchins to slide over them until they were sufficiently scuffed to meet our taste. We wanted our little club to have the appearance of being much used. It inspires confidence in the patrons.'

It seemed incredible that the club was only six months old. The walls were that soft gold that only years of the patina of cigar smoke can give to white emulsion. Walter noticed my glance.

'A triumph of my partner,' he admitted. 'He had to blow cigarette smoke through a handkerchief to show the painter, a willing but limited fellow, exactly the soft pastel shade of nicotine we required. I do not smoke. I take snuff. May I offer...?'

He took out a minute silver box. I waved it away. He looked surprised but helped himself liberally.

'And was confidence inspired in the patrons?' I enquired. Walter replaced the box with a flourish. 'On the night we opened, the stool on which you are now sitting was occupied by an elderly antique dealer of our city. When he returned the next night he discovered a lady sitting there and was quite put out. "Madam," he said, "you are sitting on my stool. I have been using that stool since the day this establishment opened!" We were both highly gratified.'

It seemed then that such perfection could not hope to last and, sadly, events were to prove me right, but I was determined, while it existed, to be part of this gastronomic Brigadoon.

'I was hoping I might be able to join,' I told Walter.

He poured the last of the champagne into our two glasses.

'You are already a life member,' he said. And we drank to that.

The door opened, a group of people moved in and Walter, bowing slightly to me, glided off to serve them. I had leisure to watch him perform and he was masterly. Some men of talent write symphonies or novels, paint pictures or design noble buildings. Walter scorned such external evidence of artistic inclination. He was his own work of art. I came to realise later that he saw his small world behind the bar counter as a stage on which he acted brilliantly. I wondered what he had been like before he created himself, for every gesture, though it came from a happy and generous heart, was studied. His conversation, or rather his monologues, for he brooked few interruptions from the audience of club members, was as polished as the dialogue in a witty play. His snuff box was flourished, not taken, from his pocket, and his eyebrows must have been exhausted by the end of the day. Every gesture, every inflexion, seemed to be saying 'Whatever the rest of you are doing in the twentieth century, I am attached here only for the purpose of rations and accommodation.'

I'm sure that if Sam Johnson or Sheridan had walked into the club they would have recognised Walter's stamp at once.

If Walter, as I had persuaded myself, was English watercolour, his partner, Tony Garrett Anderson, was Flemish oils in every brush stroke. I met him later that morning and I noticed at once that, although he was a large man, he filled much more of the room than the space taken up by his body. Traces of a profile that had once been Greek could be discerned under layers of high living. He wore an immaculate navy Crombie coat, but a button was missing and the bridge of his horn-rimmed glasses was bound with fraying insulating tape. He was tall, with wide shoulders and immense girth, but his hands were tiny and seemed uneasy on the ends of arms that he spun in conversation like windmill sails.

'Have you eaten?' he asked, when Walter introduced us.

'No? Splendid, we'll lunch together. Walter: a bottle of Dom Perignon.'

We had a crisp Sancerre with our first course, scallops mornay, a deep-throated burgundy of impressive age with the rib of beef that followed and a Chateau Yquem with a pudding that was princely. When I saw the Stilton an elderly waiter was escorting to our table, all caution flew and I ordered a decanter of '27 Dow, closing my mind's ear to mewings of my bank manager. I remember the jar of potcheen that presently appeared but much of the rest of the day is obscure. I took little part in the cascade of talk that accompanied our extended lunch but Tony was not perturbed. I had congratulated him on his club and that was obviously enough.

'So glad you like it,' he boomed like a benevolent bittern. 'When I came north to take over the family business I was distressed to discover there was not one presentable eating-house in the city. I had to open one as a matter of pure self-defence or I should have starved to death. This,' he confided, 'is prawn cocktail land. I doubt,' he went on, 'if the citizens of this city would recognise anything as a meal that did not include roast Norfolk turkey and rum babas. What is a rum baba? Some species of amusing child, I assume?'

Much of his later conversation I missed, partly out of drunkenness and partly out of blind panic at the thought of what my share of the bill was going to cost me. Plainly, the twenty pounds that I had in my pocket and which represented one third of my worldly capital was going to be laughably inadequate. When the meal ended at last, I was surprised that no-one approached with a bill. Later at the bar, as I slowly drank an Irish coffee in which only a thin layer of coffee kept the whiskey from biting the thick circular blanket of cream, I approached the subject nervously.

'Er, what do I owe you?' I asked.

Both Walter and Tony were shocked.

'Owe?' asked Tony. 'Whatever for?'

'For lunch,' I said. 'You must at least let me pay my share.'

'Share?' Both men were plainly outraged.

'But you were my guest,' spluttered Tony. 'We never take money from friends. That wouldn't do at all, would it, Walter?'

'Not at all,' said Walter primly, snuffing expressively in his embarrassment. 'Tut, tut. No, indeed.'

He took more snuff and moved a little way down the bar.

'But this is nonsense,' I insisted. 'I'll never dare come here again if you don't let me pay something.'

Tony was not pleased, I could see. He was vaguely aware that customers should not be driven away although he clearly saw no reason why he should take money off them when they came. The problem engrossed him for several seconds.

'Oh, very well,' he said at length. 'As it's your first visit... would two pounds be out of the way?'

He would not hear of me going back to my hotel when at last we ricocheted out of the club. 'You must come home with me,' he insisted. 'I want you to meet my wife.'

I pointed out that it was by that time 3am. But he was equal to that.

'Then you must meet her at breakfast,' he said. 'Jill loves meeting people for breakfast.'

I thought privately she must be from a different strain from the sort of woman I usually married. Bleary-eyed breakfast guests, indeed any sort of strangers at the breakfast table, were liable to get eaten before the cornflakes in the houses I had inhabited. But I had long ago ceased to struggle against the giant waves of his personality.

When we got down to the street Tony discovered that his Bentley had been stolen. It worried him not at all. On the way to his house he stopped a passing policeman.

'If you see a Bentley, licence number BG 289, would you stop it? It belongs to me. I'm afraid someone seems to have borrowed it.'

'Just as well, Mr Tony,' said the policeman tolerantly, for my friend was obviously a well-loved local figure. 'I should go home if I was you, like a good gentleman, and I'll send one of my colleagues round in the morning.'

'Capital!' beamed Tony. 'Not too early, mind. The dog is not an early riser, I fear.'

The promise extracted, we bade a civil goodnight to the policeman and continued on our way.

Tony's house was a pink-washed tall Regency building by the river. We opened a gate that led into a high-walled garden, tip-toed gently over a flagged terrace and through French windows into a long, high-ceilinged room.

'My music room,' Tony explained, as he poured brandy into two tulip shaped glasses. 'Had to have one. You know Milton's *Lycidas*, of course?' I did.

'I'm setting it to music,' said Tony. 'So I had to have a music room. Absolutely vital.' He handed me a glass and led me to the wall to examine a series of exquisite prints of Regency musicians.

'Bought 'em yesterday. So important for a composer to have the right sort of atmosphere, don't you think?'

It really was a gem of a room. Over the mantle shelf there was an oil depicting St. Cecilia, the patron saint of music, playing an organ. The mantle shelf supports were wood and carved with a motif of instruments and the chains that held the chandelier in the centre of the room were brazen notes of music. Only one thing was missing.

'Which instrument are you scoring your music for?' I asked.

'The piano,' he said. 'Initially, that is. But I see it, really, as an oratorio for an organ and massed choirs. I hope to have it performed in the Cathedral. They have a passable choir.'

I realised then what was missing from the room. The only musical instruments of any kind were the carvings on the mantle board. 'There isn't a piano,' I said.

'I take my first lesson on Monday,' replied Tony with grandeur. 'But first things first. One must have somewhere to sit.'

I am a light sleeper and I woke at six the next morning. After the first moment of panic that always grips me when I awaken in a strange room, for I've always been convinced that I will one day be hanged and whenever I wake in any bed but my own I think, for a terrifying second, it is a condemned cell, I began to worry about my morning calls.

The morning calls are the most important of the day for any freelance. You learn everything you need to know about the disasters of the night and the profitable prospects of the day ahead. The house was silent, if I discounted the cavernous snores that were coming from the room across the hall which was occupied by Tony. I had no dressing gown but it seemed certain that the household would not be rising for some time yet. Wearing only a singlet and briefs, I tiptoed downstairs to the hall where I had noticed a telephone. I was bare-footed, the hall was tiled and the cold struck through the soles of my feet; I could feel my legs going an unattractive mottled blue as far as the knees as I rang the first of my calls. I was half-way through my opening sentence when the doorbell rang.

Three courses of action were open to me. I could answer the door, a stranger to the house, dressed in a skimpy singlet and short underpants that verged on the downright bawdy; I could ignore the bell and carry on with my call, or I could ignore it and race back upstairs before anyone else rose to answer the door.

The third course seemed immediately attractive and I was about to replace the receiver when I heard something that reduced me to gibbering panic. There were footsteps on the stairs and they were obviously feminine. I was standing in my brief underwear in the hall of a strange house and the lady of the house was on the point of coming into view. I was frozen into complete immobility when Tony's wife appeared on the scene and, between my blushes and my blue, goose-pimpled legs, I resembled nothing so much as a furtive aubergine.

She passed me where I stood, rigid, with the telephone clutched in my frozen hand, nodded graciously, and opened the door.

'Good morning, madam,' I heard a voice say. 'I am Detective Sergeant Bracket, CID. I understand that your husband's Bentley was stolen last night. I wonder if I could ask you a few questions?'

'Of course,' said Jill, holding the door open. 'Won't you come in?'

13

The detective saw me the moment he stepped into the hall and we stared at each other in mutual disbelief as a completely different set of questions than the ones he had originally intended leapt into his mind. Jill, like a gracious Edwardian hostess presiding over a tea table, sought to put us at ease.

'This is Sergeant Bracket,' she told me, and then she paused... 'I'm afraid I don't know your name.'

I told her, under the disbelieving gaze of the detective, as she led us into a drawing room, motioned us to a settee, settled us down, switched on an electric fire which she considerately placed nearer to me than to the sergeant, and withdrew to the kitchen to make coffee.

Left alone, perched on either end of the large settee, the sergeant and I eyed each other for a long moment.

'House guest,' I said, at last.

'Oh, aye,' said the sergeant, his official glare sweeping from my purple toes to my tousled hair. 'That's nice.'

I was glad when Jill came back with the coffee.

Some days later Tony rang me in a state of high excitement. 'I think I've got a little story that may interest your readers,' he told me. 'I intend to rehabilitate the oyster.'

I told him that I did not know the oyster had been *un*habilitated, but he wasn't listening.

'I thought you might make a Hickey paragraph out of it,' he told me.

I knew that I could get two pounds for gossip paragraphs and I estimated that if I met him for lunch, as he was now suggesting, I would only be eight pounds out on the day, so I said: 'I'll see you at two-thirty in the Customs House,' naming a pub that was only one hundred yards from his club.

It was a mutually agreeable choice. Tony would not have too far to walk and I would be able to duck gracefully out at 3pm when they put the cloths on, thus salvaging part of the day from the marathon drinking session that would develop if I met him in the Symposium.

'Can I get champagne here?' he asked when he sailed into the pub, looking so irresistibly like a man-of-war in full sail that I expected any moment the flaps of his waistcoat would drop and four small cannon would pop out to fire a broadside. He could not get champagne, I was happy to discover, but he made enthusiastic inroads into several pints of Guinness before he brought the meeting to order.

'I'm organising an oyster festival,' he said. 'Nothing too grand. I plan to hire three of the Bithells pleasure launches and take a party, say one hundred or so, of the county set sailing down the river to a barbecue. I thought I would have steak and oyster pie. Do you know it? Delicious! And I'm arranging for our suppliers to send along a few score barrels of oysters. We could have them with this excellent Guinness. I must ask the landlord to arrange an outside bar.'

'Sounds great,' I said. 'Who is coming?'

'I thought I'd ask the Duke,' he said. 'He's been in the club. Oh, and the Pools family. Nice people, I'm very fond of them. And the odd earl, perhaps.'

I said it was shaping into a nice Hickey story, and it was. He was delighted.

'Thought you'd like it. I thought I might get Ossian Ellis to sit in the prow of one of the launches playing Gaelic songs on his harp. Oh, and Siobhan McKenna, the film star, is coming. Knew her in Dublin. Charming girl. And I must ring Michael MacLhiamhor. You'll love Mike. A dear man. Do you think you might to be able to do something with it?'

In my trusting innocence I said that I would do an advance story that day and a follow-up on the day of the festival. It was commercially sound. The fees from two stories would almost cover what I had spent since he had joined me.

Hickey did not use the piece I wrote but it got a splendid show in the *Herald* and a few days later Neville, the news editor, rang to ask me for a follow-up. Tony was delighted when I told him.

'I'd better start organising it, then,' he said. As I came to know him better I began to look on his schemes like cold swimming baths. The further you got into them the colder you got. Tony's last remark had me like ice in seconds.

'Start? I thought you'd organised it. You said...'

'No, no, my dear. Just thought of it that morning when I rang you. Trying the biscuit on the dog, as it were. Splendid publicity for the club.'

I swallowed hard. 'Let me know if you have to take on extra staff. I may need the work.'

Curiously, although Tony was by several stones the burliest of the partners, it was Walter, the exquisite, who was the more active. He had hunted big game in Kenya, although, predictably, his safari had innovations that must have come as a surprise to his White Hunter. He dressed for dinner every night in the bush and his safari equipment

15

included two cases of wine. One, a robust Chateauneuf du Pape, was for drinking with his meals: the other, an indifferent Spanish burgundy, was to marinade any game that fell to his gun. Sadly none did.

He was also a keen mountaineer although, here again, his equipment would have puzzled the orthodox climber.

'I understand,' he said one day, and his voice had the tone one would use to a friend who kept snakes in the bath, 'that you have a motor car?'

I admitted that I had.

'I wonder if you would help me. I'm going mountaineering at the weekend. Do you think you could give me a hand with my equipment to Camp One?'

I am the fortunate possessor of a reasonable mix of cowardice in my blood and I am so uneasy with heights that I always wear low-heeled shoes. But, happily, Camp One proved to be his picturesque name for the semi-detached house in the suburbs where he was to rendezvous with his climbing companions and I was able to comply with his wish.

The equipment was a surprise. For one thing, it was all gathered into a large brown fibre suitcase of impressive age. It consisted of a bottle of brandy, a large bone cylinder which contained at least a month's supply of snuff, a tastefully bound copy of the Folio edition of Scott's *Last Expedition* and a similar edition of Shackleton's expedition to the Pole. 'For inspiration,' he explained. I could see that, but I wondered what he wanted with his academic gown and a leather-bound copy of *The Young Visitors* by Daisy Ashford. They seemed of less use than the huge *Flora and Fauna of the Tibetan Uplands* that he also carried. There was a Bowie knife, a pair of Moroccan leather slippers and a dressing gown, but I could see no sign of pitons, climbing boots or even rope.

'Rope?' He was astonished at my question.

'My dear fellow, we haven't any notion of tying each other up. This is a serious expedition.'

Walter brought a touch of the bizarre to all his outdoor pursuits. He was a man who kept love in its proper place. Some time earlier he had discussed the problem of a lonely old age with an unmarried lady who was a member of the club. They had many deep conversations at a deserted corner of the bar and he was much chivvied about it by the other members.

'It's perfectly simple,' he explained loftily. 'We have come to An Arrangement. If neither of us has married by the time we are fifty we have arranged to marry each other.' He paused. 'Subject to contract, of course.'

My own arrangements were short term and centred, at that time, on another sultry young member whom Walter had christened La Belle Sauvage. He made a little song that he used to chant archly as I left the club with her.

'You would dearly love to ravage,
The winsome La Belle Sauvage'

Naturally, this put the natural order of things back by several weeks, but I had high hopes when another member offered to lend me his cabin cruiser for an afternoon so that I could take her on the river. Walter was delighted when I told him of the plan.

'What fun,' he said. 'I'll come with you and bring a picnic. I will lend respectability.'

It was not what I had in mind but La Belle Sauvage, a cautious minx, welcomed the idea.

We set off on a glorious August day. A band was playing Gilbert and Sullivan in the wrought-iron bandstand in the river groves and the water was crowded with boats. Presently the rowing boats fell behind us and the expostulations of the engines of the drive-yourself speedboats were half heard explosions in the distance. Walter was sitting diplomatically in the prow with a glass of Chablis, chatting idly with the fish and I knew that only the large pleasure launches ventured so far up-river. In the stern I settled down to the serious business of unwrapping La Belle Sauvage.

I was having a modest success when she suddenly stiffened in my arms.

'Passion?' I mused. 'How very nice.' And then I noticed that, far from being dark pools of emotion, her eyes were standing out like chapel hat pegs as she stared, transfixed, at something over my shoulder. A little astern of us, but catching us up rapidly, I could see one of Bithells forty-foot pleasure launches, crowded with elderly ladies on their annual river outing. For some reason they were cheering wildly and pointing excitedly towards the prow of our cruiser.

I looked round quickly. Walter, who until that day I had never seen discard so much as his umbrella outdoors, was standing on the prow in a graceful diving stance and he was stark naked. I howled my dismay and his voice came back across the noise of cheering.

'It does not matter,' he called with immense dignity as he launched himself into the water… 'I am a philosopher.'

Something elemental stirred in La Belle Sauvage. In marginally less time that it would have taken me she had stripped to an unbelievably

17

brief set of bra and panties and joined him in the water. For the only time in my life, as I sat in the stern sipping reflectively at my wine and clutching her recently vacated dress, I regretted that I was unable to swim.

The real power in the club was wielded by the head-waiter who was called Jimmy the God by everyone who did not call him sir, and that included some of the new members with whom he was very severe.

'I was trained, sir,' he would tell them in a ripe cockney accent, 'at a little coffee shop called Claridges; so I'm not really used to serving that wine with that dish.'

Presiding over his spirit stove, creating a crêpe suzette, he was like some Wagnerian troll in striped trousers. Although a small man, his magisterial air never left him and his jowls, asphalt in aspic, quivered awesomely. Two members, who were avid readers of cookery books, were arguing one day, as they watched him chafing at the dish with a veal cordon bleu, about the ingredients that went into that classic. Jimmy listened with growing impatience until he could restrain himself no longer.

'I hope, gentlemen,' he told them at last, dashing down the chafing dish and producing a wad of notes like a baby's fist, 'that you have a considerable sum of money about your persons. Because I will venture a handful of notes that you don't know what the 'ell you are talkin' abaht.'

An older member leaned over from the next table.

'I wouldn't, if I were you,' he told the other diners kindly. 'He's never lost a bet yet. There's five pounds of mine among that bundle.'

We were all dismayed, if not surprised, when some time later Jimmy had a heart attack but he was back at his station within a week. He was full of praise for the doctor.

'Spotted it in a minute, the cause of me trouble. Asked me what I drank. It's that gin and tonic, he said.'

Since Jimmy got through at least a bottle of gin every waking day it did not require a miracle of diagnosis on the doctor's part, but Jimmy had faith. From that day onwards he did not touch a drop of gin. He changed to whisky and tonic in exactly the same proportions and his faith in his doctor sustained him through the second, inevitable attack. But he returned a determined man.

'I know what it is,' he told us. 'It's that tonic water. When they took a sample out of me arm, me blood frothed.'

We asked him if he was sure that the tonic water was to blame.

'Stands to reason. It's the common denominator, isn't it?' he told us, and he did not touch another drop of tonic water until the day of his death.

Jimmy was equally ready to advise the rest of his staff in any kind of difficulty, and when the manageress asked him why he thought a young commis waiter was forever borrowing her lipstick, Jimmy saw the problem in a flash. He took the young waiter into his cubby-hole in the kitchen, poured him a bottle of ale, sighted him over the rim of his own ample glass of whisky and asked him bluntly:

'Got tendencies, 'ave yer?'

In the early sixties being a homosexual had not quite the social value that it has in these enlightened times. Indeed, there were some unhappy young men, the commis waiter among them, who would far, far rather have been normal.

'I can't help it, Mr God,' he said, tears starting in his eyes. 'It just comes over me.'

The cure was obvious.

'What you want,' said Jimmy, 'is a bird. Ever placed one, 'ave you?'

The young commis admitted that he had not.

'There you are then, nobody likes whisky not till they've 'ad their first sip. Same with sex. It's an acquired habit. And, if you'll take my tip, you'll acquire the 'abit at your earliest convenience. Come an tell me 'ow you get on.'

All the waiters had total faith in Jimmy the God and the young commis put his boss's advice into practice the very next day. Between three and nine days later he was seeking a further interview to ask for time off to attend a clinic. When we remarked on his absence Jimmy told a small group of us the story and we were all very cross with him.

'It's not your place to interfere,' he was told severely. 'Problems like that are a matter for the boy's father, not you.'

I do not think any of us had meant that Jimmy should advise the boy to tell his father of his tendencies, but he did. And, once again, it never occurred to the boy to question the advice. When next he came in he had a purple black eye and much bruising of the cheek.

'I did what you told me,' he told Jimmy. 'I thought he was goin' to kill me. As it is he's kicked me out of the house.'

Full of contrition, Jimmy began to speak, but the young commis interrupted him:

'Mr God,' he said politely, 'don't give me no more advice, please.

19

I've taken it twice and now I've got a dose and I ain't got nowhere to sleep. I fink I'd rather be queer.'

Jimmy considered the point quietly for a moment and then he came to his decision.

'Go an' arsk Norah if you can borrow her lipstick,' he advised. 'And I'd get a bit of powder for that cheek.'

We all thought that Jimmy was a fixture in the club and that one day his spirit would haunt the club as in life the club's spirits haunted him, but it was not to be. The affair of the Stilton cheese introduced the iron into Jimmy's Claridges-trained soul.

The club was so popular with the free-spenders, who, in those far-off days, made up much of the population of the city, that it seemed that not even the combined generosities of Walter and Tony could prevent it from making a profit. Even now it is difficult to see how they achieved it. But achieve it they did, and the day came when certain economies were advised by the unhappy man who did the accounts. Predictably, the economies that were made had overtones of the downright bizarre. At any given time the kitchen staff and the waiters outnumbered the diners; Walter bought a drink for every one of his friends among the members and Tony continued to invite anyone who took his capricious fancy to gargantuan feasts. It seemed unlikely that the club could be brought back to a profit-making footing by serving the Stilton cheese in portions. But that was the decision that was taken.

In the event, it reduced the overheads by the sum of Jimmy's wages. Not even the offer of an extra fiver a week, as self-defeating a piece of economy as can be imagined, would persuade Jimmy to serve Stilton cheese in portions.

'In the little coffee shop where I trained,' he said 'we were always taught that "cut high, cut low and cut middle" was the only way to serve Stilton. And always from the whole cheese. Wrapped in a linen napkin for preference.'

'Quantity control,' Tony told him firmly – he had obviously been reading a catering magazine – 'is essential if any restaurant is to make a success.'

'Cut high, cut low, cut middle,' muttered Jimmy. Indeed, he said little else for the rest of the day until it sounded like an incantation and made Walter jump nervously. From that moment he refused to serve cheese at all and winced visibly when he saw the wedges of Stilton passing him on their plates. By the end of the week it had become too much for his noble soul.

'I am afraid I shall have to give notice,' he told Tony on the Friday. 'But I should like to make one request.'

'Anything,' said Tony who loved him. 'Anything. What is it?'

'I'd like to become a member,' said Jimmy.

'Certainly,' said Tony. 'I'll propose you myself.' And he did.

When Jimmy left, Tony took over the job of head waiter, and watching him at work became the consuming passion of those of us who knew about the dire straits in which the club found itself.

The menu had always been a minor work of art. The size of a tabloid newspaper, it was illustrated with genuine Rowlandson cartoons, which Walter had bought in bulk, taken from their frames and stuck onto the front cover of the Bill of Fare. The choice inside was Lucullan. There was suckling pig and guinea fowl, quails and steak and oyster pie, syllabubs and summer puddings, blinis and sole stuffed with smoked salmon. The vegetable column, even in the deepest winter, was a messenger of spring. The hors d'oeuvre trolley was a meal in itself, and frequently used as one by the impecunious. Alas, as the creditors became more demanding, the kitchen matched less and less the promise of the Bill of Fare. One by one, and always reluctantly, because by this time the partners had become objects of fascination and affection to them, the suppliers began to insist on cash before every transaction.

It was then that Tony achieved his finest hour. The fact that the cupboard was bare he saw as a challenge and the Bill of Fare became a script from which he refused to depart. At the end of a meal one was left wondering whether to leave a tip or an Oscar, for Tony was a gastronomic Gielgud and every day produced an award-winning performance. Not one item was removed from the list of dishes. Dinner was no longer possible because of the mechanics of the new system, but luncheon continued as stylishly as ever. There were modifications, but Tony saw it as a sacred duty to keep the bad news of the club's plight and the customers at some distance from each other. The commis waiter was permanently stationed in the kitchen now, mackintoshed and fleet of foot. When diners entered Tony would himself advance on them like a genial duke.

'How very nice to see you, sir,' he beams at the host, escorting the party to the table and handing the ladies into their chairs. The menu is produced with a flourish that is pure Irving and the weather discussed at length.

'I think we'll begin with the sole stuffed with smoked salmon, Tony,' says the customer.

21

A judicious knitting of Tony's brows follows and an 'Mmm' that speaks volumes.

The query 'Is something wrong?' is the cue for Tony to lean forward confidentially, torn between his duty as a man of commerce and his personal affection for the diner.

'I could not in conscience recommend the smoked salmon,' he whispers. 'I have spoken to the supplier but we are getting towards the end of the side and it is just a thought stringy. One should indeed put it forward, but to a man with your knowledge of food? Well, really sir, I think not.'

It never failed. Praise from a restaurant proprietor is the headiest kind and from that moment Tony could have had the customer nibbling at the napery. With an air, the diner always surrendered the menu at this point.

'You know what I like..' – men of the world meeting in trust by now – 'What do you suggest?' Then, to his admiring guests: 'They always do me rather well here.'

A graceful acknowledgement from Tony, a dismissive wave of the hand to deflect the compliment, then, modestly: 'May I suggest an asparagus starter in a hot-butter sauce, and then the lamb cutlets, perfect at this time of the year, our man kills his own, you know? And vegetables in season?'

'Are they fresh?'

'They have yet to be gathered.'

It was quite true. Tony had an arrangement with a snack bar further up the street to buy portions of ready-cooked vegetables at cost. It was owned by the commis waiter's auntie, an endlessly obliging lady. But Tony always smiled when he said it as though he was joking and he managed a subtle blending of superiority and deprecation which never failed.

'An aperitif, sir?'

We all listened carefully now because this was the tightrope act and we didn't want to miss a single nuance. The future of the meal depended on the choice of aperitif. A round of orange juice and Tony was sunk. But there was no hint of the danger in which he was standing when Tony spoke next.

'A bottle of the Widow?'

They might have balked at the word 'champagne' which just sounds expensive. Translated into the Veuve (or Widow) Clicquot, even more so. But 'a *bottle of the widow*' had wicked Edwardian connotations and few diners-out like it to be thought that they do not know the vocabulary of the man of style.

'Excellent! The Clicquot it is, then...' to the admiring glances of the guests.

It was at this precise moment that Tony administered the *coup de grace*. With a slight bow he would walk away from the table and then stop dead. A change came over his manner. The air of the benevolent millionaire sat uneasily now on his huge shoulders. When he turned he looked embarrassed, like a host who has suddenly remembered there was a poodle in the guestroom.

'I'm so sorry,' He was back at the table pawing the ground in perfectly simulated dismay. 'Such a nuisance.'

'Tony, what is it?'

'It's these damned accountants, sir. We've got to have separate bills for the drinks and for the food. Alas, I cannot put your bar bill on the same account. I wonder... could I trouble you to pay separately for the aperitif? It's a damnable nuisance but one's hands are tied.'

It never failed and moments later Tony was in the kitchen passing the fiver to the waiting commis.

'Four lamb cutlets from the butcher, a tin of asparagus and half a pound of Irish butter from the grocer's, then ask your auntie if we can have four portions of peas, four portions of carrots and some crisp chips. Tell her to cut them thin, we have our standards to consider. And you call back for them in half an hour. They must be hot.'

The commis was back in minutes and the tin of asparagus popped into a waiting pan of hot water while Walter plied the diners with champagne and amusing chatter. It was a masterpiece of timing, and as they munched happily at their asparagus, the diners could watch approvingly while their chops were broiled on the charcoal stove by Walter and Tony decanted the inoffensive claret he had successfully recommended.

I have seen Tony manage seven tables simultaneously in this way and never once make an error or serve food that was badly cooked or not piping hot. But it made heavy demands upon his inner resources and when the lunch hour was over it required several glasses of something red and not too dry to return him to his ebullience.

'God knows what we will do when the wine runs out,' he used to say, and then he would brighten. 'Never mind, something is bound to turn up.'

'Bound to,' agreed Walter.

And they both drank to that.

They were an interesting study. At university they had burned with Pater's well-known hard, gem-like flame. They had been arbiters of taste and no end of dogs. Dublin rang with their exploits and they were consulted endlessly. They had their own table at Jamay's and were the prime wits of their generation. The sadness was that after university there was nothing left to do. They had conquered too early in life and everything beyond was an anti-climax. But I could not help feeling that they had won more from life, as the infant prodigies of fortune, than many to whom success came later and lasted longer.

Everyone tried to help. One member, a major shareholder in the largest hotel in the city, took to standing in the hotel foyer and waving his stick at would-be diners.

'Don't eat here,' he used to warn them. 'Eat at the Symposium. Much better.'

Inevitably the crash came and the club was closed by the Official Receiver yet, even in their hour of tribulation, the partners behaved with their wonted style. Their farewell dinner to members, on the house of course, was still talked about in the city twenty years later. The *piece de resistance* was a centrepiece of the highest art. An entire orchestra of lobsters, dressed in tailed coats and white ties made from icing, played marzipan musical instruments of every kind. There were cellos and violins, golden saxophones and thin black clarinets built round tooth-pick frames. The conductor was a miraculously stiffened sea-trout, his flippers of flake gelatine, who looked uncannily like the late Sir John Barbirolli. Chefs, who had left when there were no longer funds with which to pay them, returned to pay tribute with their skill to their late employers. There was pheasant from the estate of one of the members, a peacock in its plumage and a boar's head armed. Even the game chips were sculpted in whirls like barley sugar sticks and the sprouts were cut into delicate florets, like green blossom, with baby carrots for all the world like rosebuds. The cellars were emptied of their fine wines and battalions of bottles of the Widow flirted endlessly with the guests. Only the cunningly fashioned sugar baskets that were brought to each table, cornucopias of petit fours endlessly varied, produced a hint of criticism.

Teddy Brabazon was of that rare breed of classic drunks to whom alcohol was the rocket fuel that propelled the imbiber into inter-stellar fantasies. He once explained to me that his ambition had been to live by the river that flowed through the centre of the city.

'No use, though,' he told me. 'I'm scared stiff of crocodiles.'

Anxious to help, I told him there were no crocodiles in English rivers but he only looked at me from the depths of a massive sadness.

'You mayn't have seen them,' he told me darkly, 'but that don't signify. You haven't seen any eels either but the river's full of 'em.'

Now, on the last evening at his favourite club, a great morose wave engulfed him. The *petit fours* proved the last straw. Each basket was wrapped in a gossamer web of spun sugar and Teddy's eyes ballooned as one was placed before him.

'What the 'ell, is that?' he demanded, as his nervous fingers became enmeshed in the fine skeins of the sugar. 'It looks like the pubic hairs of a fairy.'

Teddy never really settled after The Symposium closed its doors for the last time although it should be said that his efforts to find a congenial replacement were Herculean.

He buttonholed me one night in a bar in the city with a plan that had all his kindly spirit alight.

'I'm a bit worried,' he admitted, 'about the starving millions in India.'

I said that a lot of us were but I did not see what we could do about it, things being very quiet at the time in the newspaper world.

'Well, I can do something,' he said. 'I'm going to have one of those War On Want dinners. I've hired the banqueting room of that new club out in the sticks and everyone's invited.'

'It's a great idea,' I said, and then a thought crossed my mind because I knew the table d'hote of such meals was not Teddy's normal grazing.

'You do mean the ones where everyone pays five quid and sits down to a plate of rice and a glass of water?' I asked him.

He was very shocked.

'Do I hell!' he said. 'I can't ask my friends to drink water!'

Plainly there were some things that could not be managed, not even for the succour of the third world.

'I've ordered a nice bit of turkey and a drop of booze to wash it down.'

'But that's not the idea at all,' I explained. 'What you do is charge five quid a head for the rice and send the proceeds to War On Want.'

I had obviously gone down several notches in his estimation and he looked at me now as though I were quite mad.

'Five quid a head for a bowl of bloody rice?' he demanded. 'You'll get me talked about. It's War On Want, innit? I'm not going to charge them anything.'

25

'But your friends aren't in want,' I argued. 'They're all loaded and those that aren't can borrow from you. How is it going to help the starving Indians?'

I could see that Teddy was about to say bugger the starving Indians if it meant giving rice to his friends but he was far too kindly for that.

'Tell you what,' he said. 'They can come too. I'll get some of them chapatis. They'll like that.'

I shook my head.

I knew from experience that Teddy would be deaf to mundane logic, something more was needed.

'When are you having it?' I asked.

'Tomorrow,' he said.

'There you are,' I said.

'Where?' he asked, baffled but interested.

'Who is going to look after their water buffaloes while they're away? They'd never get anyone at that short notice.' He looked at me admiringly.

'You're right,' he admitted. 'Never thought of that. Tell you what,' he said. 'The meal is a fiver a head. I'll send another fiver a head to the Indians. Provided,' he added firmly, 'that they don't spend it on water. 'Ave you seen what it does to kettles?'

Teddy was a wealthy man, which was just as well, for the most lavish War On Want banquet in history set him back a packet and afterwards he dropped a few hundred more in the casino that was part of the new club's attraction.

But, good as his word, before he went to bed that night, he made out a handsome cheque and sent it to War On Want.

He was tired after this exercise of good will and decided to stay the night at the club, which was residential. He awoke early next morning with a mouth like a vulture's sandpit and set off in his winceyette pyjamas in search of a cup of tea.

It was only 5am and in the kitchen the breakfast chef, who had also had a difficult night, was wincing at the explosions the eggs made when he cracked them into a bowl. He was in no mood to be polite when the door opened and Teddy, a dapper if tousled figure, demanded: 'Make us a bloody cup of tea!'

The chef's reply was of the order that is usually written on a piece of card and passed up to the magistrate.

In answer, Teddy lurched forward, picked up the bowl of raw eggs, emptied it over the head of the chef and ambled out of the kitchen in search of more congenial company. Incensed, the chef threw down his beating spoon and marched up to the manager's bedroom. His hammering brought the manager leaping from his bed to be confronted by his breakfast chef, wearing a fetching bonnet of congealed egg with a gradually increasing veil of albumen.

'What the hell...' he started. Then he stopped and began to sniff. It was unmistakable. 'Fire!' he shouted. 'The bloody club's on fire!'

And they both dashed down in the direction of the pall of smoke that was now weaving up the stairs.

In the dining room Teddy was standing in a ring of flames that were leaping from the burning furniture he had arranged in a semi-circle. He looked up at the two horrified men serenely.

'Now will you make us a bloody cup of tea?' he said.

It has always seemed significant to me that out of all the scholars and poets, philosophers, kings and magistrates, God, when he decided to have a Flood and start all over again, chose to save only a happy drunk, Noah; and you had only to spend a little time round Teddy to see why. There was not an ounce of vice in him and he was at his happiest when he was giving something away.

The city in which he lived was the last refuge in a busy world for the blades and, while it made for a very amusing and exciting life, it created havoc with the liver. All the action went on in the pubs and clubs with which the city abounded. In the morning when I stepped out of my hotel I could riffle through the watering holes in my mind to decide in which of the many pockets of resistance to boredom I would pass my day. While this was very good for the soul, it did little for a freelance reporter professionally. I tried ordering soft drinks but when you did nobody took any notice. A subterfuge was necessary. Mine was to strike a bet with my friend, Robin, that the first one of us to take a drink for a month would pay the other one hundred pounds. Since Robin managed the biggest hotel in the city we had a saving clause inserted in the bet that drinks with meals were permitted. The plan worked admirably with most of my friends, to whom wagers were sacred, but I had no chance at all with Teddy.

He had been buying drinks all round for some time in a favourite oasis and was fretting visibly at my tonic water.

'You aren't ill, are you?' he inquired concernedly.

'No, Teddy, it's a bet, that's all.'

Two tonics and considerable frets later, he asked the terms of the wager and I told him. He was interested at once because it presented a challenge to his generous heart. I did not notice him leave the bar, because he was never a noisy man, but presently he returned and said : 'The Joe Baxi is outside. Come on!'

I had no idea what he was talking about but the idea offered diversion, the tonic water was burying daggers into the wall of the throat, so I went with him to the taxi he had summoned to the pub.

After a number of the sort of bizarre diversions that were inevitable on any adventure undertaken in the company of Teddy we arrived at a Chinese restaurant.

In a city of big spenders Teddy stood shoulder-high and we did not have to wait too long for a waiter.

'Two plates of fried rice and a bottle of brandy,' said Teddy, and when they came he smiled happily for the first time for several minutes.

'Now you can drink with a clear conscience,' he said.

Then he looked at the rice despondently.

'Did I ever send that money to your friends in India?' he asked.

I poured us two generous measures of the brandy to take away the taste of the rice.

'You wouldn't forget,' I told him, 'not you.'

'Nice people, are they?'

'I shouldn't think so.'

'Aw, well. Mox nix. Want some of this rice?'

The battle, meanwhile, was not going well for Tony and when I next called at his house by the river the scene that met me could only have been reproduced by Cruikshank. There were patches of clean wallpaper where pictures had been, the telephone had been disconnected and the carpets were rolled up against the walls. Tony was in the drawing room. The electricity had been cut off and the only light came from a single silver candlestick on a coffee table next to a half-empty bottle of South African brandy. Tony looked the picture of dejection as he waved me to a chair and pushed the bottle towards me. 'Oh, Skiddy,' he sighed. 'What am I to do?' He was a good friend and, if I could, I would have given him a cheque to settle his debts right there, but there was not that much money in the account. I doubt if there was even that much money in the bank so all I could give him was sympathy.

'Don't worry, old chum,' I said, trotting out the clichés. 'The only way now is upwards.' He gave me a puzzled look.

'What the hell are you talking about?' he said. 'Up? What's all this Up business?'

'Well, you know…' – 'No, I don't.'

'I mean you're on the floor now but you can beat it. You can fight back, you can ...' My voice trailed off when I saw the expression on his face.

'I'm not talking about that,' he said, dismissing his problem. 'Jill wants to go to Spain but it always gives me bad guts. I'd rather we went to the South of France.' I was aghast.

'But you can't be thinking of holidays now!' I told him in a shocked yelp.

He looked at me, pityingly.

'Can you think of a time when I will need one more?'

Some weeks later I went to the station to see him off on the London train. It was late, of course, the day was drizzling and tendrils of mist wrapped themselves round the piled luggage on the trolleys.

Tony was standing at the end of the platform. The velvet collar of his coat was curling into the dank curls at the back of his neck and the button was still missing. His Russian wolfhound was shivering unhappily at his side, as it always did when confronted with outdoors in any proportion. The lead, a piece of red solicitor's tape unwrapped, I supposed, from a writ, was clutched in his left hand and tied to the hound's collar. It did not look a very substantial lead but it always took massive encouragement before the dog would move anywhere and I suppose it merely served to prevent it from falling over. Under his left arm he had a delicately carved Adam fireplace and his smile when he saw me lit up the whole of the station.

'How very nice of you,' he said. 'I was feeling a bit lonely.'

'How are you?' I asked.

'Never better,' he assured me. 'I have very high hopes for the future. When we get back from the South of France I've got an interview for a job with EMI.'

'Marvellous, I said. 'I'm very glad for you.'

'Yes,' he said. 'They are looking for a new chairman.'

He did not get the job, which surprised both of us.

Take Two

When The Symposium closed its doors for the last time we floated from bar to bar for several weeks seeking a congenial background until we settled at last for the Little Rubber. I cannot recall the name that was printed on the club notepaper because nobody ever called the tiny club on the top floor of a two-storey milk bar anything else but the Little Rubber.

The argot of the racetrack was the lingua franca of our world; a mixture of Hebrew, rhyming slang, Romany and inventive wit. A gin was a Godfrey Wynn, a girlfriend whose name was Pearl was always known as Disaster because that was what Pearl Harbour had been and 'Lillian Gish and a Bundle of Jockey's Whips' sounded somehow more exotic than 'fish and chips for one'. A club was 'Rubber-Dub'.

The leader of our band was a bookmaker, Willie Birchall. The worst time of all for Willie and his friends was the hard winter of 1962-63 when all racing was called off and they were reduced to betting on such bizarre sporting events as Jimmy Wilde's annual walking race round the city walls, or how long it would take Cloggy Andrews, a local character, to carry a hundredweight of coal round the racecourse at a brisk trot.

I had been out doing a Hickey piece about the local hunt which began its season with a steeplechase. It was always good for three paragraphs because all the riders were either dukes, millionaires, belted earls or very senior army officers. When I got back to the club Willie, who was at the bar, handed me a welcoming nod and a small Scotch.

'What have you been up to, my son?'

I told him and his interest was awakened.

'Steeplechase?' he asked. 'With real horses?'

I nodded.

'When does this sporting engagement take place?'

'Next Tuesday before the opening meet.'

'I'll make a book on it,' said Willie.

I gave him a whole handful of reasons why he couldn't and ended by saying if he did I'd write a story about it. I could imagine the salty comments I could collect from the local blue bloods when they found themselves written up at short odds on a blackboard in the window of Willie's betting shop. Though I must say that Dandy Nat made a very fine job of the lettering and I was interested to note that the Duke of Westminster had attracted odds of two to one on. My friend Lollipop, a gambling man with a computer mind, thought that Willie had been less than generous in offering Lord Leverhulme at evens but we agreed that, at three to one against, Major General Howard-Wyse was the nap selection of the day.

The news of the race attracted much interest among the excitement-starved punters of the city and I got gratifying shows in every daily newspaper. Even the *Financial Times* carried a paragraph. The next day I heard the sequel from Dandy Nat, who acted as the Damon Runyon of our little world.

'I am sitting quietly, bothering nobody,' says Nat, 'when the office door opens and a blinding flash of silver has us all shading our eyes. It is a young officer in one of those cavalry regiments. And my sympathy goes out to any horse that has got to carry that amount of silver chain, stars, spurs and armament. Including,' says Dandy Nat wonderingly, 'a sword. I thought we were using guns these days. And it is funny about the spurs, too, because I know he comes in a jeep.

'Anyway, the moment Willie lamps the sword he's down behind the counter in less time than it takes Lollipop to work out a Yankee and you can see only his eyes peering over the top. And then this chap with the sword begins to speak. "I am ADC to the GOC," the young man tells us.'

Nat is an excellent mimic and we can see the young man as he speaks. 'And Willie says, "Oh, aye." Everyone is talking initials. It is like swimming in Alphabet soup.

'"The General is very upset about that notice board in your window, the one that is making a book on the Hunt Steeplechase," the officer says. This is an unhappy choice for openers. Criticism of their business activities displeases bookmakers because it is not all that long ago that all off-course betting is illegal and many spend far too long in damp doorways taking furtive bets to relish any attack on their new status.

31

'"I am a licensed bookmaker," says Willie. "And as such I am entitled to offer odds on any sporting engagement I choose which concerns the running of horses, dogs, or, for that matter, young men in rowing boats. And if the General wishes to test the truth of this I suggest that he takes me to the Rooms for arbitration."

'At this point,' said Dandy Nat, 'the young soldier holds up his hands and I can see he is embarrassed.

'"Don't be upset," he tells Willie. "It's not that which is making him angry. You've got him on offer at three to one against and he reckons on his form over the last hunting season he should be evens at worst.

'"Although, personally," says the young officer – and we can see now that he is one of the boys – "if you are going to accede to the General's request I would like a slice of the three to one before the price changes."'

Lollipop had been an interested party to the narrative as it was unfolded by Nat. But the last remark brought an angry snort.

'Isn't that typical?' he demanded. 'There's always one in the stable can't keep his mouth shut. I seen the General out cubbing. Going very well, too. I intended to make a further modest investment myself. But the price is no longer attractive.'

Dandy Nat was very understanding at this outburst of Lollipop's, even though it took some of the shine off the end of his story. Everyone knew that Lollipop's dedication to racing was total. He was a man who did not relinquish an evening easily while it still held promise and there were times when he got home with the dawn. But seven a.m. would find him wide awake with a mug of tea, poring over the form book for two hours until the paper boy arrived with his *Sporting Life*. When he could be prised away from the study of form he was a shrewd observer of life and his advice was always penetrating. Once, after a successful run of stories, I thought I would go respectable and rent an office, perhaps even a typist who could make excuses for me to callers. Lollipop advised against it on the grounds of unnecessary expense.

'Exes ruins all games,' he said briefly, and I have observed a number of nourishing businesses going bankrupt, and countries too, which might still have been with us if that motto had been inscribed over the boss's desk.

For many years the Spring meeting at the local track was the high spot of our social season and we always met half an hour before the first race at Willie's stand on the course. But one year Lollipop, on the eve of the meeting, gave me some surprising news.

'I may have to miss the first race tomorrow,' he said sadly.

I was astounded. He never missed the first race.

'Why?' I asked.

'I'm getting married at two o'clock,' he said. 'It'll be about quarter to three before I can get away.'

'Naturally, I am not going to the reception.'

'Naturally,' I said.

Lollipop's special friend was called 'Bo-Bo', from his habit of falling asleep within five minutes of sitting down anywhere at any time, although on his feet and awake he was as sharp as anyone. Neither looked after his health with any great attention and when another friend died the hint that Time's winged chariot was goosing them brought both men to sober thought. I sat in the back row of the church with them and with Dandy Nat who, though older than any of us, was always the picture of health.

Lollipop, plainly worried, leaned over to me.

'Nip across and ask Arthur how he bets on us.'

Arthur L, who was sitting across the aisle, was a bookmaker whose betting shop was unique in that it was staffed entirely by beautiful girls. It was an eccentricity the other sporting gents viewed with mixed admiration and disfavour. Once when Nat had one of his rare bust-ups with Willie he announced he was looking for another job.

'Come and work for me,' offered Arthur, who was a kindly man, but Nat would have none of the suggestion.

'Work for you!' he said. He was a volatile Geordie whose first job clerking had been at Blaydon Races. 'Work for you? The only feller that has got a chance of a job with you is Danny-La-Bleedin-Rue!'

Arthur made room for me in his pew across the aisle and after I had identified the only girl in the congregation that he did not already know he turned his attention to my request for a show of odds on our party.

'Bo-Bo? Two to one on, although he sleeps so much we may have to have a saliva test,' he told me judiciously. 'Lollipop. Mmm. Carrying fourteen stone, doesn't look after himself too well. I'll give evens, tell him.'

'But what about Natty? He's older than any of us?'

'Natty? Two pints every evening. Home. Feet up. Out for the last hour. Bo-bo's by midnight. Live for ever. Ten to one against.'

I was returning across the aisle with the information when a thought struck me and I hurried back. 'You?' said Arthur, patting my billowing belly. 'You're joint favourite!'

Willie never went to anyone's funeral, he was far too involved in life, and he took a very jaundiced view of anyone who tried to pull down the curtains before the last act. The unluckiest punter in the city, after an appalling run of luck, decided to end it all by hurling himself from the highest buttress of the city walls. It was a carefully thought out demise because a canal flowed at their foot and the punter reasoned that if he did not dash his brains out on the rocks below the walls he would roll into the canal and drown. In the event he broke his arm on the rocks, rolled into the canal and was saved by a passer-by.

'Poor kid,' said Willie when he was told. 'Can't even back a winner committing suicide.'

He did rip up all the punter's IOUs and give him extended credit for the future because that was the way he was; but his tongue and his heart were strangers to each other and he could be very harsh in conversation. The manager of our local football team once asked Willie if he was going to watch that weeks' home game.

'Why should I?' Willie demanded. 'They didn't come and see me when I was bad. I'll tell you the truth, my son. If they were playing in our front garden, I'd draw the curtains.' He was equally caustic when Lollipop broke the news that he was marrying for the second time.

'My son,' he told him, 'the man who marries twice didn't deserve the good fortune of getting rid of the first one.'

He once had trouble on the phone with a lady secretary in a binocular firm. Courteously he asked for the manager to be brought and he told him: 'I've just been talking to your beautiful secretary.'

'How do you know she is beautiful? You've only talked to her over the phone?' the manager asked.

'There is no other way she could have got the job,' Willie explained bitterly.

During the middle ages Richard II had hired men from our city, as I came quickly to think of it, for assassination and intimidation. In reward, the city that bred these medieval mafiosi was declared outside the law and a brisk trade was done in providing lodgings for some of the worst cut-throats of the period. As a result, some local criminals could trace their pedigrees back for nearly five hundred years, and the probation officer had a private Debrett of the hundred best criminal families. Their unquestioned leader – and one of the most agreeable of companions – was called the Count because of his resemblance to an Irish singer of his day who had been elevated to that office by the Pope.

The Count was self-educated and a mine of the esoteric scraps of knowledge that this system produces. One fact, which he had read in a book by Hemingway, had worried him all his life and coloured his subsequent social activities. Hemingway wrote that the maximum number of ejaculations the human male could achieve in his life was one million, and the Count calculated in his fifties that he had only seven hundred left. This made him very careful and he spaced his amatory encounters according to a very strict rota, although when he died in prison his closest friend, a confidence trickster with a do-it-yourself knighthood, 'Sir Edgar Rogersby-Vane', claimed that the Count was heavily overdrawn.

'Sir Edgar' for many years made a handsome living by running away with elderly unmarried sisters of some of the best families in our part of the world, although he was always careful to let their relatives know the wedding date and place in plenty of time for them to buy him off. I got to know him when he hit upon a profitable little sideline by tipping off Sunday newspapers so that they could be on hand when he was unmasked. As the years went by I attended so many of these unfinished ceremonies that on one occasion he invited me to be his best man.

He executed many coups which were minor classics and was only once arrested. When he did appear at the Assizes he had luncheon sent in every day to the court from the best hotel in the city, and after he was sentenced a case of claret was delivered to the judge's lodgings with his compliments. The only time his poise ever deserted him was on the day of the Great Train Robbery. He was furious when he came into the Little Rubber.

'Nothing but a set of savages,' he stormed. 'Slashing those mailbags like that!'

We all said that we found his reaction surprising. 'You wouldn't,' he told us with dignity, 'if you'd sewn as many mailbags as I have.'

Sir Edgar invariably represented himself as an Old Etonian and he had memorised the names of the pupils of the time he claimed to have been there from an old year book. He did his homework so well that few of his victims, though themselves frequently Old Etonians, would ever believe that he was not what he said he was.

I often used to think that if some of the higher class of criminals in the city had applied themselves with the same diligence to lawful activities as they did to crime they would have become captains of industry. The 'Professor' was a prime example. He spent every afternoon of his life in the public library reading law because he had a low opinion of local advocacy and preferred to defend himself. He was so successful that often when his companions appeared in the dock and were asked to name their legal representative they asked for 'the Professor', which always made the judge cross.

The city was proud of its Guilds of Freemen who represented every trade that was practised there. In imitation, the thieves had their own informal guild which operated under the guidance of the Head Thief, a resourceful man I used to meet occasionally in the canteen of the magistrates' court. On one occasion I innocently mentioned that I was thinking of buying a TV. He was outraged.

'Don't buy one; I'll get you one from the lads.' He was a very muscular thief and while I did not wish to have to hide the TV every time detective friends called at my home for a drink, I did not want to offend him, either.

'What sort?' I asked, hoping he would name a set I could refuse on technical grounds.

'What sort do you want?'

'What sort have you got?'

'Listen,' he said. 'We don't steal one till we got a firm order.'

Sadly the permissive sixties ate into this mercantile discipline and I realised that my personal immunity was over when my car was broken into and the radio stolen. I sought out the Head Thief and complained.

'I dunno what's happening,' he told me brokenly. 'D'you know, they had my rear reflectors last week. I leave the jam jar at home now and come in on the bus.'

It always amazed me, as I got to know my city, the infinitely varied ways in which its citizens earned their daily bread. Every morning at nine the roads would be jammed with cars and buses bringing the clerks and the shop-keepers, the estate agents and the lawyers, the policemen and the soldiers, to their places of employment. Some time later the rainbow world would emerge for coffee and light refreshment.

My own favourite was Midget Mahoney. I met Midget when his daughter was temporarily blinded in a road accident. With other reporters I called at his terrace house to check certain facts we could not get from the police. It was nearly Christmas, there was no fire in the grate and Midget was avoiding work with impressive diligence. We felt sorry for the child and, as we left, each of us folded a ten bob note into her money box.

I was a bit surprised when a week later one of the tabloids rang to ask me to do an exclusive follow up.

'Apparently,' said the news editor, and I could tell he was deeply moved, 'when the little Mahoney girl received the gift of sight her first wish was to see a circus. All the time she was blind she kept dreaming of a circus she had seen in happier times and it was her great regret that she might never see the tumbling clowns, the lions, the elephants... '

'She was only blind for forty-eight hours,' I interrupted, trying to be helpful. It was a mistake.

'Have you no heart?' he demanded. He was a very sincere person. 'Forty-eight hours, forty-eight years. What does it matter how long it was before she emerged once more into God's good light? Get her a circus. And don't forget the Arab horses. She is very strong on Arab horses.'

'Who told you?'

'Her father. A man of great sensitivity. He could teach you a great deal.'

I knew then that Midget and I were going to see a great deal of each other in the future. For I remembered reading the day before of a crippled girl in London who had been taken to the ballet by the *Daily Express*. Midget had good script writers.

'What do you want me to do?' I asked, admitting defeat.

'Take her to a circus?'

'Take her to a circus? We are a national newspaper not a bloody theatrical ticket agency. I want you to bring a circus to her. I want the street outside her house filled with the gay throng of circus. I want clowns, tumblers, acrobats. And don't forget the Arab horses...'

'I know,' I said. 'She's very strong on Arab horses.'

All circuses employ advance publicity men who precede the show into a town to get publicity by any means available, and my friend Barney Carn was the best of them. If Barney had been about in biblical days he would have hustled a much better show than Exodus got for Moses in the Old Testament, and probably pictures too, especially of the incident at the Red Sea.

When I put my problem to him and told him that the story and pictures were booked for a double-page spread Sunday for Monday, he offered me my pick of the show. The lions were out of the question, of course, but we were able to come to terms for an elephant, a llama, two clowns, a juggler and assorted show girls.

'How about Arab horses?' I asked.

'You sure it's getting a double-page spread?'

'Sunday for Monday, guaranteed.'

37

'Friday for Saturday is better.'

'Small papers, Saturday. Too much competition for space. You'll get a better show Sunday for Monday.'

'You can have two and I'll throw in a Shetland pony that tells fortunes,' he agreed.

'Done,' I said. And I was.

Midget's daughter slept through the show we put on in the street outside her house but we were able to wake her up for the pictures. By some panchromatic miracle the yawn she produced as the camera shutter clicked was transformed when the picture came out to an expression of wide-eyed wonder.

But Midget enjoyed the show hugely and I could see he was itching to get back to his *Daily Express* to see what further stunts he could adapt to his own end.

When I read in the *Express* that a drowning man had been saved in Scarborough harbour by an angler who had cast his fishing line out to him and hauled him in, I knew that phone calls were imminent.

'We've got this good tip,' the *Daily Sketch* man told me. 'Somebody's been saved from drowning in your river. Apparently some angler threw his line to him. Funny, it seems familiar somehow.'

I could have told him why, but an order meant three pounds so silence really was golden.

Midget was nowhere to be seen when I arrived at the river bank but I saw a group of people surrounding a frogman who was waving his arms and shouting.

'*Daily Sketch,*' I told him. 'What happened?'

There was steam coming off his wet suit and his face was ochre with rage.

'What happened? What happened? I'm swimming along under water bothering nobody when all of a sudden this fisherman cast his line out. It wrapped round me like a tentacle. I couldn't move me arms. Then the silly bastard let go of the rod and the rest of the line wrapped round me legs. I nearly fucking drowned. That's what happened. And if I can lay my hands on the stupid sod I'll rip him to pieces.'

When the fuss died down and the crowd moved away I picked up the discarded rod and walked up the groves looking for Midget. I found him pressed against the wall of the public lavatory block, peering furtively round the corner to make sure the frogman had flipped off.

'I believe this belongs to you,' I said, handing him the rod. 'And if you ever do anything like that again, I'm going to assemble this rod and insert it inch by inch up your jacksie. And what's more, I'm going to leave the hooks on.'

'Don't you think it will make a story, then?' whimpered Midget.

'It will if I tell that frogman who it was nearly drowned him.'

The next time I saw Midget he told me that he had given up the tipping game.

'They sent me five quid for that last one and I've invested the money in a camera. I'm going to be a freelance photographer. But don't worry,' he added magnanimously, 'I'll not steal any of your markets.'

Midget's debut as a photographer puzzled five picture desks and caused considerable confusion to many. His diligent study of the *Daily Express* had shown him that pictures of animals were held in high esteem. It was logical, therefore, that his first call should be at our local zoo.

'You're a what?' asked the Curator of Mammals, Reggie Flowers.

'A press photographer,' insisted Midget, brandishing his Kodak Brownie as proof.

Reggie's surprise was understandable. Nobody could accuse press photographers of over-formality of dress, but even by their standards Midget was no Brummel. His hair was surmounted by grease so thick that it served as a hat. In fact if Midget had dived in after the frogman I could have written a story about an oil slick threatening the swans. His stubble might have done duty as a beard but I could see where Midget's habit of wearing two raincoats, summer and winter, would have thrown a man as fastidious as Reggie. However, the zoo had a tradition of helpfulness to all press photographers and Reggie was not about to turn one away on sartorial grounds.

'There's not much in at the moment,' he told Midget. 'But we are expecting six white rhinos next week. Like to come back then?'

'Roger,' said Midget, because that is what he had heard a photographer say.

'Reggie, actually,' the curator told him helpfully. I had a call the next week from three puzzled picture editors and their query was identical.

'D'you know a freelance called Mahoney?'

I said carefully that I had met someone called Mahoney: why?

'He's just offered us a picture of six white urinals. Do you think he's taking the piss?'

Sadly Midget did not make it as a photographer, nor did he marry a princess, nor experience any of the other nice things that constantly seemed to be happening to photographers, some of them much scruffier than Midget, about that time. But for years after I could trace his progress by the sort of stories that news desks ordered. When he was temporarily employed at the barracks there was a rush of army stories. Then, abruptly, just about the time the CO was muttering dangerously about commies in the camp disclosing military secrets, I was sent on a number of minor scandals in local government and I knew that Midget had joined the council. In those years I became an expert on the city's parks, the aircraft factory in the suburbs, the steelworks, even, improbably, the army recruiting centre across the road from my flat.

'Not joined up, have you?' I asked Midget when next we met. I had become by this time very fond of him.

'Temporary civilian clerk,' he said.

Midget, according to his own lights, was an honourable man and as the years went by he would always ask my advice before putting up a tip and I was able to censor some of his wilder ideas. In the end he became a useful informant and he discovered many very good stories. By this time I had built up a fairly comprehensive information service of my own in return for judiciously placed bottles of good cheer and little green pictures of the Queen. It did not always work to my advantage.

'Thanks for that accident tip,' I told a road sweeper one day. It hadn't made the paper but I prepared to hand over a ten shilling note as a gesture of good will.

'Don't pay us,' he said. 'Just give us half a dollar apiece for the kids.'

'How many have you got?'

'Eight,' he said.

Informants were necessary because I was getting a great deal of aggravation from the local linage pools. Things got so bad, indeed, that I used to go often to Chester zoo and play with a baby gorilla who became a fast friend. I would buy him the odd ice-lollipop. He liked the ones that were chocolate-covered best, but friendship is never cheap, and we would play about and wrestle on the green lawn in front of his quarters on long evenings after the zoo had closed.

'You're very fond of him, aren't you?' asked Reggie Flowers.

'He's the only bastard in this city who ever looks pleased to see me,' I told him.

I always had bad luck with animals, the baby gorilla apart.

'It's a diabolical liberty,' said Paddy, who hired out rowing boats on the river. 'My caterpillar's been banned from that pub on the river.'

He showed me the caterpillar. It was all of seven inches long; it had a face like a hung-over rhino and looked like a mobile phallus.

'Kid found it and I swapped it for an hour on a rowing boat. It gets lonely down here and I've always fancied a pet,' he explained.

'How did it come to be banned?'

'Diabolical liberty, if you ask me. When we closed last night I took it down to the pub when I went for me gargle. Put it on the bar and three punters left their drinks and scarpered. Next thing I knew me and the caterpillar are both out in the street. Landlady said I was bad enough on my own without bringing a caterpillar to help me frighten away custom.'

'Tell you what,' I said. 'Take it down again tonight about six o'clock. I'll arrange to be there a little before you and I'll do a story.'

The landlady came over as soon as I formed up at the bar.

'Thought you'd be here as soon as I threw Paddy out. I suppose you're going to do a story?'

I admitted my intentions, pointing out there was no such thing as bad publicity.

'There is if it's a managed house,' she said. 'My area manager'll be down on me like a ton of bricks if I get in the papers for banning anyone. Even that horrible monster.'

'Paddy's all right,' I defended him.

'He isn't, but on this occasion I was referring to his caterpillar,' she explained. 'Do me a favour. Get it banned somewhere else. What about your mate, Arthur, at the Bear? He's a tenant. He can do what he likes.'

Now I'm very fond of the Bear and Billet but Arthur had customers that would frighten any caterpillar in the universe and I doubted if Paddy's monster would even be noticed. My worst fears were realised when I rehearsed Arthur in his part.

'Bar Paddy? Why?' he asked. 'He's a nice feller. Besides, I like caterpillars.'

'You like everyone,' I told him crossly, and explained my reasons for the request. At length he agreed on the understanding that Paddy would realise there was nothing personal meant.

Things went wrong from the very beginning.

Arthur, when he raises his voice, is a formidable creature. 'Get that bloody thing out of here,' he roared. 'It's horrible.' And two of his regulars immediately stood up and hurried their birds out of the door.

'I'll have no bleedin' trade left,' said Arthur, aggrieved.

In the end I was able to get enough for a piece and I put it all round in time for the edition. Everything would have gone perfectly except that the *Mirror* rang up the pub for an additional quote from the landlord. Unfortunately Arthur's elderly mum answered the phone and she was very upset; when they asked her about the ban on the caterpillar.

'Oh, you don't want to take any notice of that,' she assured them. 'It's just one of Skiddy's little jokes.'

I had a hairy five minutes the next morning explaining my little joke to the news editor and it was some days before I could bring myself to go near Paddy's landing stage. When at last I did he waved me over.

'Been looking for you everywhere,' he told me. 'Got a good follow-up to the caterpillar story.'

'Tell someone else. I'll give you the phone number of the linage pool.'

'No, it's straight, this. The morning that story appeared I had a phone call from this zoologist at Liverpool University. Apparently the caterpillar was a very rare one and the moth is even rarer. The trouble is, according to this zoologist, the moth is so big and it flies so fast few people have caught one. It crashes right through the bottom of their butterfly nets. So I've let them have my caterpillar and they're going to try to keep it until it hatches.' It sounded too good to be true but when I checked with the zoologist he confirmed what Paddy had said.

'If they don't break through the net they hit it with such force that they are useless as specimens,' he explained.

Worth a par, I thought. But when I rang the *Mirror* the news editor answered and I could tell he had not forgotten the earlier piece.

'What is it now?' he asked, a trifle heavily.

'Wrong number,' I said, and rang off.

Not only is the truth stranger than fiction; it's a good deal harder to sell.

I needed informants because our police force would lie blandly that all was quiet if the charge room was knee-deep in bodies.

The land agent of one of the county's better known statesmen rang me one day in a fury:

'Sir John is very disappointed that there was nothing in the paper about his stabbing,' he complained. I shared Sir John's disappointment. Apart from his position in the government and the county, he was an amiable and courteous man and no reporter ever left his door unslaked.

'I didn't know he had been stabbed.'

'Last Wednesday. Very bad, too. He's still in the cottage hospital.'

'Could I see him?'

'Why not? He's bored to death. Might cheer him up a bit.'

Sir John was in sparkling form.

'Never been stabbed in my own knot garden,' he told us cheerfully. 'Damn bad do. Came charging across the flower beds waving his knife like a thuggee. Got me in the shoulder. Inch lower, the doctor says, and there'd have had to be a by-election.'

'Bad do.'

'Certainly was, my boy. Ruined a beautiful bed of antirrhinum. Maniac, according to the police. Thought it was the Leader of the Opposition meself.'

The news caused consternation in the offices. News editors, who had long reconciled themselves to the reticence of our police force, felt that passing mention ought to have been made of the attempted murder of one of the country's leaders. A deputation was formed to take the Chief Constable out to lunch and point this out to him.

He was impressively contrite.

'Thought about telling you, y'know,' he admitted. 'Decided against it, though. Feller's a bit of a publicity seeker.'

The Chief Constable had brought a senior magistrate who was also a considerable landowner to the luncheon with him. We had brought 'Rosie' Field, a vintage crime reporter to whom everything was potential copy. The landowner and Rosie got on famously and it was not long before he was explaining his unique system of dealing with offenders in his court.

'Astrology. Beats all your probation officers and that social inquiry nonsense. Ask the feller his birthday, then put him down while I work out this chart. Tells me all I want to know about him and I sentence accordingly.'

I resisted the temptation to write a story about this unusual method of dispensing justice since it had been very much an off-the-record occasion. No such niceties restrained Rosie and that weekend his paper carried a large piece with a headline on the lines of 'No Wonder Justice Is Blind – It's Got Stars in its eyes'.

I was forced to ring the landowner for his comments.

'Don't ask me,' he said mournfully. 'Had the Lord Chancellor's office on the phone four times since breakfast,' he told me. 'If I'd known what was going to happen I'd never have talked to the feller.'

Rosie was not famous for his tact. He was not a handsome man and we were all puzzled by his relationship with the beautiful daughter of a publican.

I met them at a party once. The beautiful lady was sitting in an armchair. Rosie was perched on one arm. I sat on the other marvelling at this unlikely duo. Leaning over to borrow a cigarette Rosie could see I was puzzled.

'Not screwing her, you know,' he told me in a voice that silenced the room. He patted her arm. 'Too much respect for her.'

Take Three

Four times a year the Assize Circuit visited our city and I took my place in the press box with a sense of happy anticipation. The Assize Court was theatre at its most impressive. The judges paraded in state, preceded by massed bands, from the cathedral to the courts; there were trumpeters and a guard of honour and during the three weeks that followed every policeman in the city brought the traffic to a halt and saluted the Judge's Rolls Royce when it passed, whether there was a judge in it or not.

The little inns round the Assizes were filled with bewigged officers of the court and bemused bit players in courtroom dramas. Criminals gave impromptu press conferences in bar parlours, elderly barristers, sherry in hand and cigarette ash flouring their waistcoats, told wildly funny anecdotes with superb timing. Some, I fancy, are still telling the story of the time Mrs Weybridge decided to murder her husband.

Mrs Weybridge was an attractive, neighbourly woman in her late thirties; her husband a taciturn and untidy man. Subsequently the court was able to pinpoint exactly the moment that Mrs Weybridge first plotted his death. It was immediately after a Z-Cars episode in which a man was poisoned by the introduction of rat poison into his custard. The court knew because it heard evidence that after the episode Mrs Weybridge had called to her neighbour over the garden fence:

'Do you think rat poison would taste, in custard?'

The neighbour said she thought it would, because custard tasted funny even if you only burned the bottom of the pan. Mrs Weybridge was not to be put off. Some weeks afterwards she was at the garden fence again. This time she asked her neighbour if she knew where she could borrow a gun.

'What do you want it for?' asked the neighbour.

'I'm going to blow the bugger's head off,' said Mrs Weybridge.

The neighbour had a horror of gossip: 'Oh, I wouldn't do that, love. There's bound to be talk.'

Subsequently Mrs Weybridge told a court the reason she was so determined to be a widow.

'Dirty bugger he was. Never had a bath from one month's end to the next. Stank like a rabbit hutch.'

There was a certain amount of sympathy in the court for the deceased, because they had heard that when Mr Weybridge took the only bath that came to public notice, Mrs Weybridge wrapped the bare ends of the television cable round the outlet pipe and switched on the power in the sitting room. It did not kill Mr Weybridge but it certainly put him off taking a bath.

By one of those coincidences that happen only in real life, a new lodger moved in next door to Mrs Weybridge, a man who had just been cleared of the murder of a shopkeeper. The lodger revelled in his notoriety and it was not long before he struck up a garden-fence acquaintanceship with Mrs Weybridge. The friendship warmed, for Mrs Weybridge was an attractive woman, and it was not long before the lodger invited her out.

'Like to,' Mrs Weybridge admitted. 'Don't get much fun in my life. No chance, though. He'd play hell.' She nodded her head in the direction of her house where Mr Weybridge, that unhappy man, was understandably engaged in a never-ending inspection of the plumbing.

'Damn pest, he is. I've been trying to murder him for weeks,' admitted Mrs Weybridge.

'Don't give it another thought,' said the lodger.

That night he hit Mr Weybridge over the head as he returned from work and disposed of the body in a very professional manner. He was caught, of course, and when he came to trial Mrs Weybridge elected to give evidence for the prosecution. At the end of the trial the lodger was sent down for life and I was sent to see Mrs Weybridge by the *News of the World*. She was making tea when I arrived at her neat council house.

'Come in,' she said. 'Will you have a cup?'

'Not on your bloody life,' I told her. 'I was in court.'

She wasn't at all upset.

'It's all right,' she said. 'Look, I'm drinking it myself.'

So we had a cup of tea and settled down for a chat. Something was bothering her and she was pleased to have someone to talk it over with.

'You say you were in court?'

'All through the trial.'

'You heard me giving my evidence, then?'

'I was fascinated.'

'About trying to murder me husband?'

I nodded.

'Well, can you explain these?' she asked, handing me a bundle of envelopes. 'They came the day after my evidence was in the papers.'

'Poison pen letters?' I asked sympathetically. 'I'm afraid they...'

'Poison pen be buggered,' she said. 'They're all proposals of marriage. Aren't people funny?'

'Indeed they are, Mrs Weybridge,' I said. 'And, no thanks, I'll not have a custard.'

Our favourite judge was 'Jimmy' Harness. In his Victorian youth he had been a reporter himself, and if a jury came back unexpectedly, he would always send an usher round to the pub to warn us before he would let them deliver their verdict.

On one hot summer day he was trying a deaf octogenarian on a case of buggery. The sun had been troubling the judge for most of the morning and he had taken to propping up the back of his wig with a pencil so that he could benefit from the cooling draught to his hair. The portly warder in the dock could use no such subterfuge and he had slept heavily through most of the trial. At last it came for the moment of sentence. 'Buggery is an abominable crime,' Jimmy told the accused who was standing anxiously, hand cupped to his ear to catch the judge's remarks. 'And you will go to prison for six months.'

'Eh? Eh? Eh' said the old man in the dock. 'What did ye say? Can't 'ear yer!'

The sun had made Jimmy unusually testy.

'Warder!' he said. 'Will you acquaint...' Then he noticed that the warder was fast asleep and snoring gently.

'WARDER!'

The warder woke up with a grunt and looked severely round the court to see who had upset the judge.

'Warder,' repeated Jimmy in a softer voice. 'Will you acquaint the prisoner with my remarks.'

With massive dignity the warder turned to the accused who was by now cowering in the back of the dock. Fixing him with a magisterial air the warder told him:

'Judge, he says you're an abominable old bugger and you'll go to prison for six years.'

Jimmy raised a hand in mild protest. 'Warder,' he told him gently, 'I have no objection to your paraphrasing my summing up. But you must not increase my sentences.'

Jimmy's career on the bench had been long and distinguished. Years earlier he had served as a judge in the Admiralty Court where he had wrestled unhappily with the technical language of the sea. He had a lot of sympathy, therefore, with the Hull trawler skipper who clearly could not understand a word that was being put to him in the witness box one day during the hearing of a salvage claim.

The bones of the case were that two ships had been steaming line abreast when one had abruptly changed course and rammed the other amidships. The trouble was that the language counsel used in cross examination had totally covered the bones with verbal fat and the trawler skipper, who had been the only outside witness to the incident, was lost. He was the sort of salty skipper who, if you pointed him in the right direction, would have found a harvest of cod in a town hall drinking fountain, but the abstruse technology of the Admiralty court had him banjaxed. Jimmy on the bench realised the skipper's dilemma. He leaned forward and said kindly:

'Captain, no doubt, like me, you are confused by some of the technical terms which, quite properly, learned counsel has put to you in trying to elicit the facts of this case.'

The man who was in the press box when this happened told me that the skipper did not understand too much of what Jimmy had just said. But he recognised the kindly intention and perked up visibly.

'Tha'rt reet there, me Lord,' he said.

'Quite so,' said Jimmy, nodding his head understandingly. 'Now then. How would this be? Forget for a moment the question as it was framed by learned counsel. Tell me in your own words. When you saw one of these two ships, which until then had been proceeding side by side, suddenly change course and ram the other, what were your reactions?'

My friend said that the skipper looked like an abandoned son at the moment of reunion with a loving father. In the strange room where he had been hectored and humiliated, where everyone spoke a language to which Hull was a stranger, he had at last found a friend. He looked up gratefully at Jimmy.

'Well, My Lord,' he said, considering deeply. 'You could have buggered me through me oilskins.'

The law reform that swept away the ancient assize system took away most of the pleasure of the spectator. In the days of the assizes the public gallery was always filled with knowledgeable aficionados. Each counsel had his fans in the gallery, many had been clients and were now watching from the sidelines the dazzling display of verbal footwork that would trap and defeat a witness; somehow these displays do not seem to have survived the birth of the Crown Court. The assize was a caravanserai, which progressed at a stately pace from town to town, with a train of officials and barristers who had become masters at passing long hours in strange hotels, telling even stranger stories. I suppose the new system where the bench has become an up-market social services counter is more efficient but it is certainly not anything like so much fun for the participants. Perhaps because the sombre moments in a court are so deeply tragic, the lighter moments stand out like trees on a skyline. And there was no shortage of them at the Quarter Sessions either.

The sessions chairman, Mr Silver Gilt, QC, was to light moments what a breath of air is to feathers. They danced and soared round his head from the moment he sat at the bench.

On one occasion he was listening with well-bred disgust – for he was not a man who insulted your intelligence with any nonsense about judicial impartiality – to a case of a minor sexual assault.

He perked up when Sister Anna entered the box. For many years Sister Anna, a minute nun who looked exactly like a tiny penguin as she hustled by, had looked after the welfare of the prisoners who came before the court. She was kind, but she was no fool. If she gave evidence on anyone's behalf then the bench could be sure that there was some scrap of grace somewhere in the accused. Now she spoke warmly on behalf of the man in the dock and I could see that Gilt was impressed.

He addressed himself to the prisoner, motioning gracefully to keep Sister Anna in the box so that she could enjoy the full flavour of the compliment he was minded to pay her.

'Prisoner at the bar,' he said, and his voice was of the tomb. 'It had been my intention to put you away from the temptations which society offers you for a very long time. You are a creature of ungovernable lusts, the prey to irresistible urges... '

He paused and looked meaningfully at Sister Anna. 'However, I have been impressed – as who could fail to be? – by the impassioned words on your behalf spoken by this good lady in the witness box. It is her and her only you have to thank for the course of action I am about to take in this case. And it is to her that any reward is due. I am putting you on probation. But I want you to promise that if ever you feel these lusts mounting in your brain, these appalling sexual urges tightening their grasp, you will rush straight into the arms of Sister Anna... '

I always enjoyed Mr Commissioner Cantaur. He had been a colonial judge among the head hunters of Borneo and no experience could have better fitted him for his present job as special commissioner for divorce on our circuit.

He was a large man with the air of a scholarly tortoise and he spread benevolence over appellant and defendant alike. He was short-sighted, touchingly absent-minded, and any day that contained him also contained much of humour.

Some of the barristers on our circuit were notoriously long-winded and many of the divorce hearings lasted longer than the marriages. However, when Mr Cantaur was presiding, it was advisable to get seats pretty early in the hearing to be sure of a good place. On the last occasion I was in his court he was struggling with a cobra of a case in which a man of seventy-nine was being sued for divorce by his sixty-five-year-old wife on the grounds of adultery. The consensus of opinion in the court was that any man of his age would offer no rebuttal of such a compliment but in this case there were special circumstances. The adultery had been committed thirty years earlier with a woman who was now dead. It had never been condoned because the wife knew nothing of the lapse until, at the age of seventy-eight, her husband, understandably, bragged about it. The wife's answer was to petition for a divorce.

Next to the court was a small Georgian public house called the Golden Eagle. The landlord, Harry Daniels, had known most of the High Court judges on the circuit when they were junior barristers and his pub was an unofficial bar mess. But the law in its majestic hypocrisy could not admit to nipping out for a swift half of Bass. Only the initiated knew what was afoot when an officer of the court announced that he was about to appear before Mr Justice Daniels in the Court of Common Sense. But, fond as I was of that court, wild horses would not have dragged me out of the real court when Mr Cantaur was presiding and I think my devotion pleased him. Only two yards separated the press bench from the judge's dais and he took to nodding at me from time to time. He even gave me a special little bow after the one he made to the court every morning when he took his place on the bench.

At last came the day of his judgment in a particularly complex case, and I sat, four sharpened pencils at the ready and thought, as I always did before a prolonged bout of note taking, of my friend Petts.

Petts was gifted with the tongue of angels but he could not master shorthand. The tongue got him a job as court reporter for a news agency in the Midlands but the pen was unequal to the task. It was dreadful luck that on his first day in court the official shorthand writer should be taken ill.

Petts saw this event, as indeed he saw most events, as the opportunity for a cough and a drag, and he was just sliding off the press bench as discreetly as possible when the judge spoke. Something happens to reporters the moment they are spoken to by judges. Petts became rooted to the spot, half crouching like a hunted hare.

'Mr Reporter,' said the judge, and Petts had the uncanny feeling of a playgoer being spoken to across the footlights by one of the characters in a play.

'Mr Reporter,' said the judge, 'I'm afraid the shorthand writer may be indisposed for some time and I have been told that it will be impossible to replace him until after the lunch-time adjournment. Would you be kind enough,' he asked, 'to take his place until the replacement arrives?'

The suggestion would have upset a seasoned court reporter: to Petts it was as bad as a sentence of death. But there was no way out. He edged slowly from the press bench and shut himself in the small enclosed desk at which the shorthand writer worked. To compensate for his lack of shorthand Petts had speeded up his longhand and he was able to take a decent note as long as the speaker did not go on for too long. But barristers are infrequently brief. After an hour Petts was hopelessly lost, and wishing the shorthand writer's disease, even if it were fatal, was also infectious and that he could catch it. His only consolation was that shorthand writers were seldom asked to read their notes in open court.

At first when the judge called on him he pretended not to hear, but the words were repeated, this time a touch testily, and he thought it politic to look up.

'Mr Shorthand Writer,' said the judge, 'there is some dispute about whether the witness saw the accused or whether she merely said that she had been told of his visit. It would be of great assistance to the court if you could refresh our memory from your notes.' So saying, the judge settled back expectantly, hands clasped in a steeple before him and elbows on the arms of his chair. Petts knew as he looked down at his notebook that it was hopeless. He could not read a word he had written. The court was silent as he frantically turned the pages looking for some calligraphic landmark he could recognise. Finally he closed the book and looked wildly round the court for a friendly face. He saw amusement and impatience but no sign of compassion.

'You appear to be in some difficulty?' asked the judge.

'I-I-I'm afraid I'm not used to this,' stammered Petts.

'I do understand,' said the judge kindly. 'It must be very difficult to be suddenly thrust into the limelight in this fashion. However, it is almost time for the lunchtime adjournment. Accordingly I shall rise now to give you an opportunity to transcribe your notes at greater leisure.'

He stood up. The clerk intoned: 'The court stands adjourned until 2pm' and Petts was led to a ground floor office by an usher. As the door closed behind him, Petts pictured the scene after lunch when he would have to confess that he had no note of the morning's proceedings. He looked round the room, a pleasant office on the ground floor. There were homely traces of a man who worked there; a box of matches, a snapshot in a leather frame and an ashtray with little grey hillocks of ash. Petts cursed the self-delusion that had lured him into journalism, a trade for which he was clearly unfitted. He wished he too had a little office and an ashtray with the pleasant lunchtime noises of the town floating through his window. Miserably he took a chair and stared out of the open window.

Some time later the door of the office began to open and Petts thought of what was before him. In the same instant he knew what he had to do. In a flash he was on his feet and the court usher opened the door just in time to see Petts jumping out of the window.

The last the news agency heard of Petts was a telegram received that afternoon. It read: 'Heading South. Regrets. Petts.'

'...In this case,' the voice of Mr Commissioner Cantaur broke in on my thoughts, 'I am asked to decide an issue of bewildering complexity. It is an issue between an aged gentleman and a wife who is only a little younger than he.'

It was some moments before I realised that Mr Commissioner Cantaur was waffling and that something was terribly wrong. The sight of the court keeper running out of the court confirmed it. He was a large man and he never ran anywhere unless it was to Mr Daniels' Court of

Common Sense, which rose at 3pm sharp. I caught him up just as he was getting into the commissioner's Rolls.

'Bit of a flap,' he told me. 'He's forgotten his judgment. Left it in the dressing table at his hotel. Come and give us a hand to find it.'

Although High Court judges either memorised or extemporised their judgments in criminal cases, in civil actions judgments were always written down and read.

'He reckons he can keep going till I get back but I don't want to leave the poor bugger too long,' said the court keeper as we swept out of the court precincts.

We had a police escort and we arrived at the hotel behind screaming sirens. The entry was deliberately impressive because judges are traditionally cushioned with a conspiracy of loyalty by court officials and the court keeper was not going to let the manager know about the Commissioner's lapse.

'I am the Keeper of the Court,' he told the manager sternly. 'On the instructions of the Judge I must ask you to let me have the keys to Room 14.'

He was an impressive figure in his frock coat and the manager handed them over at once.

'What's the matter?' he asked nervously, but the court keeper quelled him with a glance.

'I am not at liberty to discuss the business of the court,' he told him as we made for the lift.

'I quite understand,' said the manager, hovering round the door of room 14, watching the court keeper open the dressing table drawer.

In after years, the court keeper reckoned it was the worst moment of his life when he opened the bachelor judge's drawer and was confronted by neatly folded sateen knickers, capacious petticoats and rows of sensible lisle stockings. In his mind's eye he saw the Commissioner pursuing ample ladies in sateen knickers round his bedroom, rouged, or worse, powdered, in a shell pink petticoat, as a diversion from browsing through *The Times* law reports. The voice of the manager broke his dream.

'If only you would tell me what you are looking for...'

The court keeper was beyond pretence. 'I'm looking for some papers the judge left,' he admitted.

'Well, I don't know why you are looking in here,' said the manager. 'The judge is in room 9.'

When we got back to the court Mr Commissioner Cantaur was

ploughing on bravely but he was obviously worried and he kept looking anxiously, if a little furtively, for the court keeper.

'Much play,' he was saying, 'has been made of the wound received by the appellant on the forehead. Not unnaturally, when he examined it, counsel for the appellant described it as a deep wound. Equally understandably counsel for the defendant described it as a scratch.'

Once again a quick look round the court and then he plunged bravely on.

'I was invited to arbitrate but I could see nothing at all. That is hardly surprising. Had the wound been large enough for me to see it, then it would undoubtedly have proved fatal and this issue would have been settled in a higher court than mine.'

There was a gratifying laugh at this sally and the Commissioner beamed down at counsel. But I noticed his eyes had the desperate look of a commissioner who has totally forgotten the names of either of the parties who are appearing before him. His look of relief as the court keeper laid the judgment discreetly before him was touching to see.

I sympathised with his dilemma when I came to write up my story from his judgment. Normally I put my piece over from a phone in the corner of the bar of Mr Daniels' court but I thought that on this occasion I would write it. That would have been difficult in the pub so I walked to the quietest hotel I knew, forgetting completely that it was the same one at which the Commissioner was staying.

The lounge was deserted and after much pen sucking I got the story down to the sixteen paragraphs that was the absolute maximum I could get past the desk.

'It took three paragraphs to tell the story of the Creation,' my old news editor had always insisted. 'There's nothing you can't tell in two folios.'

As I put my copy over from the flimsy glass telephone box in the hotel lobby I was not happy; I'd missed out a great deal I would rather have left in. Halfway through the dictation I paused and looked out of the window and what I saw had me squeaking like new shoes. Across the lobby Mr Commissioner Cantaur was staring at me intently. He could obviously hear every word I was saying and he was shaking his head. I must have got the judgment wrong. I turned back quickly and gabbled the rest of the story at a speed that had the copy-taker threatening to pull the plug on me. I did not care. I just wanted to get out. As soon as I had finished I darted out of the phone box and into the cocktail bar.

My hand was shaking as I raised my glass, but I spilled most of it when, over the rim, I saw Mr Commissioner Cantaur in the doorway. He was still shaking his head and I knew that he was keeping an eye on me until the tipstaff arrived. I drank what little whisky was left in the glass and darted out past him. But his voice followed me.

'You, young man,' he said. 'Just stop a minute.' Instinctively I obeyed him because he was a judge and I had covered enough courts to know his powers. I waited, trembling, until he came up to me.

'You know,' he said, 'I'm absolutely sure I've seen you somewhere before. But for the life of me I cannot remember where it can be.'

Take Four

Very few people got the better of the Wicked Squire, and that included the Japanese High Command, two generations of poachers, practically every department of government, and the floor-walker in a very smart London department store.

The Wicked Squire, his own nickname for himself, affected to be puzzled at his reputation as a force to be reckoned with. He would sit in his chintz armchair – 'Don't sit there,' he always warned visitors. 'My kennel, you know. Like a dog. Don't feel easy anywhere else' – and gaze out of the drawing room windows across the acres of park and the home farm, which he had fought like a tiger to free from the encumbrances inherited from his ancestors.

'A child could have its way with me,' he assured us, at which his young wife, the prettiest woman in three counties, would snort amiably; 'Provided it was nine feet tall and carrying a sub-machine gun.'

The Squire's great talent was a gift for getting in the last crusty word. It was never better used than it was in the matter of the floor-walker. Floor-walkers in London department stores, in the days when the Wicked Squire entered the lists with one, were daunting men of enormous presence who wore frock coats. And the Wicked Squire was a stripling at the time, which I think entitles him to extra points.

He had been complaining about some omission in service at the store when the floor-walker came up and said with glacial dignity:

'Can I help you, sir?' And you could tell that the 'sir' had been tossed in as an afterthought.

'And who might you be?' inquired the Squireen, equally iceberg-like.

'I am in charge of the floor,' the floor-walker answered in the tones of a Charlemagne.

'Then I should get it swept,' the Squireen advised. 'It's filthy!'

Staying with the Wicked Squire was an undiluted pleasure. There was a bottle of whisky in every bedroom, Malvern water, a selection of crisp new novels, writing paper, hot-water bottles in beds as deep as the Atlantic and, in the dining room, a series of delightful weddings between claret and grouse, port and Stilton, and other such happy unions.

The Squire never believed in placing a duration on a guest's stay. When he considered that both guest and host had extracted the maximum enjoyment from the visit, his manservant, Grout, was sent to the guest room with a book, which he placed on the table.

It was a copy of *Bradshaw's Railway Guide*, and it always worked.

The Squire's great dilemma was that he was very fond of the pheasant, an agreeable bird when not harassed, and he hated them to be shot. Unfortunately, his neighbours had been shooting over his land for centuries and the Squire was very conscious of inherited responsibility. His compromise was to allow shooting over the rest of the estate but to forbid guns in the park that surrounded his house. This accommodation leaned heavily in favour of the pheasant, a sagacious creature, who, sporting men aver, reads the *Shooting Times* and knows exactly when it is safe to parade in the sight of humans and when to make itself scarce. Accordingly, when word got about among the birds on the estate, many made their home in the woods round the house.

This happy arrangement had continued for several seasons until one bright morning the Squire was appalled to hear the crack of a sporting gun, practically under his window. The morning paper he had been reading had scarcely fluttered to the floor before the Squire was down the stairs, out of the garden door and creeping through the woods in the manner that had brought him much respect from Japanese soldiers in Burma. It was not long before he came across the poacher; not one of the country variety for whom he had considerable respect, but what he later described as 'an oily, townie sort of feller, all winkle-pickers and hair grease'.

The Squire believed in civility at all times, but especially in the moments before the kill. 'Good sport?' he asked amiably. He is deceptively slight and the poacher saw no danger in his presence.

'Fair,' he admitted. 'Missed that one, though.'

'I'm sorry to hear it,' the Squire assured him. 'Nice gun, too. Mind if I look at it?' I doubt if a rural poacher would have fallen for it but the man was clearly lulled by the Squire's amiable manner and he handed over the firearm. The Squire examined it appreciatively.

'S'pose you've got permission to shoot here?' he asked.

'Oh, aye. Old chap who owns it is a friend of mine.'

I imagine it was the phrase 'old chap' that put the cork in.

'I doubt that,' snapped the Squire, 'because I happen to be that old chap. And even if you were a friend of mine, which is so unlikely as to be laughable, you still wouldn't get permission to start a shooting war under the windows of my house.'

At this point the poacher leaned forward to grab his shotgun but the Squire was too quick for him. There was a tree stump nearby and, holding the gun by the stock, he brought the barrels sharply down on its edge.

When telling the story afterwards the Squire always lingered lovingly over the next bit. He would not allow television in his house because he claimed it was all trash, but he was a secret Western addict, and on the evenings when a particularly good vintage Western film was being shown, he would 'harrumph' quietly to himself for at least a quarter of an hour by the drawing room clock and then, five minutes before the film began, he would announce to the company that he was just stepping down to the housekeeper's room to look at the drains. The housekeeper had no drains, of course, but she did have an elderly TV and was so used to the Squire popping his head round the door at such times that she always had an extra glass of whisky waiting on the TV table.

When the film was over the Squire would return to the drawing room and explain, with the martyred air of which he was a master:

'Damned woman insisted on me watching some rubbishy TV thing. Awful bore but one really cannot afford to upset a good servant.'

'John Wayne, dear?' his admirable wife would ask. Though she loved him and loyally bolstered all his fictions, she did not wish him to think her a fool.

'Who? No idea. Some damned American thing, I suppose.'

But he really gave himself away when he was telling about the poacher in the wood.

'Just like a John Wayne film. Shotgun came down with a crack you could hear in Derby. Barrels spread like a showgirl's legs, 'mazing thing. Cheap gun, of course.'

What the Squire had not realised was that the poacher was not alone, and a second later his companion burst into the clearing, brandishing a second gun which he rammed into the Squire's stomach. 'I'll blow your bloody guts out,' he threatened.

But the Squire had looked down a barrel or two in his day.

'Do,' he said, '...kill me, why don't you?'

'I bloody will,' shouted the second poacher, but he was sounding less sure of himself.

'And do you know what will happen?' asked the Squire.

'What?' The tone was sullen now.

'I'll tell you what will happen. I'll go to heaven with no pain at all, but not you. They'll hang you. You'll be sitting for three weeks in a little cell and then one morning, very early, a priest will call and they'll take you for a walk to a little wooden shed. And they'll stand you on a platform and Albert Pierrepoint will put a noose round your neck, they'll pull a lever and you'll dangle like a broken yo-yo.

'And I'll sit on my little pink cloud and I'll laugh and I'll laugh and I'll laugh... '

'Here,' said the poacher. 'Have the bloody gun.'

Only one fly had worked its way into the amber of the Squire's content. Whenever he prosecuted a poacher his request for costs was always denied.

'Can't expect the county to support men of property,' was the magistrate's invariable reply. 'Request denied.'

It was not the money; it was the principal of denied justice that annoyed him. Personally I've always been grateful to the magistrate because his ruling introduced me to the Squire and brought me a friendship valuable beyond price. For the Squire decided that in future he would cut out the court and fine the poachers himself, sending the money, less his costs, to the charity of the defendant's choice. And I was sent to write the story.

The Squire's approach was unvarying. When he saw a man shooting over his land or fishing his trout stream he would open the conversation with a courteous inquiry about the quality of the sport. It must also be said that if the man was into a fish, or about to take a shot, the Squire would wait until the action was over. Then he would explain his private system of justice and invite a contribution.

It took a brave man to deny the Squire and I wrote the story of the only one who did. He was an assertive man from the Midlands, and since he was safe in the centre of the stream, he refused the Squire's request. When the Squire apparently took his dismissal and left, the angler no doubt thought himself the victor, and as he drove home that night he probably rehearsed the story he would tell his friends.

Certainly he did not notice the large black Bentley motor car that followed his return route. Safely home, he was halfway through his supper when his wife drew his attention to the odd goings-on in the garden.

'There's a man!' she said. 'Eating sandwiches! On our lawn!'

A certain inaccuracy can be permitted the lady. The man was not eating sandwiches. The Squire had set up a small picnic table on the lawn and was spreading pâté on a thin slice of cold melba toast, while his uniformed chauffeur stood at his side pouring a decent little claret into a horn travelling cup.

The Squire waved his toast amiably when he saw that he was observed from the house.

'Evening,' he said. 'You spent all day in my garden; I thought you wouldn't mind if I spent the evening in yours. And, by the way, you've got greenfly in your roses.'

'I'll call the police,' stormed the discomfited angler.

'Wish you would,' answered the Squire. 'Want to give you in charge for poaching. Magistrates round here might take a more sensible view in the matter of costs.'

The angler began to panic.

'How long do you think you're going to stay here?'

'Depends what time you go to work in the morning,' the Squire told him. 'I plan to follow you there, too.'

The prospect of a life spent in being dogged by an outraged landowner was too much. The angler admitted defeat and came out into the garden.

'How much?' he asked resignedly. The Squire thought for a moment.

'Costs are going to be a bit heavy,' he said. 'I've got an expensive Bentley motor car to keep. But I won't charge you for meals; I brought my own. Say a fiver costs and a fiver to the charity of your choice. Gardening advice free, of course, but I really would do something about those roses. Devil of a thing, greenfly.'

'I will,' the angler promised. 'Now, for God's sake, will you go away? The neighbours are beginning to come out.'

'Work of a moment,' the Squire assured him as he trousered the pound notes. 'Just give me a hand with this table, will you? Pop it in the back of the car.'

And raising his hat to the spectators, he strode off down the path.

He waited placidly in the car while the angler stowed the table in the boot and fastened it securely then, with a friendly nod, he waved the chauffeur into action and his motor car glided smoothly down the road.

'You see,' he told the chauffeur, 'there is absolutely no need in life for unpleasantness. I find if you put your point of view with quiet civility the other chap is always ready to see it. Quiet civility. Always been a favourite precept of mine.'

'Yes, Colonel,' said the chauffeur. 'Very true.'

The Wicked Squire was no less severe with authority than he was with the lawless and this was at no time more clearly demonstrated than in the Case of the Customs and Excise and the Shirt-tail.

The Squire lived in a forty-roomed house, his table was of the best and there were blood horses in his stable. But he was, he would tell you with pride, a thrifty man, and when the collars wore out on two sports shirts after only four years' wear, he was incensed. His letter to the manufacturers crackled on the page and the reply was suitably humble. Sadly, the Squire had bought the shirts so long ago that the pattern was out of print, but his humble servants expressed themselves willing to take the amount of cloth needed for repair from the tails of the shirts, replacing the cloth in the tails from existing stocks. The Squire was graciously pleased to accept this ingenious solution and was very pleased with the repaired shirts when in due time they arrived. He was less than pleased with the bill, modest though it was, and expressed himself strongly in a subsequent letter.

'Pray tell me,' he wrote, 'by what flight of bureaucratic avarice I am being dunned for the quite monstrous sum of sixpence-half-penny in customs duty for "replacement cloth for making collars"? I must remind you that the cloth used was taken, as it were, from my own hind quarters.

'This savours of the worst excesses of the *Merchant of Venice*, though I doubt if even Shylock would have insisted his unfortunate creditor pay customs duty on the pound hacked from his living flesh.

'I enclose my cheque in settlement of your bill, less the sixpence-half-penny, which I refuse to pay.'

At this point the shirt-makers' nerve must have broken, because the next letter came from the Customs and Excise, and enclosed with it were four booklets containing the relevant Acts of Parliament governing the sale of cloth. The documents were heavy and the Squire was delighted to note that the postage came to half a crown. He wrote back at once:

'Sir, I claim no great mathematical gift, but it seems to me that you are already showing a loss of one shilling and eleven pence half-penny

61

in your absurd efforts to collect this wholly unreasonable claim. I, too, am out of pocket in the sum of five-pence in stamps.

'May I suggest that this correspondence should cease before you plunge the country into bankruptcy and my estate into irretrievable ruin?'

The correspondence ended then, but it was not a total loss. The Squire used the documents to line the broad bean trench in the kitchen garden that winter, and the next year there was an excellent crop.

We had the first pickings for luncheon and ate them with some ceremony.

'A valuable lesson, my boy,' said the Squire, who was in excellent spirits, 'in how many beans make five.'

The Squire was a man who gave full rein to his teeth and one of his happier offices was the presidency of a venerable dining club.

Once, prompted by some inner gastronomic gypsy, the Club, which for many years had eaten in the same superb restaurant, decided to hire a British Rail dining car for a summer luncheon. The Squire was delighted and personally donated a case of remarkable port to the cause.

The problem of transporting the port, so that it should be in a settled state when the time came to drink it was a thorny one. Finally, after much thought, the Squire decided that I should drive him over with the port some days before the luncheon, leaving it in the station master's office to rest before its great moment. This incident occurred in the days when the station master donned a silk hat to greet members of the peerage and this particular station master raised his in deferential greeting as we approached. Arrangements to store the port were inspected and pronounced satisfactory, but the Squire still looked troubled.

'Is there something else?' the station master asked.

'Matter of fact, there is,' the Squire admitted. 'I wonder, is our engine driver about?'

It was a charming foible of the Squire to become personally possessive of any activity he joined. There would be three or four hundred people on the train, besides the Club, but already it was 'our' engine driver. In the unlikely event of his ever getting on a bus, I am sure that the Squire, on being asked his destination, would give his address. I'm also reasonably sure that the bus would take him there. As it happened 'our' engine driver was about and we were taken to meet him.

'Mornin',' said the Squire. 'I wonder if you could help me.'

He explained about the meal and the port. 'As you know,' he continued winningly, 'we mustn't shake the port or it will be absolutely undrinkable. So I was wondering, when you come to any points, d'you mind going over them slowly?'

And the odd thing was that he did.

The aristocracy do not always get the last word. I was interviewing Anne, Duchess of Westminster, once and the despicable habit of dumping litter in the countryside came up. There had been a recent correspondence in *The Times* in which readers had been advised, if they saw a dumper, to collect his rubbish, drive off after him and hand it back at his house door. The Duchess thought this a very bad idea; the only time she had tried it had been a disaster.

She told me that she had been fishing in Scotland and returned to her car in time to see a family party in an ancient saloon finishing off a picnic in the lay-by. As she watched, the picnickers wrapped their egg shells and crusts, paper plates and mugs into old loaf wrappers and threw them into the hedge. As they drove off the Duchess leapt from her own vehicle, gathered up the debris and set off in pursuit. Some miles down the road she came upon the car, waiting in another lay-by, while an assortment of children did what children always want to do the moment a car starts.

Drawing up behind, the Duchess stepped regally from her own car, the bundle of scraps and rubbish held disdainfully before her, and marched to the car where the driver, a small Glaswegian, was enjoying a cigarette.

'I believe,' she said imperiously, 'that these things belong to you.'

The Duchess is a formidable lady and strong men have been known to quail in her presence. But the little man in the car was not the quailing kind.

'It's all right, hen,' he told her generously. 'You can have them, we've finished with them.'

General Sir Napier Crookenden had a similarly unhappy stroll down the perilous path of good intentions.

The General had organised an exhibition of military silver in aid of the Army Benevolent Fund and he was showing a group of press men round when he stopped before a very expensive-looking golden sword that had been presented to a regiment by a Sultan whose generosity was a legend.

'Can't stand the feller,' the General admitted, and a slight shudder passed over his frame. 'Always giving away gold watches.'

'Not a bad fault to have,' said the man from the *Express,* and the General told us the story.

'I commanded a regiment out there some years ago,' he explained, 'and I was very hot on winning the respect of the local population. When a couple of my soldiers were caught urinating against a mosque wall I threw the book at 'em. Very sensitive about their mosques these Eastern wallahs, and my worry was that news of their dreadful behaviour would get back to the Sultan. Lord knows what would happen then. Holy War at the very least. I thought a bit and decided the best thing was to be the first in, before the Sultan's spies could give him a garbled version. So I sent the prisoners off, under escort, with a note explaining the offence and my punishment, to apologise in person to the Sultan.'

He paused, shaking his head at a painful recollection.

'Unpredictable lot, foreigners. The prisoners were beaming all over their silly faces when they came back. Apparently the Sultan was so struck by their gentlemanly behaviour at owning up to urinating against his mosque that he gave them a gold watch each. Gave one apiece to the escort, too. Bloody fool!'

'Sounds a very decent chap,' protested the man from the *Express.*

'Decent chap? Decent chap?' the General spluttered. 'At my next orderly room there were eight soldiers all charged with urinating against mosque walls, trying to earn themselves gold watches. Went through the regiment like an epidemic. You couldn't step out of your quarters without being confronted by urinatin' soldiery.'

Another general provided me with what I still think is the finest attention-grabbing opening to an after dinner speech I have heard in my life.

'Gentlemen,' he once said at a press dinner as he rose to address us, speech in hand, 'this is the second time today I've got up off a warm seat with a piece of paper in my hand...'

Press conferences were frequent happenings in our ancient city, but those that the Bishop held to announce new endeavours were the most agreeable of all.

'They tell me,' he said, meeting me at the door of Bishop's House on one such occasion, 'that one of the consolations of high office in the Church is the quality of ecclesiastic sherry. I do not drink myself, but pray let me offer you a glass.'

It was not a glass, it was a crystal well, and he filled it until it was brimming, as is the way with people who don't drink themselves and think all liquid is lemonade. I took it apprehensively because the new breathalyser laws had come into force that morning and I wanted them to shake down a little before I tried them. I was sipping cautiously when a bishop from another diocese came over to chat. He eyed the sherry with surprise.

'What on earth are you doing with that?' he asked. 'You're a whisky man!' And before I could protest the sherry was succeeded by an equally large glass, again brimming, but this time with whisky.

The mixture was beginning to settle when the Suffragan Bishop, a homely man, appeared.

'You wouldn't like a bottle of beer, I suppose?' he asked wistfully. 'I can't stand short drinks, but it would look a bit odd if I'm the only one drinking beer. If you asked for a beer, I could have one as well.'

How could I refuse? Minutes later a third party joined the two warring factions in my stomach and my head began to swim.

'Hope I get breathalysed,' I told the man from the *Mirror*. 'Just imagine the magistrate asking how I got into such a disgusting condition. I'll tell him I was drinking with the Bishop of Chester, the Bishop of Birkenhead and the Suffragan Bishop of Stockport.'

The purpose of the press conference had been to announce a series of important changes in diocesan strategy and a full complement of clerics had been summoned. When we were shown into the long room where the conference was to be held, it was already filled with a fair spectrum of the Church from elderly, ascetic, scholarly clerics, through harassed vicars in shiny suits, to trendy young priests. Trendy clerics make me nervous and I looked in relief at the Chapter of elderly Canons who were seated in a row on a bench under the long windows that ran down one wall of the room. They were identical, small, round men, with shiny bald heads. They sat placidly, beaming good will, as the spring sun, its heat magnified by the windows, warmed their pates and they began to doze. The first one succumbed almost at once. His eyes drooped, his head fell forward, and he was away. Sleep spread down the line like easy money. Heads nodded in succession, until each canon was giving off little explosions of contended snores.

Fortunately, the Bishop had his back to them as he announced a series of crusades and a new plan for worker-priest units with which he intended to bring his diocese into the twentieth century. His statistics were impressive, his delivery impeccable and his ideas visionary. When he was finished he offered first his general staff and then the priests the opportunity to add their own ideas. Finally, before it was our turn to ask questions, he bethought himself of the canons. But when he turned to offer them their chance, they were all asleep, sighing in little rills. At his voice addressing them, they awoke, as they had gone to sleep, all in a row. They looked confused and very boyish, as disturbed sleepers of great age always do.

'Perhaps the Chapter has some suggestions?' asked the Bishop at his silkiest. Lesser men would have been caught, but the littlest canon of all knew how to please his Bishop.

'Would it be a notion, my Lord,' he piped in a voice like a drawn sherry cork, 'would it not be a good idea to ah... ah... have a press conference?'

Dignity was not the sole gift of princes of the church. Poochy Bobbin was a man of immense dignity who had worked his way up, greatly assisted by strong drink, from being a foreign correspondent on a quality newspaper to operating the night switchboard of a garage in the next city. The incisive blade of his mind had become dulled but his dignity never deserted him. He lived in a small, mean room at the top of a rickety stair in a tumbledown Victorian slum house, only a few streets away from his office. The only appointment of his decrepit home which troubled him was the lavatory. It was three flights down from his room and it was something less than luxurious.

'When standing above it and looking down into its grimy depths I seem to see Charon rowing across it in his boat,' he confessed. 'Though how he would negotiate the cigarette ends is beyond my comprehension.'

Not wishing to add further navigational hazards to that unfortunate oar, it was Poochy's habit to run-off each night against a lamp-post that a thoughtful council had placed before his front door. He was so occupied one winter evening when a policeman arrived on the scene.

'You can't do that,' the policeman said. 'It's against the law. I can 'ave you for that,' he added, drawing out his notebook.

Poochy ignored the constable until nature had run its full course, and they must have made a pretty tableau under the glow of the lamp. Finally he buttoned himself and with impressive dignity turned to the policeman.

'But, officer,' he said, 'this is my lamp-post.'

Few people were proof against Poochy in his pride.

'Sorry, sir,' said the policeman, returning his notebook and buttoning his pocket. 'Didn't realise.'

And touching his helmet, he strode off. I believe he even said 'Evenin' all' but that may have been an embellishment of Poochy's.

Reporters are compulsive embellishers as well as being collectors of apocrypha.

The most popular of them all turned up in Oldham, in Bristol, indeed, it seemed at one stage to turn up in every large town in the country. It was the story of the housewife, so engrossed in stripping paint from the bathroom door that she was only brought back to a sense of passing time by the sound of her husband's car on the gravel of the drive. Realising his evening meal was unprepared, she threw the paint-stripper into the lavatory bowl and hurried downstairs, shouting the housewife's immemorial battle cry: 'Your tea will be a bit late, I haven't had a minute all day.'

The husband was a philosophical man. Collecting his evening paper, he made for the bathroom to spend a reflective five minutes en-seat, reading the news and smoking. Summoned at last to the table, he folded the paper and dropped the cigarette between his legs into the bowl below. Unfortunately, the cigarette ignited the paint-stripper and a column of fire shot high into the air, severely burning the luckless husband in an area not normally exposed to naked flame.

One of the ambulance men who presently arrived in the bathroom was of an inquisitive turn. 'How did you do it?' he asked, as they carried the husband out of the bathroom on a stretcher.

Unfortunately, the husband told his tale just as they reached the top of the stairs and the ambulance man laughed so much he let go of the stretcher, the patient slid off, tumbled down the stairs, and was admitted to casualty suffering from severe burns and a broken ankle.

So widely circulated was this story, that when a lady of my acquaintance told me about The Man In The Hospital Bed, I was doubtful and, did not follow the story up.

The lady had been visiting a sick friend in the city infirmary. In the next bed was a figure heavily swathed in bandages.

'Know who that is?' the sick friend asked.

'Tutankhamun,' hazarded the lady.

'Charlie Harris from next door,' said the sick friend. 'You've met him. Plays snooker every Wednesday afternoon in the club. Big feller. With an Alsatian.'

67

The lady did know him and, compassionate lass, she turned at once and bent over the other bed.

'Whatever happened to you, Charlie?' she murmured.

She told me that Charlie was so heavily bandaged only his lips protruded from the yards of white gauze. They moved now, imperceptibly, and although the voice was faint she detected a faint sound of hysteria.

'Don't ask me, for God's sake,' said Charlie.

The lady withdrew at once, both from good breeding and an ardent desire to get the facts from the other bedridden party at the earliest convenient moment, which was then.

I have always believed that wives learn certain phrases at their mother's knee. 'You use this place like a hotel' or 'You wouldn't come home at all if you didn't have to change your socks' or, again, 'I've been staring at these four walls all day', perhaps even, 'My mother said to me "I'd rather carry you out feet first than see you marry that man",' will be familiar to most husbands. The one Mrs Harris had employed to drag Charlie back from the brink of sleep as they lay in bed one summer dawn was a perennial favourite. It was:

'Psst. Wake up! Burglars!'

There are many counter ploys to this remark. Feigning sleep, a placatory 'it's the dog' or 'shut up you silly cow, you're dreaming'. One of my friends even suggests placing a caressing hand on the wife's thigh. He claims that always sends his wife straight back to apparent unconsciousness, but I don't know. The point is that none of them works permanently, and the fourth 'Psst. Burglars' forced Charlie out of the bed.

During the summer, Charlie slept in the buff, which is no sort of condition to face a burglar, so he slipped on his short rather snappy dressing gown and tied it round the waist as he crept out of the bedroom.

Charlie's Alsatian slept in the kitchen, and reasoning that was the least likely room in which to find an intruder, Charlie naturally looked there first. He was relieved, when he opened the door, to observe that the dog was fast asleep.

Bravery growing with the realisation that there wasn't a burglar in the house, he searched every downstairs room diligently. By the time he reached the dining room he was even ordering imaginary assassins not to dare move.

He was crossing the hall to return to bed when a shadow crossed the far side of the fluted glass front door. There was indeed a burglar, and he was in the garden.

Charlie was reluctant to open the door. A preliminary recce through the letter box would dictate further action, he thought. Unfortunately, the letterbox was in the lower half of the glass door and Charlie had to bend to reach it.

In his haste to find the burglar, Charlie had left the kitchen door open and his subsequent movements had awakened the dog. It came out now and padded silently up the hall to see what all the fuss was about.

In bending down Charlie's dressing gown had exposed much of him to the outside world, and when the Alsatian gave him a welcoming nudge with his nose, it struck bare flank. Healthy dog it was, too, with a cold nose, and the shock to Charlie was so great that he jumped straight through the glass door. When his wife found him he was lying in the porch, bleeding badly from the neck, and of the burglar there was no sign.

As I say, the story seemed too strange to be true so I did not make an inquiry. But I did not forget it either, and when next I was one of a party of reporters and detectives examining that year's crop of apocrypha, I modestly entered Charlie as my contribution.

There was a gratifying laughter from all except the head of the county CID who snorted :

'Apocryphal be buggered,' he told us. 'I remember that. I was out on it all night, we thought it was an attempted murder.'

Take Five

My only concession to physical fitness in those happy days was lifting heavy glasses and riding work for Curly Beard, a veteran show jumper and trainer who lived nearby. My favourite mount had been Skipper Jack, a hunter which I took out three times a week on gentle exercises for Major Black, a brewery chairman. When one day out hunting the horse jumped into itself, the trainer knew exactly where it was going to spend its retirement.

I was enjoying a bout of flu in the pleasant drawing room of my house at the time. I had taken every possible medical precaution. There was a bottle of whisky by the sofa, flat racing on the T.V. and a thoughtful friend had delivered the *Sporting Life.*

I always have flu in the good weather so that I can get the maximum of enjoyment out of it. The windows were open. In the distance I could hear the soothing litany of a lawnmower that someone else was pushing and Peter O'Sullivan was cooing gently on the television. All was well with my world when it was interrupted by a third sound, less pleasing than the rest. Curly had a voice like a rusty Bosche bayonet.

'I've got a horse for you,' he said, poking his head through the open window.

'It's O.K.,' I told him, 'I'm doing Gay Charmer in the 2.30 and I may invest a modicum on... '

'Not that sort of a horse, you bloody arab,' he said. 'A real one.'

Ten minutes later I had become the nervous owner of Skipper Jack.

Now Skipper Jack, after a hard day's hunting, was a quiet, amiable cit you could give children rides on. Sadly, a few days' rest turned him into a dragon with hooves, and after I had blossomed from every hedge for miles round my house, we signed a peace treaty. I did not ride him and he, in return did not throw me into every hedge he thought deficient in blossom. I now had a horse I could not ride; the bloodhound with no sense of smell came later.

'You've got a big garden, haven't you?' asked Neville Stack, news editor of the *Daily Herald,* and I admitted that I had, though, for recreational purposes, it had lost much of its charm the day Skipper Jack moved in.

'Only, a neighbour of mine is moving into a flat and I'm trying to find a home for his bloodhound...'

If ownership of a horse one cannot ride has problems, they are as nothing compared with the custody of a bloodhound with no sense of smell. Unfortunately, Druid was also slightly deaf and his eyesight was so bad he kept bumping into things. This deficiency of the senses meant that when I took him for a walk I had to stay within three inches of his quite useless nose. If I stood at any greater distance behind he could neither hear me, see me, nor smell me. His immediate thought at such times was that he had been deserted on an empty planet and he took the only course of action open to an animal in those distressing circumstances. He sat down and howled in anguish and as a result I was twice reported to the RSPCA.

I can blame nobody for the cowardly bulldog that next joined our happy band. He looked fierce enough and I was very proud of him until the day a cat chased him up a tree. When Kerry, an adorable whippet with a weak heart, joined us our cup of neurosis was full. I now had a horse I could not ride, a whippet that could not run, a cowardly bulldog and a bloodhound with no sense of smell.

On balance Druid was the most difficult of my patients. The eye of a bloodhound is so constructed that it magnifies everything that comes into vision to an enormous size. Thus, the bloodhound believes that it is the size of a chihuahua in a world of giants, and Druid was constantly trying to curl up on my knee. In consequence, I spent several hours trapped in an armchair when I should have been out earning money and I know what Curly meant when he warned me 'If you're going to keep a bloodhound you need deep pockets and wide knees'.

The cost of keeping these animals, a long series of unstuck favourites and the high price of lubricants soon had me in trouble with the bank. Obviously I had to earn money quickly and the best way was to accept some day duties as a 'casual' reporter. When I had first become a freelance I was determined never to set foot in a national newspaper office for the rest of my life. Closing down my paper had left an ugly wound and I was disenchanted with newspaper politics. I saw myself as the fortunate possessor of a journalistic Chiltern Hundreds, a sort of newspaper remittance man cast up on a far rural shore. But, plainly, the time had come for change and some days later I reported to the news desk of a Sunday paper for the first of a long series of Saturday shifts.

It was a chummy office. During the week a daily newspaper was produced there but on Saturdays the small group of hedonists who staffed the Sunday moved over for Production Day. They scorned the long rows of desks at which the daily reporters sat, instead making themselves comfortable in a small group round the news desk. The news editor, who was much given to gracious living, brought two bottles of Burgundy each Saturday and we took it in turns to supply *a fete champetre* of out-of-season delicacies from an old-established grocers we found nearby. Some weeks I earned almost as much as I spent but I never complained. The pace was unhurried and I later calculated that I earned more for reading *The Sun Also Rises* during my shift than Hemingway got for writing it.

Ours was the old-fashioned sort of Sunday newspaper, written for the reader rather than the Press Council and the Honours List. We specialised in revelations of private lives, the pranks of incautious clergymen, the diabolical schemes of small-time crooks, and every week we were able to find someone somewhere who was changing sex. We flattered ourselves we were a campaigning newspaper and we were constantly warning 'Rats' to 'go home' and pompous public figures to 'Spare a Thought For Mrs Windersleg at 33 Arcadia Grove'. In every sense of the word we were old-fashioned and since my life has been a constant pursuit of the nineteenth century I enjoyed myself enormously. The sort of stories we wrote were not the kind that invited return visits to the subjects and we could find ourselves in embarrassing, often violent, situations when such a thing occurred.

I had been exposing an international conspiracy in the sale of Darts Final team places when I was ordered over to a Yorkshire town to chronicle the doings of a runaway chorister and a lay reader. A photographer was being sent over from head office to join me and I arranged, through the news desk, to meet him at the Gryphon, the only pub I knew in the town. When he joined me, he looked taut and his message was brief.

'Drink up and let's piss off,' he said.

'Why? I've just ordered a sandwich.'

'If you don't hurry up you'll have nothing to eat it with,' he said. 'We did this pub last week.'

The story was not a pretty one. The World Cup Final had been played in Britain that year and there were more than the usual number of foreign visitors to be seen on the streets. The landlord of the Gryphon had chosen to organise a lunch-time striptease as an extra attraction on World Cup day, starring a doctor's wife from the south coast. We had chosen, the photographer told me, to see this as an affront to our great country.

'This disgusting show must not be allowed to continue,' our paper had thundered. 'Is this how Britain chooses to represent itself to the world?'

'Thousands of foreign tourists thronged our streets this week,' the story read. 'They hoped to see British sportsmanship at its best.'

I do not suppose more than eight of them had visited this particular town but ours was not a paper to involve itself with trifling facts of that sort.

'…But the strip they saw at the Gryphon had got nothing to do with football!!!!' the story continued. We were very strong on exclamation marks.

'The only lunchtime engagement the Gryphon customers are interested in is a lascivious display of poorly concealed erotica.'

Apparently, we had continued with a searing attack on the landlord's morals and the obligatory veil-by-veil description of the strip act.

'The trouble is,' the photographer told me, 'the landlord is built like a block of flats and I don't fancy getting me camera smashed.'

At this point my attention wavered because a large black shadow had darkened the bar counter before us. I looked round to see the largest publican I ever hope to avoid glaring down at us.

'I know thy face,' he growled, pointing with a finger like a saveloy at the likeness-taker. 'Tha's been here before.'

'We were just going,' I said. 'We have to be back behind the counter at Woolworth's by one-thirty. Perhaps that's where you saw us?' I added hopefully.

'I dunna know thee,' he said, which was something. 'It's thy friend.'

He paused and then a great light illumined his face. 'Th'art bloody newspaper chap, is t'a?'

The poor photographer was beyond speech by this time and he just nodded miserably.

'Wait there a bit,' growled the landlord, wagging his saveloy menacingly. He shuffled off like a purposeful Yeti. 'Dunna dare move,' he called over his shoulder.

'Let's sod off,' the photographer pleaded. But I was fascinated.

'Gerroff,' I said. 'I've not finished my beer. Besides he doesn't want me, it's you he's after.'

The landlord was back within seconds clutching our paper in a fist so big the pages peeped out like a frill at each end. Shouldering us aside, he smoothed it out on the bar and the article in question stared up at us accusingly. Tracing the line with his finger, the landlord read the damning sentences. He was not a gifted reader and it took him some time to reach the end of the story. But when it was finished he looked up and stared at the photographer in silent thought.

'I've only one question to ask thee,' he said at last. We waited apprehensively.

'Is there any chance of doing me again next week? The day that came out the bloody pub was crowded. Best lunch-time we've had since Christmas Eve, and a party of Germans rang up from London to try to book in for the week.'

'In fact,' he said, 'my mate down the road at the Horse and Jockey says he'll buy you all the beer you can sup if you'll go down and expose his smoking concert next Thursday. He hasn't got strip, of course, but his auntie was a tassle dancer in Scunthorpe and if you'll tell him what time you can come he'll get her to do a bit of a turn.'

It took all sorts to make a page lead in our paper and not even the highest in the land was safe from our probing inquiry. When the lobby man heard a whisper that Macmillan was planning to fly in a Heron of the Queen's flight to visit Her Majesty at Balmoral, it seemed a reasonable bet that something serious was afoot. I was sent to meet him when he flew into the airport at Aberdeen, and put the obvious question.

I waited in some apprehension on the tarmac, for in those days statesmen had done nothing to diminish the awe in which they were held. Prime ministers were for cheering at, not talking to, and when the plane landed I walked nervously towards the gangway down which Macmillan was gracefully descending.

'Excuse *me*, Prime Minister,' I began hesitantly. He stopped and smiled encouragingly. 'My paper would like to know if the purpose of your visit is to dissolve parliament.'

That urbane statesman looked down at me, considering, then the smile broadened impishly. 'Don't you think I ought to tell the Queen first?' he said.

I have never had a lot of luck with politicians since I fell foul of

Aneurin Bevan on my evening newspaper in the fifties. The day after he had denounced the press as vermin he came to Doncaster, where I worked, to address a miners' rally on the Hexthorpe Fields. When I saw that I was down on the diary, not only to cover the meeting but also to interview him for a feature piece, I made urgent representations to the news editor.

'He thinks we're all vermin,' I pointed out.

'Prove him wrong,' said the news editor, an unsympathetic man, who claimed I had given him ulcers.

Aneurin Bevan was holding court in the centre of a group of councillors and aldermen in the long bar at the Danum Hotel. He was not difficult to spot. He had that aura of celebrity that surrounds certain people like shiny perspex. His hair was cut with the negligent skill that only the most expensive barbers can give, a soft cream shirt separated a nourished neck from the collar of a navy suit, which glistened in the light, and his shoes were soft and expensive. Uneasily, I hovered round the edge of the group, coughing timidly. He turned at once and his warm sun of a face burst into a friendly grin. 'Whassa matter, boyo?' he beamed. 'Lost something, have you?'

'I-I'm from the *Yorkshire Evening News,*' I stammered nervously; I was very young. 'They want me to interview you,' I said.

He waved an expansive arm of welcome. 'Come into the body of the chapel, boy,' he said, sweeping away an alderman or two and leading me up to the bar. 'What are you going to 'ave?' He had a Valleys accent, one of the friendliest in Britain, and he used it admirably.

'Could I have half of bitter?'

His eyebrows climbed in horror as though trying to get out of the way of this surprising request. 'Bitter? Bitter? You cannot dip the pen of eloquence into the watery ink of bitter beer.'

He waved the arm again, this time displacing at least three councillors and beckoning the barmaid. 'A large Scotch for my literary friend,' he told her. In those days we had whisky only at Christmas and nobody had ever called me a literary anything before. I found myself nodding condescendingly at an alderman I knew slightly. He glared frostily back.

The next quarter of an hour was among the most pleasant of my life. Bevan was a brilliant talker and he had a rare gift of listening, too. He was in turns wildly funny and deeply, movingly, serious. When I wrote it down afterwards, I found that he really had not said anything at all, but while he was saying it, I felt I was sitting at the feet of an Oracle.

When the interview was over, he bought me another large Scotch and asked me what my plans were for the rest of the day. I told him that I was going on to report his speech at the Miners' Gala.

'Jasu, they want their pound of flesh from you. Tell you what, boy. When we've finished our drinks we'll walk up to the field together. Always a privilege to talk to a member of the press.'

At the time I paid no attention to the sudden gleam in his eyes and I was deeply flattered when he cleared a way through the throngs of miners and made a space for me directly beneath his rostrum. 'Got to be where you can hear, boy,' he explained. 'Always stand in the eye of the whirlwind.'

While he waited at the back of the platform to be introduced, he winked down at me in the friendliest way and the change did not come over him until he was halfway through his first sentence.

'Brothers!' he shouted, arms open wide, and the ten thousand miners were immediately silent. It was a tremendous achievement because it had been a hot day and the Barnsley bitter was throbbing under the roseate foreheads of that vast crowd of the most militant miners in Britain. 'Brothers!' he repeated. 'The enemy is not the capitalist in his London hotel suite. No. The enemy is not the international financier in his Swiss chalet... No... Do you know where the enemy stands?'

They didn't, so he told them. Dramatically his arm swept down and his finger pointed accusingly at me.

'There is the enemy!' he said. 'There he stands in his villainy.'

I could not believe my ears. I felt like a favoured son who had just been kicked in the crotch by his father. It began to rain but I was not sure whether it was the rain or tears that was making the writing swim and dissolve on my note book page.

'The prostituted press of our great country. The Lackey of Capital. The Foe of Labour...'

I heard an angry rumbling behind me as ten thousand bitter-washed throats began baying like starved wolves. It was only a question of moments, I knew, before they started to rip me into little strips. I tried to shrink into my raincoat but I knew there was no escape. I wondered what they would say about me in the newspaper that night. 'Ian Skidmore, described as a journalist (they always said that when any of us died) was torn to pieces on Hexthorpe Fields today...'

I need not have worried. With consummate skill, Bevan produced another target out of his magician's bag and in a second the mob had forgotten my existence.

When the speech ended, I trudged from the field. The bright, wet grass, churned into mud now by twenty thousand pit boots, was a network of long gouges in which I slipped and stumbled. An arm came out and grabbed me by the shoulders, steadying me. I looked up and saw Aneurin Bevan beaming down at me. 'Well, boy?' he demanded heartily. 'What did you think of the speech, then?'

I was sunk in a deep trough of total betrayal. My idol had feet of steel and he had trampled on me with them. Brokenly I managed to gasp out my protest.

'Mr Bevan, I think you're a right bastard,' I told him. The smile broadened and the grip on my shoulder tightened.

'Don't take it like that, boy,' he told me with a friendly wink. 'We both got a job to do. Come round to the Labour Club and have a drink.'

Sunday papers specialised in sex investigations designed for reading in bed. One reporter was sent to disclose the awful goings-on in a suburban house where the mistress had advertised health-giving vibro-massaging in a colourful magazine to which we subscribed under a nom-de-plume. His instructions were explicit.

'Let her get as far as your knees and then sit up and say: "I am from the *People* and this is a disgusting exhibition",' he was told by the news editor.

Later that day he presented himself at the house. The operator of the implement that was doing such remarkable things for the health of the nation was a nubile German lady. She admitted our man wearing a see-through short nylon housecoat over fetching lingerie. When she took the coat off and stretched up to hang it on the highest hook in the room, her brief flame panties stretched across taut buttocks like a flame-coloured membrane. She was wearing high heels, a suspender belt and seamed stockings, too.

'Take off your clothes and lie on that bench,' she instructed our man.

'Oh, you already have,' she said, when she turned round. 'That's nice.'

'She'd the touch of a randy nun,' the reporter told us afterwards, wonderingly. 'And every time she bent over the couch it was like standing in Inverness and looking down the Great Glen.'

Desperately, the reporter repeated the incantation to himself that would end this thrall. But with every thrilling minute the words seemed less effective. There was a sound like bees breaking wind in a flurry of wing-beats as she turned on the massager. Seconds later the bees seemed to have grown into a great swarm and it was as though they were in turn biting his toes and brushing his ankles with their wings.

Unhappily, the reporter muttered to himself the words 'I am from the *People* and this is a disgusting show,' but they were becoming less charged with meaning as every second passed. The swarm of deliciously nibbling, voracious bees had reached his legs now and he could feel their wings fluttering against his skin. The stirrings he had felt when he had first seen the lady were insistent demands and alarming changes were taking place in his structure as the machine went about its work. He made the first attempt at his duty as the machine reached his lower knee, dropping coyly to the soft skin at the back.

He sat up on the bench and started to say, 'I am from the...' but it was no use. The nibbling was insistent and he sank down onto his back. He made his second attempt when the machine reached his lower thigh.

'I am from the Pee ...' but greater forces than his own will were at work and once again he sank back into deep pools of sensation.

He made one last, desperate grab at the coat tails of his fleeing duty. Gritting his teeth he forced himself once again onto his elbow in the attitude so nobly captured by the chisel of the sculptor of the Dying Gaul. His voice was hoarse and there were beads of perspiration on his brow. 'I am from the...' he began, desperately trying to think of his grandmother's funeral, work out his expenses, remember his last Butlin's holiday – anything to clear his brain. But it was no use and the last words came out in a despairing sigh. 'Bugger the *People*,' he muttered as he sank fathoms deep in an ocean of languor.

Many Sunday newspapers' best-laid schemes and noblest endeavours to rid Britain of sin ended on similar notes of pantomime. When one of our rivals learnt that an enterprising pimp called Tony the Malt was organising sex parties for visiting businessmen, it was resolved that a small group of reporters should pose as executives from out of town and attend, from the purest of investigatory motives. The London office, which always masterminded our wilder follies, ruled that at least five reporters should go, make the usual excuses, and leave when the party reached the home straight.

Normally the news editor of this paper, a dignified and happily married man, disdained to take part in field work of this kind, but the office was in the grip of a flu epidemic and there were only four reporters working. The nature of the job made it unwise to employ freelances and the news editor was forced to make one of the number.

He was a man who embarrassed easily. As the evening wore on he became less and less in command of himself, gulping unhappily at his drinks and refusing with shocked insistence even to waltz with the small group of ladies who had been assembled for their pleasure.

'I'm not going with any bird; not into a bedroom,' he told a colleague halfway through the evening. 'I'm a happily married man.'

'You don't have to do anything,' his colleague told him. 'Do what you always tell us. Make an excuse and leave.'

'But she mightn't take any notice,' he pointed out desperately.

'Stick a tenner down her bra,' he was advised. 'Tell her you're ill – she'll be glad of the rest.' But no advice would appease the news editor.

'You get me out of this or I'll have you on nights so often you'll have to sleep hanging upside-down from the ceiling.'

These were hard words: the midnight to four a.m. shift was the terror of all. There was no chance of a drink and you had to play poker with the editor who would have started three gunfights a night in Dodge City. He was considering the implications when Tony the Malt came beaming over.

'Right, gentlemen,' he said, 'we've got things nicely sorted out.'

'You are to accompany Jeannette,' he told the reporter, and then he turned winningly to the news editor 'and Charlene has just said how much she is looking forward to knowing you better.'

'I-I-I...' the news editor stammered, and Tony looked at him in surprise.

'Sorry, mate,' his colleague told Tony. 'Don't bother for my friend. He's not like that. You know how it is... ' Tony was full of apologies.

'Say no more,' he said. 'Not a word. Quite understand.' He turned to the news editor, his arms wide in a gesture of total understanding.

'All I want,' he beamed, 'is that you should be happy.'

And with a broad wink he left us. The news editor's face flooded with relief and the high crimson died on his brow. 'Thanks,' he said shortly. 'You just saved yourself a lot of sleepless nights.' It was noticeable that now the emergency was over he was slipping back into his better-known, hard-boiled self. But it was a short-lived transformation.

'Excuse me,' a voice said behind him. It was Tony again, but he was not alone. At his side stood a slim young man in a cerise shirt, pencil slim cavalry twill trousers and the sweetest suede chukka boots.

'This is Jeremy,' said Tony. 'You want he should show you his photograph album? I know he's longing to meet with you.'

79

There was one reporter who refused to have anything to do with stories of that sort. He was the archetypal Britisher and his code of behaviour was rigid. So deeply did he loathe abroad that I was greatly touched when he agreed to spend a weekend with me in Amsterdam. In a bar by the docks we met a friendly burglar who insisted on taking us on a tour of the city. I was fascinated by the red light district where the whores sat smiling at us from behind plate-glass windows, but astonished when my colleague, in his deer-stalker and sheepskin, left our little party and approached a passing street-walker. I hurried after him.

'Excuse me,' I heard him address the startled lady, "can you tell me where one can get a pot of tea?'

A pal once told me about an executive in a newspaper who treated plane crashes, bombings and murders with cool competence. Only food brought the flush of excitement to his moon of a face. As a result, he was only marginally taller than he was wide and he moved about as little as possible. But he was by no means the jolly fat man of legend. He was bred from stern stock. His father, a mill manager, had been forced to sack the father of nine one day during the depression. The next day the man was waiting tearfully at the mill gate.

'Eeh, Mr Walter,' he told the night news editor's father, 'I've been crying all night.'

'Ah, well,' Mr Walter answered, 'tha'll pee less.'

Especially favoured reporters were taken to his delightful home for gargantuan suppers. One, even more favoured than the rest, was invited on the night that a family speciality, plate mince pie, was on the bill of fare.

The night news editor was a hospitable man. Throughout the journey to his home he endlessly described the plate mince pie.

'It's the wife's speciality,' he said lovingly. 'What a cook! Touch of a master with pastry, has the wife. Make you weep to watch her in the kitchen. I sometimes wish I had three sets of teeth and four stomachs.'

The early part of the evening went swimmingly, the wife dimpling happily under the compliments her husband paid her. At the table succulent course followed course and the evening looked like being an enormous success. At last the great moment came when the pie was borne in.

As it was placed before him, a change came over the host's previously benign face and he began to quiver with suppressed emotion. Finally with an angry bellow, his host seized a carving knife and hacked the pie into four ragged portions, glaring at his wife, who was by this time cowering in her chair. 'If I've told you once…' her husband roared, and taking a portion of the pie on his knife end, he flicked it accurately onto the wall behind his wife's seat where it ran damply down the expensive paper.

'If I've told you twice...' A second piece of pie hurtled from the end of the knife, whistled over the reporter's head and flattened itself against the piano.

'I've told you a thousand times…' Scorning the knife, the host picked up the last remaining portions of pie and hurled them with deadly accuracy at a Medici print on the only wall in sight that was pieless.

'Don't put sugar on me plate mince pies!'

The rest of the evening passed somehow and when it was time to go the reporter left his host slumped in an armchair, still muttering about the culinary iniquity. The wife followed the reporter to the door where she helped him into his coat. While being handed his hat the reporter was surprised to see that the wife was smiling proudly.

'Very faddy about his food is my hubby,' she said as she let him out of the door.

Occasionally, when our night news editor was off-duty, the editor would put me in charge of the news desk and I began to understand why night news editors behaved oddly. It was not the stories that were the problem; it was the cranks.

'I am being pursued by an international gang,' an educated Scotch voice announced early on one such morning.

'Really?'

'Aye,' said the voice. 'A very highly organised gang who follow me from town to town.'

'I'm sorry to hear that.'

'Oh, I can always spot them,' the voice reassured me. 'The silly fellows all dress exactly alike. Mind you, I have to admit it's playing havoc with my nerves. I've been under the doctor for nearly five years.'

There was a pause before the voice continued in a stage whisper.

'There's one outside the phone box now and he's listening to every word I'm saying.'

I began to get alarmed for the caller.

'Look here,' I said, 'you must put the phone down at once and ring the police. They will know exactly what to do.'

The voice changed to a tone of withering contempt.

'And who do you think it is that's following me about?' it demanded.

Take Six

During the week I worked casual shifts on the daily papers. Freelances were often used so that editors could keep down the size of their staffs. It cost more to employ freelances, of course, but they went on the linage budget, not the salary budget which the board of directors saw. And, seeing, were astounded that the editor was able to manage a great newspaper with so few people helping him.

I didn't mind. The pay was good and I got some nice trips. Once I even got to Dublin...

I was leaning over a bridge and looking down at barrels of stout being winched onto a barge below me on the Liffey. The bargee was wearing a seaman's black jersey and across his chest in white letters I read the legend: *SS Guinness.*

'Cast off, for'ard,' shouted the bargee impressively. 'Cast off, aft.'

With an impressive clanking of chains, the barge chugged into mid-river and headed gently down the Liffey to the next quay, an Odyssey which was all of seven hundred yards.

Everyone in Dublin is an actor and the bargee had star quality. He stood at the stern, sleeves rolled to his elbows and tattooed arms folded across the chest. His white sailor's cap was tipped over his eyes and a cutty pipe jutted from his Jack Hawkins jaw. He looked like the master of a nineteenth century sailing ship. It was all too much for the urchin who was leaning over the parapet beside me.

'Bring me back a parrot, mister!' he bawled derisively.

It was always good to be in Dublin.

'It's me ambition to spend me holidays cruisin' on one o thim Guinness barges,' said a voice behind me, and I turned to be grabbed by my old paper's stringer, Toby Galloway.

'How's your man?' he said, squeezing my elbows as though he

wanted to bring toothpaste from my mouth and wrapping me in a fragrant cloud of second-hand stout fumes.

'Thirsty,' I said.

'Whin were ye not?' he asked, and he led me to the Pearl Bar where the rest of the Dublin press were drinking as though the front of the pub was on fire.

The barman had a spatula to scrape the creamy golden froth of the stout from the top of the pints. He waved it in greeting at us, sending bubbles of stout flecking into the faces of the drinkers.

'May ye be in heaven half an hour before the devil knows ye're dead,' he shouted, and pushed two pints towards us.

'May God give your enemies twisted feet so you may know them by the way they walk,' I told him in answer, for toast swapping was a favourite game with us.

The drinks looked like black ice-cream sundaes in glass cones and we sighed happily as we carried them to a table. Toby grinned.

'Not lost your taste for it?' he asked.

'Heaven is a chip shop,' I told him, 'with four pints of this down you after an evening at the Festival Ballet.'

'Ballet? That's nothing but puffs' football,' said Toby.

It's a funny thing. At any ballet performance the stage is filled with girls, hand-picked for their beauty and grace, with legs on them to make your hair curl. At most there are a couple of male dancers but they are the only ones that get noticed. It has always seemed to me that people who notice one man when there are twenty-four birds to look at could get themselves talked about but I said nothing of this to Toby.

'How's your bird?' I asked. He was engaged to a neurotic actress whose highly publicised suicide bids usually coincided with slow news days.

'She's just taken her third under-dose this year,' he said.

'Her priest has threatened to excommunicate her but I got two page leads and a deep caption in the *Sunday Pic*. If she ever succeeds I'll be out of work.'

'Now then,' he said some time later, 'what brings you to Dublin this time, the Guinness apart?'

'I'm freelancing like you, since the paper folded. I was doing a casual shift and got lumbered with this job.'

Toby looked at me for a moment in the narrow way that one freelance always looks at another who appears on his territory for any reason whatsoever. Then he grinned and said:

'What the hell. What's the job?'

I told him and he groaned sympathetically because I was the last of a long line of reporters who had arrived for the same purpose.

The Irish Horse Scandal was one of the most successful campaigns the newspaper I was working for had waged. Stringent regulations prevented the export of horses from Britain to the continent where they were slaughtered and eaten. Eire had no such regulations and a thriving trade had built up in the export of British horses to the continent via Ireland. It was this trade which the paper that had sent me was fighting and its campaign had been masterly. Reporters from the 'Heavy Brigade' had followed a consignment of horses from a Midlands' fair through two sea voyages and a long continental train journey to a Paris slaughter house. A reporter had successfully posed as a horse trader. His usual office wear, which gave him the air of a warned-off jockey, had inspired such confidence in the dealers that not only had he been able to travel with the horses as an ostler, he had been tipped by the French dealers, which was very rare. My own part, which I had just concluded in a shower of confusion, had been less than constructive.

A picture of a girl in a bikini in its pages is enough to get a paper banned in Eire and artists are kept in constant employment with an airbrush painting clothing onto bathing beauties. Over enthusiasm has its hazards. Once an artist painted out the domestic equipment of a prize bull which had been very much in evidence in a picture taken at a county show. It did little to enhance its creative fame as a breeding animal and the owner successfully sued the paper.

Even so, it was an unusual week that did not find one national or Sunday newspaper banned in Eire. When one of this paper's leaders blamed the Pope for not intervening in the horse scandal a ban was inevitable and the circulation manager said as much to Jack Spratt, the night editor.

He could hardly have chosen a worse time. The night editor was examining the first edition, in which the whole front page was devoted to an open letter to the Upper House demanding that they intervene in 'this callous trade'.

'Dear Senator...' was the headline, and the night editor looked round in anguish.

'What's the use of sending a letter to the Irish Parliament if we can't get the paper into the bloody country?' he said. His eyes went wide as the ultimate disaster took shape in his mind. 'I can see this lot finishing up on What the Papers Say.'

'Why don't we smuggle them in?' suggested his assistant. It was meant as a joke but the night editor was soon ablaze with the idea.

'That's it!' he said. 'That's it! We'll fly some in by charter plane. We won't need a lot, just one for each senator. We could post them in their pigeon holes in the Senate.'

'You would never get them past the customs,' the assistant said, by now wishing he had never made the joke.

'Fly a reporter in. He can carry some in a suitcase and wrap them round his body.'

'Sixty papers?' The assistant was doubtful.

'He can wrap some of them round his legs under his trousers. Who's on late?'

'We've got a freelance, Skidmore, doing a casual,' said the assistant, offering me up for my martyrdom.

'Couldn't be better,' beamed the night editor. 'Won't even affect the duty rota.'

I was called in and told of the plan.

'I'll get five years,' I croaked.

'You'd get three months at the most,' the night editor told me comfortingly. 'And don't crease the papers. You had better not sit down after you've wrapped them round your legs.'

I was prepared to argue further but I was interrupted by the assistant night editor who was looking unhappy.

'The FoC wants to see you,' he said, taking all the pleasure out of the night editor's evening.

Newspapers like to believe that printing originated in monasteries. For this reason we do not have union branches, we have chapels, and the shop stewards are all Fathers of the Chapel. The most powerful of these was not the editorial Father, nor the typographical Father. The important union was the one that controlled all the satellite trades. In those days it was called NATSOPA and its FoC was much feared. He was a machine minder by trade but he would have gone much higher in medieval Florence where he could have given Machiavelli three blacks and still beaten him.

'I understand certain arrangements beyond the scope of house agreements have been entered into re the despatch of papers,' he said as he walked through the door. He was a large fat man in a boiler suit and he rubbed his hands on a rag of self-righteousness.

'????????' said the night editor.

'In specific terms I refer to the proposed despatch of newspapers to

85

Eire in a manner that goes far beyond that which my members understand as acceptable practice.'

'????????' repeated the night editor, with more emphasis.

'I mean,' said the FoC with weary patience, 'your plan to fly a quantity of newspapers in breach of certain agreements between union and management. We can't have it.'

The night editor was beginning to understand the sense, if not the sentiment.

'It's true,' he admitted, and his eyes had gone wary now, 'that a temporary member of the editorial staff is being asked to take certain copies of tomorrow's newspaper with him when he goes for a normal tour of duty in Ireland.'

It was like rhinos brawling and I watched the cumbersome sparring which was essential to the ritual.

'Precisely,' said the FoC.

'That should be in no way described as being in any sense an admission that agreements have been, or are about to be, broken,' said the night editor, who was now talking like quite a different man from the one I knew. 'I should point out that he is a freelance and as such not bound by any house agreement.'

'Newspaper deliveries are undertaken by the transport department of this company,' the FoC reminded us all. 'Save in certain specific situations, ie the distribution of a limited number of copies to city police stations which is done by a reporter, by agreement with my union.'

'Exactly!' said the night editor triumphantly. 'And Skidmore's deliveries can and should be interpreted in that light.'

I was fascinated by the FoC because I had never met a man who said 'ie'. I had only seen it written and I wanted to know if he said 'eg' as well, or even 'ab'. I was glad when he ignored the night editor and continued.

'...and in those cases the aforementioned reporter is always transported by the editorial driver who is, of course, a member of the appropriate trades union.'

They were coming into the straight now and the FoC was leading by a short head.

'My members in their wisdom have given me a mandate to express to you the gravest concern of all departments at this departure from accepted industrial practice which cannot but be damaging to the good will that exists in this building. Or had existed heretofore between management and labour. And,' continued this new Cicero, 'if you try it on we're all out, no bloody danger.'

'Be reasonable,' said the night editor. 'He's only taking sixty papers in. 'We've got a letter to the Senate on page one and we can't get the paper into the country so they can read it. Surely there is some way round it?'

'Reserving the right,' said the FoC, who was ruffled at the way the night editor had broken into non-jargon, 'to take the appropriate action in another place in rebuttal of your assertion that my union is in any way unreasonable... Reserving that right, I say, I am authorised to negotiate a solution.' He paused and continued only when the night editor looked suitably grateful. 'We will be content with the token presence of one of our members on the flight to assist in the transport and delivery.'

'Of course,' said the night editor. 'Who do you suggest?'

'Adult Messenger Tintwhistle,' said the FoC, and I knew then that he wished me ill.

In ancient Egypt Adult Messenger Tintwhistle would have been seeded as Eleventh Plague. He was a tall, disputatious Scots ex-policeman, a veteran of World War One and many verbal assaults.

When I went to collect him from the canteen he was waging his favourite word-war on the comparative merits of Manchester City and Manchester United.

'See that City coach?' he was saying. 'See him? Coach? They couldn't make a coach out of yon man if they knocked all his teeth out and filled his mouth with bus seats.' He broke off when he saw me and nodded a welcome. For some reason he saw me as a kindred spirit and he was delighted when he heard he was going to Eire.

'It'll be a relief tae get away frae the missus,' he said. 'That woman could make a bloody fortune doing holiday relief in Loch Ness.'

The merry quips of the charter pilot did not help either, when I dropped my trousers in order to wrap newspapers round my legs.

'Get the strength of the prurient round you,' he sniggered.

'If you like I'll drop you by parachute and you can release the papers over the city like doves of pornographic peace.'

When we landed, I had twenty copies of the paper in my suitcase, two wrapped round each limb, another ten in the fold of my mackintosh and Tintwhistle carried the rest. As I walked across the tarmac I felt, and looked, like a cardboard robot.

'Bit stiff from the flight?' asked the customs man sympathetically. I nodded and the papers in my suit crackled like kindling. By the time I had finished telling the story of my arrival, the Pearl Bar was heavy with that choking laughter that transcends sound.

'Ye don't know the best of it,' said Toby, eyes streaming, when he could speak. 'There's no ban on the paper at all. Sure, you can get it at any news-stand in the city.'

I swore savagely and then took refuge in ritual.

'That back bench,' I said. 'Couldn't organise a piss-up in a brewery.'

'Nor a bunk-up in a brothel,' intoned Toby, supplying the formula response in the Gregorian chant of our despair at the world.

After bringing all my professional acumen into play on the problem of getting my newspapers into the Senate without being shot by the *gardaí,* I reached my conclusion: there was no way I could sneak sixty newspapers into the Senate House without getting shot by the *gardaí.*

I took my problem to Toby and he took us both to the Pearl Bar where we discussed it at length. Happily the more stout we drank the less insoluble the problem became. I had always known drink was the finest and cheapest cosmetic in the world because if you drink enough any bird looks pretty. But I had not realised how good it was at solving problems.

I had the notion to creep in quietly, but Toby said that would be a mistake because nobody did anything quietly in Ireland and it was a sure way to draw attention to myself. So we went up the steps boldly the next morning, with our bundles of newspapers under our arms, and a porter helped to carry them down the hall. We folded them neatly and posted one in each pigeon hole where senators' mail was left, and then we took our places in the press gallery to wait the arrival of the Senate.

When they came the sight would have gladdened the heart of our circulation manager. To a man, they were brandishing copies of the paper. Most were reading it, although not all of them had delayed over the letter; they had passed quickly on to the pin-ups, uncensored in Ireland that morning for the first time in years, which were a feature of page three. By the standards of today, pin-ups in the fifties were over-dressed, even prudish, but at that time they were considered bold and provocative. Some senators, I could see, were impressed, others shocked, but none was indifferent, and it took longer than usual to call the Irish Upper House to order that morning. After prayers, the first senator shot to his feet. He had white hair, eyebrows like hedgerows and a nose that curved out in a courtly bow to his jutting jaw. He had been put together on the same assembly line as the ancient Greek orators and he knew it. He swept the Senate with a piercing glance, then raised his eyes to the rostrum where the puzzled *Taoiseach* was trying to discover why every senator seemed to have bought the same newspaper that morning. Several of the younger senators groaned audibly when they saw the old senator grasp his own lapel with an orator's passion. When he spoke I was expecting the rumble of an outraged Zeus, but, disappointingly, he piped in the high whine of the Far West.

'Distinguished members,' he began, 'Sodom lives. Gomorrah thrives in our midst.'

His news seemed to cheer the younger senators considerably but they went back to their papers with his next sentence.

'This is Ireland's blackest day,' he declared. 'The days of the English atrocities are with us again. Once again the filthy Saxon hand lies athwart the emerald soil of the Auld Sod.'

'When I entered this noble building this morning I came, as I always do, with a sense of humility and of purpose.

But what did I find?'

His eyebrows leaped and hid in his silver thatch. He awaited their return and when they were properly settled over his eyes he continued. Raising a hand, in which a copy of our paper was gripped like a bedraggled fasces, he continued:

'I found my pigeon hole crammed with pornographic literature; pedlars of filth, fellow members, move about us even in these sacred portals.'

He went on to list, page by page, story by story, and picture by picture, the obscene horrors which, according to him, oozed from our innocent little newspaper. I will say this for him, he was a thorough reader; he had obviously gone through the paper from cover to cover.

'I will not,' he ended, in tones of thunder, 'take any further part in the business of this house on this evil day.'

With a look of unutterable disgust, he hurled our newspaper to the floor at his feet and swept out of the chamber.

The door had scarcely ceased to swing behind him before he was back. With great dignity he returned to his place, picked up his newspaper, smoothed it, folded it and walked out with it under his arm.

After that everything about the trip was anti-climax. The paper was banned the same day, the Pope declined to intervene in the horse trade, English dealers increased the price of horses for the export trade and, on the continent, happy families ate dead horses. Back in my own peaceful rut, I wrote up my expenses for the trip, sent them to the paper in Manchester and received in return a biting memo from the news editor.

'I am well aware,' it read, 'that the moment you set foot outside this office on our behalf you pass your days digging into cans of Beluga caviar, with your feet on the running boards of two taxis, hurling gold coins at passers-by. However, the accounts department is intrigued to know how you could possibly spend £20 entertaining 'a member of the Irish Parliament' without apparently learning his name. Please re-submit this delightful work of fiction which you laughingly call an expense sheet. And this time name the member of the Irish Government with the appetite equal to that of an entire Indian village.'

The only Irish I knew was *Póg ma thoin* which means 'kiss my arse' and I provided the phonetic rendition: Poag Mahon, which sounds sufficiently like a Gaelic name, and I am not at all unhappy that for years that paper's accounts clerks thought it was the name of an Irish Government official.

I just hope that on holidays in Ireland they never asked to meet him.

The early editions of the paper were the responsibility of the Manchester and Glasgow offices but after midnight everyone had to follow London. If London put a story on page fourteen then Manchester and Glasgow had to do the same. The cry of 'What's London doing?' punctuated every night and I have been told that recently, in one Manchester bomb scare, a senior editorial executive was asked whether the building should be evacuated.

'What's London doing?' he is said to have replied.

Some night editors were grateful for this release from responsibility but Jack Spratt hated it. He was a red-braced individualist, with eyeballs to match, and his hobbies were opera singing and cricket. He was a very good cricketer.

Some nights Jack relieved the frustrations of having always to follow London's lead by holding an impromptu smoking concert in the editor's office at the end of the night shift. He led a choir that consisted of the sports editor, the night picture editor, the night news editor and the late duty reporter, who had to collect the whisky from the Press Club and was therefore made an honorary member of the Executive Choir.

The night news editor took part in these concerts reluctantly because he was not a good singer and whisky made him sick, but the night picture editor and the sports editor, one of the finest cross talk acts of the day, were superb, and on one occasion, this harmonious gathering was the launching pad of a very successful career. One of the night editor's jobs was to lure talent from opposition newspapers. Because of the nature of the operation, daylight interviews were out of the question, and little notes were sent to the chosen, inviting them to drop into the office at the end of their night shift. We were battling with 'On With The Motley' when one such applicant arrived. He was a tall, earnest young man and he brought with him a portfolio of impressive cuttings. He has since faced most newspaper crises without turning a hair and he puts this down to opening an editor's door and finding the entire senior night executive with cups full of whisky, wringing their hands and issuing the heart-rending sob that is the most gratifying part of that well known aria.

The night editor was very fond of that sob and nothing would induce him to end it before its season. He sobbed on, at the same time looking quizzically at the new arrival, from eyes that had been pulled out of shape by the exertions of the lower jaw. It was a horrifying sight and people usually took a heavy pull of their whisky just before it was due. It mesmerised the new arrival and he was unable to move for some moments after the sob had died on the air. The first words of the night editor demoralised him entirely.

'Tenor,' he asked, 'or baritone?'

'I've got these cuttings…' the other started, but the night editor cut him short.

'We don't want a gardener, we want a baritone,' he said. 'We've got a tenor,' he added quickly, because he was unreasonably proud of his voice and did not wish for competition.

'I've been copy-tasting for seven months now and before that I was a foreign sub…' the applicant continued desperately.

'Tenor?' asked the night editor, whose temper was short and showing: 'or baritone?' The picture editor silently filled a cup with whisky and passed it to the applicant.

'If you want the job never mind the cuttings,' he advised. 'Sing!'

This applicant took a last baffled look round the room, drained his cup and burst into song. He had a pleasant baritone voice and a smile spread across the night editor's face when he discovered he was not a tenor.

'Eighteen hundred a year all right?' he asked.

The applicant broke off in mid-bar and looked at the night editor severely.

'D'you mind,' he said, 'not interrupting me when I'm singing.

91

PART TWO

Prequel and Sequel

Take One

It was raining. A sea the colour of wet dustbins stretched to a soggy horizon that was hazy with fog. White fingers of foam picked listlessly at the damp sand and on the promenade seagulls, deterred from flight in the wet wind, stumped crossly through the puddles, shoulders hunched, wings crossed behind their backs, muttering mutinously.

A solitary small round figure with a stomach like a spinnaker, wearing an incongruous sky-blue plastic mackintosh, I clutched the promenade rails and looked about sourly at the visual hangover that was midsummer day in Blackpool, 'Queen of the North'.

Our star columnist Noel Whitcomb coined that one and used it endlessly, announcing the *Daily Mirror's* 'Funtabulous Week of Free Frolics', its 'Surf-eit of Seaside Fun', along with other descriptions he dreamt up in the office the preceding winter to describe the summer annual circulation boosting promotions the *Daily Mirror* funded in Blackpool.

The slogans, translated onto placards lashed with gales and wet with rain, returned to haunt me as I trundled unhappily round the rained-on resort in the wettest British summer on record – up to the 1950s, anyway.

When Hugh Cudlipp, the original Welsh Dragon from the Valleys, arrived later that morning he would no doubt blame the paper's executive for the weather. With reporters within earshot, of course. Cudlipp only pulled the wings off his butterflies when there were caterpillars watching.

On the face of it, my assignment was enviable. Every day the paper produced a four-page supplement telling the holidaymaker, often in spite of the evidence, what fun he was having. The supplement was written by a travelling circus of columnists who were dragged up to Blackpool hyperboling away. Columnists and holidaymakers rarely met. Three dog-eared reporters, Jack Stoneley, Frank Howitt and I, were the intermediaries, the Leg Men.

While the star writers swarmed in the smart hotels on the front, our job was to bring in quotes from happy holidaymakers that would give credence to the new words the columnists had racked their brains to invent to describe the fun they were having.

At breakfast that morning they used some pretty old-fashioned words to describe the day they were about to endure, crushed between the merciless hospitality and the dangerous bonhomie of Cudlipp on his bad-will visit. I was glad, as I listened to them, that I did only the labouring work, the interviewing of semi-celebrities, the sheep-dogging of the reader, shot-blasting from the rocks of fact the little nuggets of half-truths the writers chiselled into artistic shapes.

The next day was going to be the best of all. A day trip to Denmark with the paper's top writer Noel Whitcomb and a bunch of lucky readers. All summer the *Mirror* had been offering A Day Trip to Copenhagen, Sex Capital of the World to readers who gave the best reason for wanting to go. Tomorrow was the big day and in my inside pocket was a wad of *krone* I had drawn from the cashiers to cover expenses. Not such a bad life after all.

I did not even have to organise the stunts in Blackpool Week. That was the job of management: marketing, circulation and publicity. To them fell the task of financing the free deckchairs, to which a voucher in the *Mirror* entitled readers to an hour any time during the day so long as it was before 10am and after 5pm.

Management rode shotgun on the free donkey rides, organised the printing of the carnival hats with the motto I AM A HAPPY MIRROR READER, the talent contests, the glamorous granny competitions and the penny-off-a-pint in one of the rougher pubs on the seedy street that ran at the back of the promenade.

It had been management (Special Events) that had organised the big event to coincide with the Visit of Cudlipp. That was the Treasure Dig, on which, wrapped in an unsuitable mackintosh I had borrowed from a receptionist in my hotel, I was about to report.

As yet another welded seam in the plastic burst in surrender to my girth, I wondered where I had left my own loved and stained mackintosh. Under the seat in one of five draught Bass houses I had

93

visited last night, no doubt. I looked forward to the search for it. Meanwhile, below on the beach, the event was in full progress. A group of men in smart lounge suits, huddled under huge golf umbrellas, watched another group in assorted beachwear who were scratching at the sand like demented shrew mice. This second group did not have umbrellas and they were very wet.

As I prepared to join them, I reflected that, overshadowed and outnumbered as I was by columnists and management, I presented a very small target: too small, I hoped fervently, to attract Cudlipp's attention. I was very frightened of Cudlipp. It was nothing to be ashamed of. Every member of the staff from the managing editor downwards was frightened of Cudlipp. He was thought by many, including himself, to be the finest journalist of the 20th century, one of three brilliant brothers. The others, Percy and Harold, edited the *News of the World* and the *Daily Herald.*

Cudlipp looked the Hollywood image. White belted raincoat, electric blue suit, with a cigar only marginally smaller than the pier, he had the air of a man who wore his trilby on the back of his head. He was born in humble circumstances in Cardiff, the son of a commercial traveller in eggs and bacon. Christened Hubert, he wisely shortened it when he took a job as trainee reporter on the *Penarth News*. In time, he became a district reporter in Blackpool for the *Manchester Evening Chronicle* where his stunts of 'creative' journalism passed into legend.

It was he who promoted the unfrocked Rector of Stiffkey who fasted in a barrel on the Golden Mile and was later eaten by a lion in a similar show in Skegness.

An England soccer player in a mess over money confessed to Cudlipp he would like to disappear for a week. Cudlipp arranged for him to join the crew of a trawler whose skipper he knew. No sooner had the player embarked than Cudlipp had a splash lead, Missing Full Back Mystery.

He was waiting on the dockside when the trawler returned. He got another exclusive with the follow up: Chronicle Finds Missing Full Back – Exclusive Interview.

From Blackpool his rise had been meteoric until there was only one man above him, Cecil Harmsworth King, the Chairman. Like most of the Northcliffes, King went mad towards the end of his career and plotted a government of businessmen, headed by Lord Louis Mountbatten, to take over the country from Harold Wilson. In time Cudlipp was to oust King using the techniques King had taught him.

King was married to Dame Ruth Railton who ran the Youth Orchestra of Great Britain and was also barking mad. When she visited Manchester the *Daily Mirror* sent seven reporters to cover her press conference. I was one and we were all instructed to say we came from different national newspapers.

No one was immune from the terror he inspired. At a Cudlipp lunch I attended, my editor Ted Fenna buttonholed me in the lavatories during the pre-lunch session at the bar on which Cudlipp insisted. Humble reporters were there because we gave him an audience when he cut our bosses down to size.

'Quick,' Ted ordered me. 'Change ties! He saw me in this one last week.'

A little later in the day, two more executives told me in separate bursts of drunken confidence what they would say to Cudlipp on the day, the inevitable day, when he sacked them. Very brave speeches. Defiant even. Roughly the same one, whichever executive planned it. Usually it began: 'I think you are a right bastard, sir...' Always 'sir'.

So far as I knew, the speech was never uttered in Cudlipp's presence. Surely, with such executives so thick on the ground, a humble reporter – and none existed more humble than I – would escape censure? A vain hope. Cudlipp's wrath was a heat-seeking missile that found even the smallest target.

With deep foreboding and a wet neck, I climbed down from the promenade and picked my way between the seaweed, the torn plastic buckets and the used condoms to the Treasure Dig.

The men in the lounge suits under the gay umbrellas were from Special Events. They had been up early burying treasury notes in plastic envelopes for the readers in beachwear to find.

The rain had not improved anyone's temper. Furious quarrels broke out between the holidaymakers when one with grit-caked fingers scratched at a territory that another had marked as his own.

The Treasure Dig was never a pretty event and I was not looking forward to the interviews with the diggers. One of the men in the group was wearing a pirate's cocked hat to show he was in charge. He was not holding his own umbrella, and the man who was held it high enough so that it did not brush against the cocked hat. The man who was wearing the cocked hat was Captain Chinstrap, the inspired nickname given to our pseudo-military executive director (Special Events) by the picture editor George Harrop.

The fact that it was a cocked hat and not just any old pirate's kerchief, like the ones the other men from Special Events were wearing, made his identification as leader positive.

This was Chinstrap Day. He was in command. His methods of retaining his position were not subtle for he was not a subtle man. But they were effective. He had learned man management as a subaltern in the Army Cadet Force. Getting people's names wrong was a ploy he used endlessly but only against underlings; people like me who could not harm him. When he saw me we went through the ritual of quickly hidden, though deeply intended, disdain, followed by loud bonhomie that passes for interdepartmental goodwill in the media.

'Slidey,' he called from under his umbrella, and he made the name sound suspiciously like Smelly. 'Not seen you since you used to chew bread for our ducks. How the hell are you?'

('Brilliant writer,' he added in a loud aside to the man who was carrying his umbrella like a punkah, in a move to take the edge off the greeting, because one day even I might have power.)

'It's Skiddy,' I said sourly. I had no umbrella to shelter under and my collar felt like a damp noose. Chinstrap's suit was bone dry and beautifully pressed. 'Going to be much longer?'

Wrenching the umbrella from his assistant's grasp and moving away so that the luckless man got the full force of the rain, Chinstrap pulled me a little way from the group, carefully stationing me just where the rain would drip on my head from the rib of the Special Events issue umbrella.

'Got to keep it going for a bit,' he confided in a low voice, 'Cudlipp's plane is due. ETA in minutes five.' He always estimated time in that way. Like the knee-length, camel hair British Warm he wore even on the warmest day because he felt it gave him a military air. 'Wanted the old boy to see the show is on the road.'

Old Boy? Love the Old Boy to hear that, I thought. Cudlipp was obsessed with youth and at fifty-plus was struggling to retain his own. His first question to a man was always 'How old are you?'

I asked, 'What happens if they find all the prizes before he arrives?'

Chinstrap smiled with maddening superiority. 'No chance of that. We've started them digging in the wrong place. The money is buried two yards to the right.

'We'll move them as soon as I see the boss on the prom.'

He nodded dismissal and turned on his heels, quite a trick on wet sand. I turned to seek more amiable company and found it in Tommy Lyons, a photographer muffled in a bright yellow anorak and tucked into vivid red socks, who was glaring at the holidaymakers. As always he was stoking the fires of an inner resentment. 'Dunno why the office sent out on this,' he said crossly. 'Never make the paper.'

It was the photographer's standard greeting. Photographers say the same thing on mass murders and department store fires. A photographer on the Ark with Noah would have turned to him as the waters rose and said 'Dunno why the office bothered to send. Never make the paper in a thousand years. And, anyway, the light is all wrong.'

'All knickers and avarice,' ground out Tommy as we watched the stretched backsides of the holidaymakers, all modesty flown in their desperate search for riches. 'Nice sort of picture to look at over your breakfast cornflakes.' Then he brightened. 'Nice little pub on the square. We're all using it.'

George Harrop, the picture editor, had once called Tommy a typographical Judas Iscariot because of his uncooperative attitude to the paper, but he was never wrong about pubs. He had the guidelines of centuries of hacks. All the pubs newspapermen use are the same pub in different towns and, indeed, different centuries: same shabby walls, curling sandwiches, flexible licensing hours, willingness to cash cheques. There is always someone who is sleeping with the barmaid, although all seem to go home together.

'Coming then? This lot'll go on for hours.'

'Can't go yet, Cudlipp is due.'

The effect was electric. 'The bastards never told me,' snarled Tommy, reaching for the camera he rarely took out of its case. The grey day was suddenly transformed by the electronic sunshine of his flash. That was the effect Cudlipp had on his staff.

Across the sands came the flat Manchester voice of Jimmy Wallace, the northern circulation manager, haranguing one of his assistants. 'You must know how many bloody lamp-posts there are between his hotel and the airport. Why 'aven't you counted the bloody things?'

A second, more adroit, assistant supplied the answer. 'Three hundred and forty-five,' he said decisively, aware that in the media business it is better to be decisive than to be right.

'And 'ow many bloody contents bills we brought then?'

'Two hundred and ten,' said the first assistant who would go through life answering the wrong questions.

'Only two hundred and ten? Two hundred and ten? Christ, boy, that means a 'undred and thirty-five empty lamp-posts. I can't 'ave 'im seeing empty lamp-posts all over the prom.'

Wallace swore fluently. Then his boxer's face brightened. 'Ere's what we do. Got your van? Good. I want them two 'undred and ten contents bills on every lamp-post from the airport, as far as they'll go. Right?'

The first assistant nodded miserably as his cleverer colleague moved out of earshot. 'Wait in your van till 'is car comes out of the airport gates,' continued Wallace. 'As soon as he's out of sight, collect the bills he's seen, nip into your van, scoot past his car and put them up on lamp-posts he hasn't reached. OK?'

'I'll try, Mr Wallace,' said the assistant doubtfully.

'Do that. I like a trier.'

I knew what Jimmy liked. I had been told in lascivious detail the night before and put his present bad temper down to the fact that, as usual, we had failed to find anyone who would provide it among the promiscuous crowds of trippers who had thronged the bars.

'The trouble is,' Jimmy had observed owlishly as we made our unsteady way back to our lonely beds, 'I never fancy any bird who fancies me. Only get going when I pay for it; and that's only because it would be a waste of money if I didn't.'

Tommy and I walked over to him. He nodded a surly greeting but made room for us under his executive umbrella, which was bigger than those Special Events were using.

At last the rain stopped.

'Boss must have arrived,' Jimmy said. He was only half joking. We laughed obligingly. But we were not surprised when, a little later, we saw the office car that had been driven fifty miles from Manchester solely to take Cudlipp the two miles from the airport to his hotel. As the assembled executives watched, the car drew smoothly up to the pavement, the chauffeur got out and ran round to open the rear door for Cudlipp.

Our editorial director was not a big man, he walked in a boxer's crouch and looked like a malevolent triangle. He never missed an appearance at the seaside promotions where he had once been a district reporter. He said he came because he liked to see his people getting in the spirit of things. It was his favourite phrase and he used it with telling effect whenever he came on them hovering over a glass.

'Getting into the spirit of things?' he would ask with dangerous sweetness, eyeing their glass in a way that suggested they were drinking too much, and left them for the rest of the day drinking a great deal more and making nervous jokes. This was an especially effective ploy against the star writers who were the most insecure. They had been reporters once and they knew that one word from Cudlipp and they would be again.

On the beach an awful silence reigned, broken only when Special Events began bullying the luckless holidaymakers. 'Go on! Dig! And look happy, for Christ's sake,' they snarled.

Chinstrap bustled up like a bespoke tug to greet Cudlipp. He was a quick mover but he still came in a poor second to Jimmy. 'Welcome boss,' said Jimmy, with a grin that was at once impish and servile.

'Hello, Jimmy.'

'Welcome sire,' said Chinstrap, winningly but not as effectively.

'Where did you get that bleedin' hat?'

Chinstrap's hand moved like a manicured snake, and in a second his head was bare, but for Cudlipp he had ceased to exist.

Tommy's flash had exploded so often the prom was bathed in a silver light.

'Tell that bloody beach photographer to put his camera away. No wonder it costs so much to run the fucking paper.'

Then he saw me transfixed in a semi-crouch. 'I hope we aren't preventing you from working?'

Wallace tried to save me. 'This is Skidmore, sir,' he said. 'Editorial.'

'Good morning, Skidmore,' said Cudlipp with deadly sweetness. 'Always come here for your holidays, do you?'

I turned desperately to the nearest human. 'I wonder if I could have your name? Are you enjoying your holiday?'

'Don't muck about,' the man said, shying away nervously, 'I'm from Circulation.'

Cudlipp turned away in disgust. 'Come on, Jimmy,' he said. 'Let's go and have some red booze.'

Chinstrap looked crushed but Wallace's triumph was brief. As the two men walked away, Cudlipp said:

'Gone a bit mad with the contents bills, haven't you? I counted one hundred and thirty-eight between the airport and here. Not made of money, you know. Spread 'em out a bit.'

The muscles on Wallace's jaw twitched as he thought of his assistant obediently tying posters to every lamp-post between them and the hotel. It was going to be an interesting ride for the office chauffeur.

Tommy watched them until the car moved off. 'Right,' he said, 'I'm off to the boozer. Coming?'

As we climbed the steps to the promenade I turned to look back. The Special Events team had dispersed and the tide was beginning to come in but the little group of holidaymakers was still digging furiously. 'No one's told them they are digging in the wrong place,' I said.

'Tough,' said Tommy as we ploughed across the rain-swept promenade and in through the swing doors of the pub.

In the bar I sank into the nearest armchair to think about Copenhagen. Tommy went to the bar where a group of glamorous girls in high heels, tightly stretched brief white shorts and amply filled navy tops greeted him warmly.

'Aren't you going to introduce me to your daughters?' I asked when he returned with the drinks.

When Tommy grinned his cheeks went high and his lips pursed, exposing his teeth, which protruded slightly and gave him in such moments the look of a lecherous squirrel. 'The Ginger Snaps,' he explained. 'They walk up and down the prom and the punters take pictures of them. The one who gets the best picture gets to take the girl he photographed to a slap-up dinner at the end of the week.'

'How many have you taken?'

'Every last one,' said Tommy happily. 'Under nine different names.' He waved expansively at the group who instantly translated the gesture into an invitation and ordered a fresh round of drinks. Tommy's eyes went wild as glass followed glass to the optic. Then the girls turned and all raised their glasses. 'Ah well,' he said philosophically. 'Cast your gin upon the waters.'

The Ginger Snaps must have been Cudlipp's idea. Swimsuits and high heels showed a touch of genius. Not much fun to walk on but bliss to follow. Like an earthquake in an apple loft. 'Ask 'em over,' I begged.

He signalled, but it wasn't the Snaps who came over. It was a small man in a tweed cap who uninvited sat at our table.

'From t'*Mirror*?'

'No,' said Tommy, '*Fur and Feather*. But don't say owt. We're an undercover investigative team. There is a nasty racket goin' on in seagulls' eggs.'

The small man laid a grubby finger alongside his nose. It was a long nose and the finger did not cover it all.

'No danger,' he said, winking owlishly.

'You've come to t'right shop. There's fellers at the bar sweating, seein' me talking to you. I could close this place down. Rackets? Ask to see a balance sheet from the outing. The landlord'll drop dead at your feet. No danger.'

'No time,' Tommy said. 'We've got to meet Frances France, the pop singer. Anyhow, a story like you've got, it's a bit big for us. Tell you what, our boss'd be interested. Why don' you go to see him? Name of Cudlipp. Staying at the Imperial. But don't let on we suggested you should. Supposed to be under cover.'

The finger was back along the nose, the eye winked.

'Stand on me. No danger,' said the little man and left us in a walk that was like nothing so much as oil snaking along a garage floor.

In return for helping judge the *Mirror* talent contest Frances France was getting her picture in the paper. Special Events had invented a story that would look vaguely like a news story. I explained it to her.

'The idea is that you should be walking along the promenade when by chance you see this bunch of children looking fed up. So you decide to give them a treat and you take them all for a sail round the bay.'

'It won't cost you anything,' I added hurriedly. Few show business folk readily spend money on others. But it was not the expense that was troubling her.

'Can't stand kids,' she said flatly. 'They make a noise and they don't buy my records.'

'You'll like these kids, I've spent the whole morning picking them, and, anyway, it will only take as long as it takes for my colleague to take a picture. Make a lovely picture too. You know how it is. Kids and dogs make lovely pictures. Every day has its dog.'

It was my favourite witticism but it missed Miss France by a wide margin. 'You mean every *dog* has its day,' she corrected me primly. She had three golden discs for singing but no hope of any kind of award as an audience. 'I like dogs, though. Couldn't I take a dog instead of all those kids? I could take Cherub, my poodle. She dies for her country and I am sure your readers would rather see a photo of her than a load of kids.'

Odd how everyone I met in those days knew how to do the job better than I did.

'Afraid it's got to be kids,' I said, 'or no picture. I'd agree in a minute but it's our sub-editor. Hates dogs.'

It was the clincher. Everyone knows about the Sub-Editor. He is the one who slants all the stories and carries out the political conspiracies the people that reporters meet have always spotted. 'It's not you,' they say knowingly, 'it's your sub-editor.'

In fact, on the blazingly socialist *Mirror*, there were forty sub-editors and they were Conservative to the last sandal. The only conspiracies

101

they favoured were the ones that got them fifteen minutes extra on their supper break. But Miss France knew about the Sub-Editor and surrendered to the inevitable.

'Oh well,' she said, 'I suppose I owe it to my fans.'

She had only one who counted. He was her manager. He owned a record shop, and when Miss France cut her first disc, he had ordered, through his shop, enough copies to make the Top Twenty. The moment that happened everyone bought the record.

'The pier at 2.30 then?' I said.

When we arrived at the pier Tommy was all gallantry. 'Miss France,' he said, advancing with his hand out in welcome.

'No, Diana Dors,' snapped the star. 'You're late.'

Tommy spread his arms wide, legs straddled, and Miss France recognised the stance. It reminded her of her manager who represented discipline. Tommy spoke body language like a native. 'My life,' – he even sounded like her manager – 'for worlds I wouldn't have had it happen. But my colleague here has just stumbled on this story. Big, my dear. Very big. He does all our big stories. Tomorrow he leaves for a most important conference in Copenhagen. But he insisted no one else should handle this important interview with you.'

'Well, if I am not keeping you,' said Miss France, only partly mollified, 'perhaps we can get on. These poor children have been waiting in the cold for hours.'

She gestured to a group of children who were waiting sulkily under the charge of the Special Events man who had marshalled them. I recognised most of them. One was the son of the group finance director and the others were offspring of the various executives who always came to seaside promotions when Cudlipp was in town. They waited at the top of a collapsible jetty that stretched like wooden vertebrae to the deeper water where an insubstantial looking boat was bobbing on an unquiet sea.

'Everybody ready, then?' I asked. 'Good. Then let's get aboard, shall we, so the nice photographer can take our pictures?'

The nice photographer belched into the wind. Miss France looked disgusted but the children were deeply impressed and, from that moment, were his slaves. Led by him, they picked their way along the swaying jetty. Inboard, the boatman was waiting for them with the happy smile of a mariner who smells on the wind the sharp tang of money. 'Having a bit of bother with the engine,' he said, but not until after I had handed him the £50 he demanded.

'Got to be back in half an hour,' Miss France said as he helped her in, exposing rather more of her than was normally available to fans.

'If I have to carry you back on my shoulders,' the boatman promised her hoarsely.

'What a picture!' breathed Tommy.

I caught a tantalising whiff of the boatman's beer-laden breath; the children thought of shipwrecks. Each with our dreams, we set off for the first empty patch of sea where Tommy could take faked pictures of Miss France opening her purse for the boatman.

The children were very good, really. The first one did not start crying until half an hour after the engine failed, beating Miss France by a short head. Her tears were pure rage.

Until it stopped I had not realised how noisy the engine was, like old bookmakers coughing. That noise was succeeded by the wet laughter of the waves as they slapped against the side of the boat, nudging its clinker ribs.

'The engine,' said Miss France unnecessarily, 'it has stopped. We are marooned.'

'Adrift,' I corrected, with the irritating pedantry of a former sub-editor. 'Marooned means trapped on a desert island. And we're not trapped on a desert island, kids, are we?' I went on, hoping desperately to get the children on my side, on the Machiavellian principle that if you can range the people behind you by creating an enemy they will do what you want.

Tommy was not impressed. 'You are great at comforting speeches,' he whispered. 'How are you at shouting for help? I am bursting for a slash.'

Odd how the moment someone else mentions it, you want to go yourself. 'Help!' I shouted. 'Help!'

'For Chrissake,' said the boatman disgustedly, 'we are only twenty yards from the shore.'

'Thank you for nothing,' broke in Miss France icily. 'If you think I am going to wade up to my fanny in icy sea water you have another think coming.'

Female stars use such language all the time but the boatman, who did not know any, was deeply shocked. 'What sort of a way is that to talk in front of children?' he protested.

The children loved every minute of this breakdown of relations between the adults but Tommy and I were past caring in our growing anguish.

At length people on the pier heard our cries and one rushed to a telephone box.

'It's all right,' Tommy said, 'we have been spotted. Help is on its way.'

It was not. A half hour went by before, through the waves of his agony, I heard the dreaded sound of a child sniffing in an exploratory way until, confident it had the attention of all the adults in the party, it began to howl. Apart from a bag of sweets nothing passes faster through a gang of children than a sniff. Once let it take hold and within seconds wailing children stretch from horizon to horizon. An ex-husband and father, Tommy knew the value of a firm voice. 'Belt up, you little brat,' he told the sniveller, before he realised it was the son of the group's finance director.

Miss France exploited the opportunity for rehabilitating her image with the boatman. 'Don't shout at the poor wee soul,' she said.

'For God's sake don't say wee,' Tommy begged. Miss France ignored him as she swept the snivelling child to the creamy mountains of her bosom. As he disappeared there was a quick gleam of panic in the child's eye. I sympathised. In mammary mountains of that size a small boy could be lost without trace.

It was no sort of country for a young boy to be lost in but my attention was distracted by movement on the pier.

The man who had been to the phone had gone over to talk to a number of men who had just arrived in a car and were running over to the jetty, where another boatman, hand characteristically outstretched, was waiting.

'They are going to tow us in,' I told the children. 'Soon be home.'

'I wouldn't bet on it. That first one is Larry Hall from the *Sun*, that's Buddy Flynn from the *Mail* and Aubrey Matthews from the *Express*. The tall one at the back is the local freelance. It must have been him the feller telephoned.'

The freelance was impartial. He had not only telephoned the opposition: he telephoned the *Mirror* as well, which we assumed was how Cudlipp got to hear about it so quickly.

One thing, I reflected as I sat on the plane for Copenhagen the next morning and gratefully saw Britain diminishing under the wing, his stunt had got plenty of publicity.

Unfortunately it was all in the other papers. The *Mirror* had not carried a line. I foresaw a difficult interview with Cudlipp.

Fortunately the take-off had been fixed for a very early hour and reporters share with other members of the animal kingdom the ability to drown the future in the pleasures of the moment.

When the stewardess came round I ordered a large Aquavit and mused on the wonders of the publicity stunt.

Take Two

People ask what is special about tabloid reporters.

Tabloid writing should be concise and composed of non-obscene short words. A story is never longer than two folios. It is always black and white. Colourful writing is for journalists.

Is there a difference?

There is, and it was best expressed in an old Hollywood film. A journalist is someone who bums drinks off reporters.

Content in a tabloid is important. There are certain essential ingredients. A very good tabloid reporter called Frank Howitt once wrote the ultimate tabloid headline: 'Glamorous dog-owning granny elopes with vicar'.

Animals are important. The *Daily Mail* sacked a reporter for not including the death of a rabbit among the thirty people killed in an air crash.

I overheard the best lesson in tabloid writing in the *Mirror* office in the fifties, which I had just joined with another Kemsley reporter called Arthur Brooks. Arthur was clothed in the invincible armour of vanity. I once heard him tell another reporter, 'You supply the facts and I will do the word-artistry.'

He invariably and oddly greeted you by rubbing his extended hands along the wings of his highly polished hair, straightening an already rigid tie and saying 'No danger' out of the corner of his mouth.

Bizarre greetings proliferated. A reporter called Rosenfeld always began a conversation with a request to borrow your comb and tuppence to ring a friend. He was cured by another very good tabloid reporter called Stringer who pressed a silver coin in his palm and said, 'Here is sixpence. Phone them all.'

On the occasion of the lesson of which I speak, Arthur had handed in his account of a murder that contained sufficient words to be published in paperback. He was called up by the news editor, Roly Watkins, who always resented people bringing him stories and so interrupting his study of the *Sporting Life*.

'Arthur,' asked Roly, 'Are you familiar with the Bible?'

'No danger,' said Arthur with a sideways sweep of the glistening hair.

'Then you will have noticed,' said Roly, 'that the story of the Creation is told in four, or perhaps five, paragraphs?'

When Arthur nodded his hair caught the light and flashed like sunlight caught in a mirror.

'Then why,' asked Roly, 'does it take you five folios to tell the story of a tatty murder in Liverpool?'

Writing about this consoles me in the sadness of knowing it is all over.

So, I suppose, is moonlighting in these high salary days. I once stood the markets with a miniature loom invented by my first father-in-law for mending holes in socks.

In my chromium-plated youth I was the scourge of housewives' purses in far-off Barnsley. I stood Grafter's Alley, as we say in the trade, in Doncaster, Thorne and darkest Mexborough, where they were said to plait sawdust and the sun only shone every third Wednesday.

Of course, that was in the days when socks were darned until they were little more than a dazzling patchwork of speedweave-darned former holes... days when, their life at the end of the feet exhausted, they were pressed into service as mittens for the young. I take a modest pride in the knowledge that in those far off days the internationally praised neatness of the collier's foot, a by-word where men of fashion gathered, was due in no small way to the darners I sold.

Curious I should make so much money demonstrating a machine. Machines and I are usually at odds. But I used to stand behind my small makeshift stall, darning the same old sock, of which I had become fond, while miners' wives flocked to buy at five bob a lump. I asked one, why?

'I were thinking that if thou can work that machine, any beggar can.'

In the Grafter's Alleys of my youth, exotics roamed, common as pigeons. There was the budgerigar that put two boys through public school with its ability to pick pieces of paper from a tray. Its owner wrote appealing fortunes on them involving the death of wealthy relatives and the coming of tall dark strangers. She advertised the bird as the only fortune-telling budgie in Britain, though I have always suspected there was another in Sowerby Bridge. Certainly in South Yorkshire it out-distanced garrulous gypsies. Tiny, a seven-foot Romany who had the neighbouring stall, reckoned his tribe was being brought to the brink of starvation with every bob of the budgie's beak.

Tiny was a pioneer of medicine. His line was hedgehog fat, a sovereign cure for everything. I helped him mix it. Two parts lard to one part butter. No one could tell Tiny's mixture from hedgehog fat, though the opportunity to render down a hedgehog came rarely in the South Yorkshire coalfield.

The odd thing was that it cured my bad back. And I knew it was margarine.

Now there are easier ways of earning a living.

It had taken four joint conferences of Special Events, Circulation and Publicity to come up with the slogan 'A Day Trip to Copenhagen, Sex Capital of the World'.

Every issue of the *Mirror* contained thirty stories, average length 350 words, about twenty-five picture captions of around 200 words each and 25,000 words of features.

Twelve staff reporters, an assortment of freelance writers and a staff of five in Features, plus an assortment of columnists, churned out this impressive wordage in twelve hours every working day. So why, I wondered, had it taken a month for the joint conferences to come up with nine words that would not fit as a headline and had to be re-cast across the centre spread? It was part of the received wisdom of the trade that the most important message in the paper, whether it was a headline or a sales pitch, should be carried 'above the fold'. That way, when the paper was folded in half on the newsagent's counter, the message could still be read and, either headline or sales pitch, it was a powerful inducement to buy.

'A Day Trip to Copenhagen, Sex Capital of the World' was as powerful an inducement to buy as the Joint Conference could devise. But it could not be used on page one so punters did not read the offer until they had bought the paper. It meant the whole expensive promotion was a waste of money. I did not understand how grown men could take part so solemnly in charades of this kind. But then there was so much that I did not understand. In the brave new world of hi-tech newspapers I felt uncomfortably like a coelacanth, beached on a foreign strand. It came, I told myself, of being the last of the non-graduate reporters. Nowadays everyone in the newsroom has read something at university and nothing at all afterwards. Their studies never had anything to do with the job. Social Sciences, Geography. One of them even had a degree in Marine Biology. Few had degrees in arts subjects and none came from Oxbridge. *They* went into television, which was some small comfort.

I had started as a copyholder at the age of fourteen. My job was to read reporters' copy to the proofreaders who checked the type that had been set on the stereo machines, vast typewriters that used hot metal in place of ribbons.

There are no stereo machines now to warm the composing room on cold mornings, no welcoming smell of boiling lead that hit you when you came to work, enveloping you, making you feel part of a vast, amiable conspiracy to keep people informed of the small local world about them.

Now the world is bigger and the paper is computer-set. Reads like it was computer-written too, and the proofreaders have all gone, because mistakes are acceptable and, in the new received wisdom, that is considered a small price to pay for increased efficiency.

Redundancy. That was my Nirvana; the paradise that always eluded my grasp.

Whenever Cudlipp decreed a new wave of redundancies I always put myself forward, the first sacrificial goat in history with a broad smile on its face and its hands clasped in supplication.

But when the list was published my name was never on it. Younger men went off clutching fistfuls of fivers, in my bitter phrase; older men shuffled gracefully into PR consultancies. But I came no nearer my Nirvana than a seemingly endless succession of farewell parties at which I made the speech as the office wit and indeed, as the years went by, its elder statesman. It seemed so unfair and in blacker moments I suspected Cudlipp of liking me, I couldn't think why. I was the only reporter on the staff of any national daily who had resolutely refused to learn shorthand.

Looking back, refusing to learn shorthand was probably the only bit of advice I had ever followed since National Service. There was a reason for this. Arraigned on a charge of assault on six regimental policemen outside the Green Dragon in the market square at Thetford, Norfolk, of which I was patently not guilty, I had accepted the advice of my defending officer at the court martial and pleaded guilty. This, the officer convinced me, would dispose the court in my favour as it would save the expense of bringing witnesses over from the UK to Germany, where I was then serving.

In the event it did not. I was awarded 56 days in the glasshouse. When the bruises healed I decided the experience had been worth the pain. It prevented me from taking advice ever again. Over the years it has saved me a great deal of hassle. The spell in the glasshouse was also a crash course in the art of survival through the exercise, in the absence of brawn, of rapidly honed wit.

The one good piece of advice I had and took was given me at the age of 13 when I managed to get past the commissionaire of the *Manchester Guardian,* indeed under his vast stomach, and find my way into the office of Cockburn, the abrasive Scots news editor. Plainly impressed by my ability to get past all the defences he had erected against job applicants, Cockburn received me kindly.

'So ye want a job, do ye? Weel, the *Manchester Guardian* has never been a paper with strict rules aboot dress but I dinna think we are quite ready yet for short trousers. However, if ye can get past the commissionaire *and* my secretary ye obviously have the makings o' a reporter. So A'm going to give ye a wee bit of advice. Never learn shorthand.'

'I thought you had to, sir?'

'Not at a'. Ye see, laddie, when you grow up and you find yourself in a newsroom, the news editor will look around for someone to send to the magistrates court. He'll ken ye dinna do shorthand so he'll say, "It's nae use sendin' him." He'll send the feller next to ye and he'll spend the rest of his bliddy life stuck in the magistrates court.

'Then he'll look around for someone to send to the council meeting and the Rotary lunch and the police press conference and a' that crap; and every time he'll pass you because you canna take a note.

'Pretty soon ye'll be the only reporter left in the newsroom. And that's when the bliddy plane will crash. You'll get sent out. And ye don't need shorthand for hard news, just the sort of cheek that got you in here.'

Incredibly it all fell out just as Cockburn had promised. Sheer cheek got me my first real reporting job on the *Yorkshire Evening News* and on my first morning, when alone in the office, a jet plane crashed at RAF Finningley. Three telephone calls resulted in a front page lead, a by-line and a wholly unjustified reputation as a hard news reporter that stayed with me throughout my career.

On the principle that one-legged men try harder, the lack of the shorthand tool sharpened my responses until, almost without trying, even unwillingly, I became a good hard news reporter. Which was probably the reason my name was always struck off the redundancy list.

My almost permanent state of tipsiness, insubordinations, apparent unawareness of office discipline and blatant raids on the 'lolly box' for advances on expenses were all overlooked and would be so long as I continued to deliver.

But it didn't get me into the rarefied strata of Joint Conferences where success came without effort and in spite of unsuccessful slogans that would not fit the space for which they were intended. Joint Conferences that were so practised at rising above incompetence that, despite the slogan's manifest unsuitability, a luncheon party was held to celebrate it.

The reporters' room was greatly in favour of the promotion. A reporter and photographer were always sent to help Noel Whitcomb, the paper's most popular columnist, chronicle the day out. They had such fun that I thought it a pity that readers were included.

This view was not shared by the readers who competed in their millions for seats on the 'Airchara', as the charter plane that flew the winners to Scandinavia and back in twenty four hours had been whimsically named.

That naming took three further conferences and was also celebrated with a luncheon party.

'Wonderful, wonderful Copenhagen' was an additional slogan which, despite strenuous efforts, the Joint Conference was unable to claim as its own.

The structure of the competition was quite complex and in consequence was bought from an outside agency, which was briefed over yet another expensive lunch to do the job for which the Joint Conference had been set up.

The competition was run separately in each of the *Mirror* circulation areas, of which there were eight. In this way, the agency spokesman explained, the paper got the maximum publicity and the winners were evenly spread over the areas where the paper sold.

This was welcomed by The Joint Conference as evidence of high creative genius. The competition itself was less complex, so that was handled in-house. The preliminary heat merely asked: 'Tell Us Your Funniest Sex Story. What put the laugh into your sex life?'

I could have won that heat at a hand canter. My sex life had been pure pantomime for as long as I could remember. I could have had a shot at the next question too. Competitors had to place in order of importance the contents of the *Mirror*. On reflection, my own priorities – holidays,

days off and expenses – might not have impressed the judges.

The next question was: 'Who would you like to spend your day trip to Copenhagen with?'

The final test was an invitation to say in fifty witty words what the competitors liked best about the paper. The answers that did the most for the super-egos of the senior executive were rewarded with tickets for two on the flight.

The competition in the editorial department for the two seats that went to the accompanying staff was less witty and even dirtier. Not only for the trip. Whitcomb was the paper's finest writer and a general good egg who always gave credit to his leg men. Careers were founded on good words judiciously placed so all ambitious reporters were desperate to work for him.

Whitcomb, a deeply fastidious man who disliked flying, had to leave his beat in London's clubland and accompany a raucous planeload of readers, whom he disliked even more than he did flying, on a drunken trip to Copenhagen which he loathed. Nevertheless, this year, as ever, a professional to his fingertips, he was waiting in the airport departure lounge to greet the readers brightly. His pigskin-cased portable typewriter was at his side and the ebony cane that was his trademark was raised in cheery salute. When I arrived with Tommy the briefing was a short, revealing reprise of the orders he gave every year.

'When I nod my head on the plane, call for the stewardess and order me a large brandy – and of course two for your good selves. The paper will pay.'

'Nice bloke,' said Tommy warmly as we jostled for seats before take-off. 'Has he nodded his head yet?'

'Used to be a reporter himself, you know,' he told me as we waited for the navigator who appeared to have got lost on his way from the crew room. 'Then he wrote this story about a bloke with an ink bottle up his backside.'

'This what?'

'This bloke, see. There was a piece about him in the *Lancet*. Some surgeon writing up an operation he had done to remove an ink bottle from a guy's Tuckers.'

'How does anyone…?'

'He used to write letters in the bath. And he used to keep the inkbottle by the bath. Happened a long time ago, of course. Before biros. Anyway, he got out of the bath, slipped on the soap, sat on the bottle and.... bingo! Right up his jacksie!'

Cudlipp used to hand out stories like that when he joined the paper and he was looking for columnists. Anyone who could write them up so that they could be used in a family newspaper got a column.

'Whitcomb passed the test,' said Tommy. 'He even got a letter from the surgeon who conducted the op complimenting him on his lightness of touch. Never looked back.'

'Was it any good?'

'What?'

'Whitcomb's story, you prat.'

'How should I know? Never read the paper. I get paid for taking photos for the rag. If they want me to read it too, I want extra.'

Whitcomb, as always, was faultlessly dressed in soft, silky tweeds. He had the cheeriest of faces in normal times but that day it was puckered with anxiety. 'Two large brandies,' he told the stewardess as she ushered me into the seat next to him.

'Very large brandies.'

'I hate flying,' he said. 'It is no accident that the swift, the bird which flies highest, furthest and longest has the smallest brain in the ornithological world.'

He lifted his glass and looked balefully at the door to the pilot's cabin. 'Nor has the distressing habit of air crews of eating the passengers after air crashes in the Andes done anything to bolster one's faith.'

The pedant who was never far from the surface in me pointed out that it was not the aircrews but the other passengers who had done the eating. It brought little comfort to Whitcomb.

'The essential point,' he continued, taking urgent swallows of his brandy, 'is that passengers were eaten. If I am to be lunch the guest list is of minimal importance. I have even thought of tattooing my body with discreet notices saying "Not for human consumption". Or of dyeing myself blue like condemned meat.'

I tried to reassure him by quoting the statistics that show that flying is no more dangerous than driving. He was not having any of that.

'Arsenic is no more lethal than cyanide,' he pointed out. 'Neither is to be commended.'

'It should be a great day out,' I said, hoping to change the subject.

'It will be an appalling experience,' he replied firmly.

'When, any moment now, as I believe, that wing falls off and we plummet into the very chilly sea below, to be eaten, if not by the passengers, then by giant cod, my only consolation will be that I have been spared the horrors of the next twenty or so hours.'

'You don't like Copenhagen then?'

He considered the question for several seconds before he spoke, thoughtfully.

'It would be untrue to say that I dislike Copenhagen. To be absolutely accurate I loathe the entire landmass of Scandinavia, including its ridiculous islands. I also dislike the sea. It is ostentatious and vulgar. I am a chalk stream man, myself. In addition, Scandinavians have the wan, hunted look of the reluctantly permissive. You feel them straining at every pore to be liberated and virile. They even link arms when they drink, like lovers. It is a country where sex is not just encouraged, dammit it's compulsory. And it shows in their haunted eyes.'

'Oh well,' I offered, 'the readers will love it.'

He looked around at the assembled readers who were keeping two stewardesses at a brisk trot serving drink.

'Could any single remark be more damning?'

'They are our bread and butter,' I reminded him.

'In the light of our earlier conversation I find that an exceedingly ill-chosen image,' he said, closing his eyes.

He did not open them again until the plane began circling Copenhagen airport.

'If this pilot manages to land us in one piece,' he said, 'it will be necessary for us to follow a plan. You clearly cannot wait to leap into the promiscuous delights of this city. I, on the other hand, cannot wait to return to England. So you and your wooden top accompany this noisy rabble on its foray whilst I wait in the airport until you return.

'I shall need from you six hundred words, mostly names and quotes. You will dictate them to me on your return in time for me to phone my copy over before the plane takes off. Do not worry about me. The airport has an excellent restaurant and I have already booked a room in its hotel for the day. How are you for money?'

'We've drawn fifty quid each from the office float. All they would let us have.'

Whitcomb took out a slim black wallet from which he extracted four twenty pound notes and two tenners. He handed them to me. 'You may need to buy a paper,' he said.

Fastening his seat belt and waving away my thanks, he added: 'As always, the paper will pay.'

He looked out of the window as the tarmac leaped up towards us. 'I shall spend some time on that dear little balcony, watching planes take off,' he told me. 'The knowledge that I am not on their passenger manifests will afford me the only pleasure available on this entire continent.'

We spent the morning with the readers, collecting names and addresses and taking pictures against easily identifiable backgrounds. Most of the quotes had to do with the price of beer and I would have to orchestrate them considerably.

I cheered up when the readers were joined by a pretty young guide from the Danish Tourist Board but they remained unimpressed.

The guide told them Copenhagen had been an important trading post since the 13th century. One of the readers, a tall, cadaverous man who had come on the trip with a small, round friend whose single conversational contribution 'By 'eck, 'Arry' had clearly endeared him to the tall man who liked an audience, said it wouldn't be a trading post much longer if that is what it charged for half of bitter.

The guide said Copenhagen had been the capital of Denmark since 1417 but that it owed much of its character and design to Christian IV who had been inspired by Amsterdam. And the cadaverous man said so were the brewers because beer was expensive in Amsterdam too.

'By 'eck, 'Arry,' said his friend approvingly.

Bravely the guide went on to show us the Town Hall, which she said had taken eleven years to build. Then she led the way through the Kongens Nytrov, which she said had been laid out in the 17th century. And the cadaverous man said it wasn't the beer that laid it out because that was like gnat's piss.

By the time the coach reached the Amelienberg Palace the guide was showing signs of defeat.

Everyone got out so that Tommy could take pictures of readers standing next to the sentries in their boxes. The sentries were dressed in uniforms so ancient they looked as though they had actually been handed down from the 18th century, instead of merely copying the period.

That was not what troubled the cadaverous reader. The guide winced as he pointed at a giant Viking.

'E's got dirty boots,' he said. 'Should be on a bloody charge.'

I led the guide out of earshot. 'Cheer up,' I told her. 'Next stop is lunch.'

'Did you know,' she replied, 'your great hero Lord Nelson is not so popular here because once he shelled Copenhagen?' She nodded her head thoughtfully. 'He killed many innocent people,' she said, 'but I still prefer him to that terrible man.'

She cheered up visibly when we arrived in the hotel where lunch was awaiting the party. I have never met a Scandinavian however small who was not a formidable eater and lunch was the one field in which Special Events were expert.

There was a bottle of aquavit on every table, which was set for four, and in the centre of the room was the smorgasbord to end all smorgasbords. Under the urging of Special Events, the chefs had done things to fish that not even evolution had managed in a million years. The guide gasped with joy as she reached for a plate.

'What an eater,' said Tommy in admiration as she joined the readers at their table, her plate piled with food. 'She's got a pile of grub there Arkle couldn't have jumped over.'

But every sign of pleasure vanished from the girl's face as she sat down and saw the cadaverous reader advancing on her. His plate, too, was piled with fish in variety. He had also included the meat dishes from the hot trolley, which were offered as an alternative. But his face held no joy.

'What does he want now?' the girl gasped.

'He's come to complain,' Tommy suggested.

'Complain? That is a Christmas Smorgasbord. I have never seen one before at this time of year.'

'Something'll be wrong,' insisted Tommy, who knew readers. There was. The cadaverous reader thrust the plate on which salmon swam in a murky sea of curry sauce and dill floated on the surface of a beef casserole from which giant prawns with frightened eyes glared in alarm.

'I'll tell thee t' trouble with that bloody buffet,' he said accusingly. 'You're spoilt for choice.'

After luncheon the now broken guide waved with us as the coach took the readers off on their great treat of the day, a visit to a city centre cinema where a heavily pornographic film was on general release in a double bill that also featured 'Bambi'. They were not to meet again until the evening when there was to be a banquet at Tivoli Gardens.

Ever hopeful, Tommy had tried to lure the guide to join him in the cinema. She declined. 'It is too late,' she explained. 'By the time they get there they will have missed Bambi.'

Cheated, as always in my case, of dalliance, we passed the afternoon, after I had tapped out the morning's work, sleeping in comfortable armchairs in the hotel lounge. We awoke just as dusk was falling. Sober again, we ambled through the city towards the Tivoli Gardens. The sleep had done us good. 'Nothing like a spot of Egyptian PT,' said Tommy, appreciatively. 'Puts a right edge on your thirst.'

When we reached the park, high in the sky above us a tightrope walker from the open-air theatre dipped and danced in a searchlight like a white moth; a boys' band, cheeks rouged and toy-box uniformed, marched and counter-marched in puppet-like precision. The music from their glittering instruments was bright and tin-like.

Across a dark and mysterious lake the floodlit facade of the Chinese Pagoda restaurant where the party were to dine looked like a giant jewel box.

'All it needs,' said Tommy generously, 'is a Yates' Wine Lodge and it'd be another Blackpool.'

Through the restaurant windows we could see the waiters, elderly, courtly men, laying the places for the readers' banquet. The waiters brought on the inevitable smorgasbord platters. With the fine dedication and deeply creative sense that only old waiters achieve they began dressing plates of individual salads. Each waiter had a tiny pot of black, fish eggs with which he was tracing an intricate design over the lettuce. It was lumpfish roe, which, to the untrained eye, looks exactly like caviar. Or rather it does to most people. To the tall, cadaverous reader it had other associations.

'Caterpillar shit, all over me lettuce. Dirty devils,' he said to his small, round friend who was also staring with repulsion at his plate. 'You'd think they'd wash t'salad before they put it on us plates. All the same, foreigners. Mucky lot. You've only to look at their boots.'

'Actually it's fish roe,' I whispered, anxious to avoid a scene.

'It's what?' the reader asked disbelievingly in a very loud voice.

I told him again and the man's lip curled in disbelief. 'Roe? Don't be soft. Roe's brown. This stuff is black.'

'Caterpillar shit,' he repeated, and followed by the small round man he began carefully and fastidiously to scrape the roe from his lettuce. His alarm communicated itself to the rest of the party. To the astonishment of the elderly waiters they all began scraping off the roe. The cadaverous man looked at me with lofty disdain before once again addressing his friend. ''E said we could eat it,' he said. ''E can eat caterpillar shit if he wants. I 'ave me standards.'

In my confusion I accidentally helped myself to salad from the plate of his neighbour on the other side, a buttressed lady with electroplated hair. 'Eat your bloody own,' she spat with little bonhomie. 'They invite you for a day out and then they eat the dinner off your plate'.

The waiters knew a potential enemy when they saw one, and to neutralise the cadaverous man they were endlessly attentive with first aquavit and then various colours of wine.

Finally mellowed, the cadaverous man leaned towards me as the table was cleared. 'Tha'rt journalist, aren't tha?'

I admitted I was.

'Nowt fresh to thee then, this abroad lark?'

These annual nightmares were the nearest I had ever come to an overseas assignment but I wasn't going to let the cadaverous man know that. 'Nowt fresh,' I agreed.

The cadaverous man peered owlishly round, anxious not to be overheard. Then he leaned forward and his voice dropped.

'This sex, like, they 'ave a lot of it over 'ere, don't they?'

'More than most.'

'Thowt so,' he said. Again he paused as though wondering whether he could take me into his confidence. 'Weere?' he said.

'I beg your pardon?'

'Weere? Weere does it go on, then?'

It was a perennial complaint that what with the readers and the aquavit I had never seen anything to justify the city's reputation as the sex capital of the world. But I wasn't going to let that get back to Barnsley. I thought of the sex spots I had known and all I could come up with was Leeds and Manchester.

'Back of the railway station,' I said.

'By 'eck,' said the man, impressed. 'Just like Leeds.'

He was plainly astonished that in a land where the excreta of caterpillars was routinely eaten anything at all could have a Yorkshire parallel.

'Fancy a bit of a walk then?" he said.

'The plane's at 1am,' I told him.

'Live dangerously,' advised the cadaverous man, 'we can get a taxi to t'plane. Put it on thy expenses, lad.'

The cadaverous man slid effortlessly into a new role as world traveller. The small, fat man and I had to struggle to keep up as he dashed out of the Tivoli Gardens and headed for the station.

'By 'eck, 'Arry,' said the small, round man, betrayed into loquacity by a display in a brightly lit shop window of leather underwear, black silk mask, brass-studded gauntlet gloves and a leather bullwhip.

'What the 'ell is that lot for?'

The cadaverous man was staring in disbelief. I answered for him.

Both stared at me in horror. 'It's bloody disgusting,' said the tall man at last, plainly bemused by a race that would fill itself with caterpillar droppings before launching on its partner with a bullwhip. The small fat man shook his head.

'Shaggin's got a long way to go i' Yorkshire,' he said.

I began to explain the purpose of other accessories but the cadaverous man refused to believe me.

'On the end of your what?' he demanded, glaring at a circular fringe of fine goat's hair. 'It must be bloody agony.'

Visibly shaken, he pushed on through the crowds that thronged the streets round the station. He walked so fast, his face rigidly set, that we were unable to keep up. I could only follow the back of his neck, now a deep, embarrassed crimson, as it towered above the throng. His size made him an attraction to the girls who were plying their trade in shop doorways. One smiled at him and, to my amazement, the tall man stopped, turned and forced his way through the crowd to speak to her. He had already retreated, face an even deeper shade of red, when we caught up with him.

'Cheeky bitch,' he said venomously.

'What's up, 'Arry?'

'What's up? I only asked her if she knew anywhere we could get a pot of tea. Right parched I am.'

'What 'appened, 'Arry?'

'She had hold of me person', the tall man said.

'Asked me if I wanted a bit of jig-a-jig. Soon put her in her place, though. "D'you mind?" I said, and I give her a look enough to stiffen 'er, "It's the wife's birthday tomorrow"...'

The tall man and his friend could not wait to get into a taxi and put this Scandinavian Sodom behind them.

As they walked into the airport lounge the tall man insisted on shaking me solemnly and wordlessly by the hand. Noel Whitcomb was sitting alone in an airport bar.

'You would be surprised,' he told me, 'how much better an aeroplane looks through a brandy glass. A fortune awaits the man who markets brandy-filled binoculars. Got anything for me?'

I handed him four folios of quotes.

'Thanks,' he said, 'I'll add it to my piece. You will be delighted to hear you all had a fabulous day.'

His voice took on a sprinkling of concern. 'What sort of a day did you have?'

I told him and ended with the story of the cadaverous man and the street girl.

'My dear man,' said Whitcomb, 'you have just supplied me with the entire piece. It's going to be a cracker.' He looked at his watch. 'Twenty-five minutes before we have to be on that damned aircraft.'

He stood up, surprisingly steadily for someone who had spent the day watching aircraft through brandy balloons.

'Come on,' he said, 'the phone is over there. I'll do the column round your man. Won't name him, of course. Wouldn't be fair, but it is too good to miss. We can add your general quotes at the end.'

He was in the booth and dialling before I could answer.

'No time to write it. I'll go straight on to copy. You stand in the prompt corner. Copy, please. Copy? Whitcomb here. Stanley, how are you? Wife any better? Good. Splendid. Now can I give you my bit of nonsense? Splendid. Good lad.'

And without a moment's hesitation he dictated his column. I had been trained on an evening newspaper so was used to dictating from notes. But that was only on hard news stories. A column was something again and I listened with admiration.

Whitcomb's copy sparkled with little jokes and he had a gift of inventing new words; omnibus words, which said three different things at once. He told the story crisply and economically. But he told it in his own special way and when it was over he had created a minor work of art.

It took just fifteen minutes. In one short paragraph he recreated the atmosphere of the red-light district so that you could see it, even smell it. He even had time to bid the copytaker a courteous goodnight before he put the phone down.

'Did you know,' he asked as we briskly crossed the tarmac, 'the correct noun for caterpillar shit is frass. I have always thought it would make a pretty swear word.'

'Is there,' he went on, 'time for a drink before we have to get on that damned plane?'

'Yes, and I'll buy it,' I said.

Take Three

Life for Tommy was a short journey endlessly repeated between peaks of intoxication and the damp, misty plain of the hangover. He had joined the RAF as a boy apprentice because that seemed the simplest way of getting through life with the minimum effort. He was not quite sure how he had ended up in the photographic branch nor why he should have been blessed with a picture sense that enabled him to win a number of quite respectable competitions. It was the discovery that you could make money by photographing girls with their clothes off, and more often than not make the girls too, which had decided his career. He had graduated as a freelance from the fringe nudie magazines, first to art calendars and finally to the tabloids. His skill was to inject his pictures with his own over-powering lust. His black and white studies, all taut skin and erect nipples, leaped from the page and became so much in demand that Cudlipp took him on the staff because it was cheaper than hiring him as a freelance.

It was a mistake.

Tommy had no interest in the world around him. He had once startled me by asking where he could buy books. Since Tommy had often boasted that he had not read a book since he left school I was curious.

'What sort of books?'

'Books,' repeated Tommy, 'you know – *books*.'

'What sort of books? Novels? Biographies? Thrillers...?'

'Books,' replied Tommy crossly. 'Y'know, like the ones you've got on your wall. They look nice and you don't have to decorate.'

That was sacrilege. To me books were a trapdoor in the pantomime stage that was life; one that I could escape through into a world where I could be an interested spectator, untouched by the tragedies, unharmed by the adventures, loved by beautiful women, the companion of the brave and the wise. For Tommy the trapdoor was drink. Sudden oblivion, redeemable suicide, all the fancy names that I gave it meant nothing to Tommy. He just liked being pissed. If he thought about it he did not even like the taste of booze. But its effect brought such relief that he sought it on every conceivable occasion.

He had grown a pencil moustache he believed essential to the glamour photographer and cultivated the manner of a successful car salesman who knows he is a wag. He had a way with women that baffled me. But what I most admired was his constitution and the way he withstood hangovers. Tommy had hangovers like other people grew prize marrows – huge, unbelievable and unpalatable. He called them Satan's Blanket from some dim childhood memory of the Band of Hope.

He was suffering from one when, on the day after our return from Copenhagen, I sought him out in his room at the hotel to bring the unwelcome news that we had been summoned to the presence of Cudlipp.

The room was in darkness, heavy with the scents of unwashed laundry. On the floor by the bed was a tray on which most of a hearty breakfast lay uneaten and pitted with cigarette ends. An egg had been smashed in its merry face by a cork-tip and another floated, dispiritedly, in a half empty coffee cup. Nevertheless there were two humps in the bed and on the pillow next to Tommy's unappetising, unshaven head were the unmistakable blonde tresses of one of the photo girls I had last seen in the bar on the day of the Treasure Dig.

'That was quick,' I said, 'we didn't get back till 3am. Where did you find her?'

Tommy, who had been looking up at me from under a protective cowl of blanket through one boiled eye, was momentarily puzzled. Then raised his head.

'Oh her,' he said without a great deal of interest, 'she's been here a couple of days.'

'Working her passage to Page Three? Here, cop for this.' I handed him the vodka and tonic I had brought up from the bar for him.

'Ta, mate,' said Tommy reaching out with an unsteady hand. Grimacing, he regarded the drink with trepidation.

'The brave don't cry,' he said. Conversation with Tommy was conducted on simple lines, the chipped pearls of slogans, picked up heaven knows where, strung on the outmoded slang of the RAF.

'Satan's Blanket, mate. Wrapped in it. Thick and hairy.'

There is a special technique for dealing with those unfortunates who are wrapped in Satan's Blanket. It is unkind to give them too much in the way of ideas. The thoughtful friend breaks unwelcome news into palatable lumps.

'We're in the shit,' I said, and waited for Tommy to assimilate.

'Us?' he asked presently. 'Why?'

'Dunno, but it could be that business with Fanny France.'

'Why? We got some marvellous shows.'

'Yes, in the other papers. That may be why Cudlipp wants to see us in an hour.'

I waited in respectful silence while Tommy prepared for the ordeal of the first drink of the day. Silent messengers ran down Tommy's arms giving courage to his hands. He looked at the vodka, then at me, then to the glass again as he raised it to his lips. He used both hands as the surface of the drink changed from a heavy swell to a Force Eight on the Beaufort scale.

'Over the fields of clover...' he sang in a thin, frightened little voice and then downed the drink. It was a saddening sight. Tommy's boiled eyes misted, his body shook and his cheeks filled. But presently he sighed. 'Got it,' he said.

It is funny about drinking. Just imagine. You are on your way to the boozer and a space ship lands in the road. And a Thing gets out with seven arms and a questionnaire in every one of its fists. And it says, 'We're having a bit of trouble on our planet and we're thinking of moving here. I'm just doing a market survey to see if it will be OK for us. Do you mind telling me what you are doing?' And you tell him you are going down the pub for the last hour and the spaceman says, 'Pub?' And you explain a pub is a brick structure where you cannot see for tobacco smoke; where you stand in front of this waist-high piece of wood with a flat top called a bar and drink a potion that will make you stagger and fall over and the next morning give you a headache and a mouth like a vampire's pantry floor.

This Spaceman would say, 'Oh, I understand. You have misbehaved and this is a punishment.'

And you say, 'No, I am doing it for pleasure. In fact I give money for this potion. You would have to explain what money is and how, to earn it, men risk their lives and go down to hack coal in holes in the ground and things like that. And the spaceman would say, 'Hang about. You do all those things to get this thing called money. Then you give it away for a substance that makes you ill? Thanks, but no Thanks,' the Spaceman would say. 'I think we will try another planet.'

A puzzled blonde head appeared behind Tommy's shoulders.

'What's all this racket?' the girl said, her voice cracked with sleep. 'Is it a party?'

'That's how I pulled her,' Tommy said as though the girl were not there. 'Mad on parties. So I stuck a few bottles of stout in the boot of me motor and a couple of bags of crisps and invited her for a midnight bathe.'

'What happened?'

'Bloody tragedy. I was so pissed I stuck them in the boot of the wrong car. Someone is in for a right surprise when he opens his boot this morning. Trouble was we only had a miniature scotch between us, me and her, and it was freezing with nothing on,' said Tommy, a master of the throwaway line, 'so when we'd had our swim we came back here and I ordered a couple of bottles of brandy.'

'Nothing on?' I gulped at the thought of a naked Tommy, his little paunch drooping, walking out of the waves like a Botticelli nightmare, waving a miniature scotch bottle. Then I thought of the girl with her huge, high breasts, marbled in the cold night, and the sea water making small diamonds as it ran down her body.

Tommy was miles away in the surf of a photographer-polluted ocean, rubbing his stubbled chin with a still shaking fist. I felt the need to hurt.

'Get dressed,' I said savagely, 'it's time to see the boss.'

Cudlipp had the Royal Suite and when I stood back to let Tommy knock on the door it was opened by his male secretary.

'Yes?'

Then he stood silently with his hands coupled before him over his waistcoat while I tried to remember of which of his maiden aunts the secretary reminded me. And I thought how you could tell really powerful men. They had men secretaries, not girls. It would have seemed a wasted opportunity to Tommy but it was one of the more subtle trappings of power. 'The Editorial Director wants to see us,' I said at last.

The secretary waited, well aware of the reason for the visit but determined to squeeze the last bitter drops from our discomfiture.

'About the Miss France story?' I ventured, and the male secretary smiled.

'Oh yes,' he said, and he made the words long and loving. 'The ED is in conference. You may wait in the vestibule.'

When the door of Cudlipp's drawing room opened we were unprepared for what came out.

'Goodbye,' the great man was saying, 'I am grateful to you, grateful. And rest assured, I will take up the matter at once. This great newspaper will look into this monstrous outrage on your behalf. Have confidence in our power and in our desire always to serve our readers.'

'Thanks, mate,' said a little voice under a familiar tweed cap as he saw me.

Cudlipp looked mystified; we looked horrified.

'It's the man from the pub,' said Tommy.

'It's the sack,' said I.

Cudlipp ignored us as he closed the door, still looking puzzled.

'Don't fret,' the tweed cap told us grandly as it passed. 'I've seen you right, fair play.'

In what seemed like centuries later a bell rang and the secretary returned. 'The ED will see you now,' he said.

We followed him into a big room furnished in the manner of Louis the 21st. Through the windows I could see a watery sun keening to itself as though it were sorry for us. Out in the bay a fishing boat was doing keel-stands in the swell and a horse tram, in which soaked tourists huddled unhappily on the open upper deck, passed slowly by on the prom, the horses' shoulders hunched against the gale.

'I have been watching your work with care,' Cudlipp began. 'It would be nice if you could get the occasional story in my paper as well.'

A shiver of pleasure disarranged the set of the secretary's jacket as he flowed through the door.

'Fortunately,' Cudlipp continued, 'by getting us all that remarkable publicity in the opposition papers you seemed to have freed Mr Chinstrap from his responsibilities in that direction sufficiently long for him to do what, in my innocence, I assumed I was paying you for.' He paused to light a cigar so long that I could have lit it for him; I was nearer the end.

'Do you know the gentleman I was showing out as you arrived?' he asked.

The denial came so quickly that Cudlipp reacted suspiciously.

'That is the man who pays your wages,' he continued, 'one of the four million trusting souls who believe that people like you spend every waking hour protecting them from crime and corruption. A man who thinks you search the world to amaze and confound him with stories of the great events of the day.

'You and I know differently, of course. We know you spend your days arsing around in boats with decaying pop singers, terrorising the innocent off-spring of my senior executive staff.' The group finance director had not wasted any time.

'Fortunately,' continued Cudlipp, 'our readers do not know that. When one of them is being cheated, what does he do? He sees the contents bills that Mr Davies has been plastering on every lamppost between here and Wick and he reads their message. "They will help," he thinks. "This is the paper that cares." And he looks for a representative of that paper, happily unaware that the sea here is over-flowing with them having their pictures taken by the *Mail* and the *Sketch*.'

'Fortunately, not all my staff are content to spend their days playing photographer's models. Mr Chinstrap, with a vigilance I propose to reward, is looking about him. And Mr Chinstrap finds the story that, despite the gold coins I hurl monthly at your undeserving heads, is the only bloody story to come out of this rain-swept paradise all week.'

He paused to draw breath. 'Now get your notebook out,' he said, and glared hotly as I dived into an inside pocket and brought out my chequebook, the back of which was the nearest to a notebook I had ever carried.

'There is a racket going on in this town; a particularly nasty racket because it is being played on the working class.' Cudlipp was very strong on the working class from which he had emerged, so long as he did not have to meet too many of them.

'This paper will not put up with that. From this moment we, or to be more precise you, with some assistance, are going to take it to pieces. Right?'

We nodded.

'I believe, and you almost certainly know, that there is a public house in the Town Hall Square called the Bull and Stirrup?'

A second, more confident nod.

'Did you also know they have an annual outing?'

Less confident nods.

'No, how could you? It seldom takes the form of a cruise round the Bay. However, an outing they have. Nothing unusual about that, of course. In this great country of ours many pubs organise these annual outings. Money is collected in a hat, draws are arranged and more often than not the landlord makes a small contribution. Am I right?'

Confident nods, but unwise.

'Not in this town, I'm not. In this town outings are arranged by one firm. In return for a round sum from each customer this firm lays on a coach, crates of ale, a ploughman's lunch at a transport cafe the firm owns, an active afternoon and, to round off a magnificent day, every man on the outing is made an honorary member of a club which is also owned by the firm. This entitles him to something called Chicken in a Basket, which I assume is a meal.'

He paused for confirmation but, fearing to be caught out twice, we remained uncommitted by head movement.

'If his stomach is strong enough he can watch girls, also presumably owned by the firm, peeling off their sweaty, G strings.'

'Sounds fun,' said Tommy, unable to resist the remark.

'Were you sitting in the bloody sun on that boat?' Cudlipp snarled. 'Supposing that on most days this firm arranges two outings and there are thirty men on each outing. Your free ticket only entitles you to chicken in a basket and sweaty tits in the eye. Drink you have to pay for. And, as you will no doubt discover with glee, you cannot get ale in this club. Only shorts at high prices, which should not be reflected in your expenses claims. On which you will go very easy indeed, if you have any sense. Because I shall personally oversee them.

'I leave you to imagine how many short drinks men who have been in the open air drinking ale all day can put away before they start throwing up all over the prom.'

He stopped and looked at my brow, which was deeply furrowed. 'You look puzzled. I have not been going too fast for you, have I?'

'No sir, it's just that I do not quite see where the story is...' I began.

'How could you? Your eyes are fixed on a further horizon than most of us see. While we poor mortals grub about in the gutters of life for stories with which to pay your inflated salary, you are out on your bleeding yacht, beating children.'

I thought that was unfair. Only one of us had a yacht and it wasn't me.

'However, I agree with you,' he continued, 'so far we have got nothing to pin it on. No one forces these men to go on the outing. But do you not think it odd that there is one old-fashioned custom that seems to have gone by default? The one where you pin up a balance sheet on the pub wall so that the punters can see where their money has gone.'

'But if the firm arranges outings all over town,' I ventured, 'it would take one clerk with a computer a very short time to write a detailed receipt.'

Cudlipp played his ace.

'Fortunately my recent visitor is not as trusting as you. This gentleman was not happy about last year's outing. He did not think he'd had value for money and scrutinising this list I am bound to agree with him.'

He handed me a grubby piece of paper. As I took it, I could easily imagine the man under the tweed cap, licking his pencil and jotting down the price of every swallow. The paper read:

```
Coach hire fee, shared......... £1
Beer on coach................... £2
Sandwiches (three).............£1.10s.
Beer (fishing)................... £2
Chicken in Basket..............£1.10s.
                 ---    £8.00s.
```

Cudlipp passed over a second sheet of paper, a small poster that read:
ANNUAL OUTING £30.
FISHING, BOOZE AND MADAME ROSALIE
Coaches collect you at the pub door for a
ploughman's lunch in a country pub and
domino knock-out competition.
Free drink on coach followed by
an afternoon's match fishing and more free beer.
(thirty minutes fishing for pleasure after match)
Followed by dinner and cabaret
in the North's most fabulous night club starring
Madame Rosalie and her
internationally famous team of striptease artistes

I read the poster and then handed it over to Tommy. I was unsure how I was expected to act.

'Want us to go on the outing and knock up a picture feature for the slip edition?' Tommy hazarded. 'Plenty of faces and quotes...'

'No I do not. We are going to have 'em. Look at the figures, man; direct on them the laser like glare that so far only I and that reader have employed. Calculate the profit. Thirty men who have already paid for their own transport, delivering themselves at your club door, gasping for drink even at the prices they are going to have to pay; bringing with them the sort of thirst that only an afternoon's fishing can produce.'

It didn't make the earth move for me, however Cudlipp felt about it. I supposed that in a slip edition that only appeared in the resort it would make a passable page lead. But the picture feature across the centre spread which Cudlipp was now outlining? I doubted it. But only to myself because Cudlipp was enjoying himself and only the deeply unwise take a ball away from a playful tiger.

Cudlipp was running to seed in a way that not even Savile Row could disguise. The waves in his silver hair were about as genuine as the ones a machine sent bowling over the surface of the swimming pool in the hotel basement. His skin had that look of powdered latex that is the hallmark of the celebrity, and power surrounded him in a nimbus that separated him from the herd.

He was just too big for me to take in one bite. The patronage he had in his gift was awesome. By a whim he could lift you from a semi-detached cottage to a Mayfair penthouse and give a writer a greater audience than many a pope gets.

He was the doorway to celebrity, to the TV chat show circuit, huge advances on very small novels, and if you lasted the steeplechase course of a career on his paper, a pension that would make your eyes water.

Any sort of power worried me. At the modest level to which I tenaciously clung, almost everyone had more power than I did. Yet I thought how frightened all those wielders of power were of the man before me. Everyone confides in the lowly, it is like talking to yourself. At events like this promotion, which were the only times I came near to senior management, the fear they all had was palpable. One after the other these powerful men were cut down. They took their golden eye-shields, spreading their incompetence over TV, or to organise similar promotions to this one, or they just faded away to retirement in seaside towns where within weeks they looked several years younger right up to the time when, so meagre were their resources, they died younger than they should have done and usually of boredom.

For all that, I had to admit Cudlipp was a newspaperman from head to dagger tip. The briefing he was now giving was thoroughly workmanlike and if only Tommy and I had been able to carry it out the job would have been as easy as he made it sound. But that is the nature of newspaper briefings. Executives give reporters detailed briefings because that is their function. Reporters go out and blunder about at the deep end because that is their function, and sometimes it works and sometimes it doesn't.

To be a successful reporter requires little or no skill. It merely requires luck. I remembered my own first steps and the advice never to learn shorthand. All had fallen out as Cockburn prophesied. Here I was, a highly overpaid tabloid reporter, listening to a briefing from the most powerful man in his industry. Or not listening, I thought with panic, and began to pay attention.

Fortunately, Cudlipp was talking to Tommy.

'...keep your camera in its case in the early stages. I don't want you lousing things up. Your job is to witness interviews. I want a reporter and a photographer on about five outings. I want to know how much is spent, how many sandwiches you have and how much the catering firm pays out. Tell 'em it's all a stunt to show people having a good time for our promotion week. When the dodgy part is over then you can bring your camera out. I don't want happy snaps, I want a series of pictures of punters with their hands in their pockets, handing over money at the bar; looking miserable.

'And I want a picture of that chicken in a basket. We'll blow it up big with a nice white on black caption and a price label showing how much it cost and how much the punters got charged.'

He turned to me.

'So, get him to take pictures exactly along those lines.'

With that simple sentence Cudlipp ruined any chance we had of getting the story we wanted, I thought. He had implied that I was in charge. Photographers are very sensitive about that sort of thing. Any reporter soon learns not to say 'my photographer' under any circumstances whatsoever. Revenge is inevitable. But Cudlipp, who must have known this, went blissfully on digging my grave.

'And do not let him take too much tit. We are a family newspaper.'

Tommy smouldered quietly.

'Who is in charge of the job?'

'For the moment, Skidmore.'

A pretty good sentence. It only contained four words. I didn't like three of them and Tommy loathed the fourth.

'You bringing someone else in?'

Cudlipp nodded.

'I have asked Manchester to send the Heavies.'

Every newspaper has a heavy team. They are always on the 10am to 6pm shift and they get a longer break at lunchtime, because they would not come back in an hour even if they did not. They are the cream of the reporting staff. Luck again. They became the cream because of the good stories they did and, since most of the good stories happened between 10am and 6pm, they usually stayed the cream until blown up by scandal. There was always a scandal.

The Heavies were already in the bar by the time we reached it. Frank Howittt leered from across the bar. It did not signify amusement. Howitt's leer never did. He lived in fear that the luck that put him in the team would one day desert him. At the beginning of the day he was always polite to the assistants on the news desk. He said good morning to each one of them in turn before scuttling to the back of the room with a pile of weekly newspapers, which he scoured for stories to develop. As the day wore on he got angrier and angrier, unsuccessfully working his way through column yards of parish council meetings. Then he got even angrier waiting for his break, which he could only take when the news editor wandered down to his desk and said, 'Why don't you nip out for a jar?'

The news editor was reluctant to do this because he knew about the morning anger but he also knew the post-prandial anger was much worse and noisier, and he spent as long as he could cudgelling his brains to think of something to get Howitt out of the office productively. Howitt always came back from the pub smouldering about some imagined slight and spent the afternoon prowling round the news desk looking with his small tight face like an angry budgie.

'It's your round,' Howitt told me. 'What's the birds like, Tommy?'

'Brick shithouses,' said Tommy, who once he had an image in his head believed in making it work. Howitt looked at him balefully, challenging him.

'Bloody woodentop.'

I stepped in to prevent a breach of the peace.

'On your own?'

'Nearly,' said Howitt. 'I've got McNally with me.'

It is impossible to be a reporter and grown up. All reporters are Peter Pans playing role games. Scratch a court reporter and you will disturb a QC manqué. Sleuths not tall enough to make the police force become crime reporters and talk incessantly of 'chummy' and 'feeling his collar'.

Like most of the CID men they work with, they are Freemasons.

In every industrial reporter a tycoon or a union leader struggles to get out. Stand next to a lobby correspondent in a bar and within seconds you are looking for the red despatch box.

McNally wanted to be an international playboy. He worked at it tirelessly. He had the looks of a dissipated guardee. Age was beginning to weary him and the years condemn but he always wore a red carnation in his buttonhole and his regimental tie stood out from his crisp white shirt like a zebra crossing. He had a suede tongue and a complexion of brushed pigskin. He had everything his role demanded except the income. He was sadly under-funded. Always.

He beamed all round as he came into the bar from the gents where he had been giving the mirror his undiluted admiration. 'G and T?' he murmured hopefully.

'Half of bitter,' I told the barman. 'How's the game?'

'Don't ask. Know what the first day of Passover is?'

He had a Jewish girlfriend and in consequence knew about these things. For the same reason he knew about St David's Day, St Patrick's Day, St George's Day, St Andrew's Day, Independence Day, Ramadan, Bastille Day, even to judge by some of the dogs he squired, as Howitt had memorably said, Hallowe'en.

'It is the day the Angel of Destruction flew over the Jewish tribes. And it's just made a three point landing in the small of my back.'

'Trouble?' asked Tommy, unnecessarily. McNally had trouble like Tommy had hangovers. Being an international playboy, even in Manchester, was an expensive pursuit and a number of banks were making a poor job of financing him.

'Phone was cut off this morning,' he said. 'Electricity goes this afternoon. Have to park my motor a mile from the flat so the HP company won't snatch it and the county court bailiff is round so often he gets a Christmas card off the neighbours.'

'See the boxing on the telly?' Tommy asked him in an effort to lighten the conversation.

'Son,' said McNally, 'if I want to watch the telly I have to go to Radio Rentals window.'

He turned to me, the office expert on being hard pressed.

'There are only three ways left to me to get to the office. I owe garages on all the others. This morning I drew a £200 advance on exes to come here. Thought I'd drop £50 off at the electricity and another £50 at the telephone, appease them a bit and leave me with a ton for walkabout money. But I had to stop at the lights at my local garage. Owner spotted me, jumped in the car and wouldn't get out till I gave him £100 off my bill.'

'Hit the bank for some,' said Howitt, who was from Leeds and close with it.

'No bloody fear. Took your advice last time and wrote them a jolly letter. Told 'em everything. Said I had made a full and frank disclosure so they could set the Hamlet's ghost of my overdraft against the Elsinore of events. Thought it struck the right lofty note.'

'Did it?'

'Manager wrote back saying, was I aware that Hamlet was one of Shakespeare's greatest tragedies as I was one of the Midland Bank's. Clever bastard.'

'Only thing you can do now,' I said, 'is to go to a solicitor. Get him to write to all your creditors explaining he would take a sum of money from you each month and distribute it amongst them until your debt is cleared.'

'Will they fall for that?'

'Never been known to fail. All credit is based on trust. Your creditors don't trust you but a solicitor is an officer of the court. All you have to do is live frugally for a few months and you will be bees in clover.'

'Skiddy,' said McNally, 'you've changed my life.'

He signalled the barman.

'You got a decent champagne on ice?'

'Frugally,' I said.

'Of course,' said McNally, 'I am putting it down to Chinstrap's account. Always do. What is his room number, by the way?'

After the bottle was empty we went out looking for a pub outing to ruin.

Take Four

'You are having a good time,' said the large man in the orange papier mache policeman's helmet with kindly severity, 'don't spoil it.'

We were on the top deck of a bus which was careening wildly round a maze of country lanes at the mercy of a driver who had consumed nine large whiskeys, forced on him with malicious glee by Howitt. Around us a small bacchanalia was coming into mid-season form and the deck below us was a trophy room of the spoils of our visits to small and, until we left, comparatively well-furnished country pubs. Howitt had set the fashion by removing from a wall a flight of pot ducks and the idea had commended itself to the gang of Irish navvies whose outing we had joined. Their sporting instincts roused, the bag grew from beer mats to a dartboard and a cribbage set, tantalisingly incomplete without its cards.

'Well,' the small cliff of a man who had stolen it explained apologetically, 'there was fellas holdin' 'em at the time.'

There were fire buckets too, a cast iron marble topped table and a stuffed stag's head. We had also collected four girls who were making the best of things, or in the case of the one who was with McNally, being made the best of in the darkness at the rear of the bus. Howitt was plying another with drink like a tiny Yorkshire Imp of Destruction. It was not a pretty sight but it was much prettier than the one I had just caught sight of in the lane behind us.

Sitting on our tail was a police car, siren wailing, horn blasting and vainly attempting to overtake us. Plainly someone in that car had a notion to bring us to a halt and launch the due process of law.

That was the sight that caused me to cry 'Stop the bus' and brought me to the notice of the large gentleman in the orange helmet. His face was flushed, indeed it ought to have been flushed away. The drink had brought his blood to the boil. It was bubbling under the skin of his face and the orange helmet looked like a very angry pimple.

'Don't go spoilin' the fun,' he said, swaying over me and waving a beer bottle in my face.

'But there is a police car behind us,' I persisted, warily eyeing the bottle. 'I, I, I think he wants us to stop.'

'No doubt he does,' said the large man sagely. 'No doubt of that at all. And wouldn't they be after supping every drop of ale we have on the coach?'

'I don't really think they want a drink,' I said, 'I think they may be a little bit upset about all those things we stole from pubs.'

'Stole, is it?' roared the man, angry now. 'And me in a policeman's helmet. Are ye an eejit or what? Oive nivir stole a t'ing in my life.'

'But all those things downstairs?' I started to ask.

'Them t'ings ain't stolen at all,' he said, suddenly pedantic. 'What doze t'ings are, in a manner of speakin'...' he explained, and paused for thought. 'Doze t'ings are de spoils of war.'

'But we aren't at war,' I said.

'Aren't we so?' he demanded, his sideboard chest heaving and the bottle disappearing in a York ham of fist. 'D'ye dare to say that and me lovely country echoin' to the tramp of the boots of de English oppressor?'

He had boots on him you could have stuck a mast in and sailed them back to Eire. Except I have noticed most patriotic exiles from any given country kick up the biggest fuss at any prospect of forcible return to their native land. Naturally I said nothing of this to him in case it would upset him further.

'You want yer stinking crib board d'ye?' asked the man in fury, his throbbing boil of a face thrust against mine. 'We'll swap 'em yez for the Six Counties.'

There was a murmur of appreciation from the large forest of men that had suddenly grown round us. It only wanted the wrong word to start World War Three. It goes without saying that Howitt supplied it in tones of malicious clarity.

'Ah tell him to go back to his priest-ridden bog of a country.'

Tommy was sitting next to Howitt, concentrating heavily on the cut and thrust of the argument as he drank his sixteenth bottle of pale ale. Plainly puzzled he asked, 'Why shouldn't a priest go to the bog same as any ordinary feller? If there is one thing I cannot stand it's religious intolerance.'

'And isn't he right the little fella?" a voice came from the depths of the forest of men. 'Why not indeed?'

They say in your last moments your whole life flashes before you. For me the events of the past twenty-four hours had been plenty. Personally I do not believe a drowning man does see his past life. I believe a man sees his past life and then drowns deliberately.

I saw us going into one respectable pub after another, trying in vain to join their outing. None wanted a group of strangers to mar the harmony of their gentle bibulous forays.

In retrospect I should never have allowed Howitt into any pub called 'The Pride of Erin'. I know what can happen in a stationary taproom let alone in a fast bus when a group of Irishmen go a-pleasuring. The Erin regulars had welcomed our company when we offered to chuck in a case of whiskey as our contribution to the outing.

Not that there was going to be a story anyway. The courier from the firm that arranged all the pub outings for the gangsters who ran them had been left behind at the first pub. The itinerary was the next thing to be abandoned and from then on things got steadily worse.

I waited unhappily for the moment when the fist would replace the tongue as a weapon of argument. As a precaution, I removed my glasses and my watch, took out my false teeth, wrapped them in a hanky and placed them under the seat. I had been out with Howitt before.

'What about Bloody Sunday?' demanded an eighteen-stone stripling of a Kerry man.

'Not as bad as bleedin' Mondays,' said Tommy with conviction. 'Can't stand bleedin' Mondays,' he explained to the Kerry man, who looked like an Indian scout who has somehow missed the Pawnee raiders, as he tried to follow the conversation.

'And which would be Bleeding Monday? There's a battle I don't remember.'

'It's the day before Sodding Tuesday,' said Howitt. I never met a man with a more highly developed instinct for self-destruction.

In the scuffle that followed I played a small and undistinguished part. When the Kerry man lunged at Howitt I got out of the way. Unfortunately in doing so I cannoned into the only amiable man in the party who had been teetering gently at the top of the stairs, looking puzzled. With a look of pained surprise he rocked backwards, brow furrowed and then slowly toppled down the stairs to the deck below.

'Did ye see that?' said an onlooker, and I was pleased to detect a note of awe. 'The little fat yin threw the Bull from the top to the bottom of the stairs without a jot of effort.'

'Yes scut,' roared another Irishman. 'A nice fella like the Bull.' He lunged at me, missed and with a roar joined the Bull on the lower deck.

'The divil of a man,' cried my invisible fan. 'Hasn't he done it again? Sure the same wee fella'll have us all down there.'

Behind us a general melee had broken out and the deck was a monkey-puzzle of arms, waving legs and feet, with fists that broke out of the scrum like so many mutton meteors. From somewhere in its heaving heart I could hear the anguished cry of Tommy.

'My camera, watch my camera. Don't tread on my camera!'

I looked for the tattered remains of Howitt, gone, I supposed, to a martyr's rest. I should have known my man better. He was sitting at his ease on a front seat of the bus, watching the battle with interest and drinking from a bottle of pale ale. He caught my glance and a malevolent smile creased his wedge-shaped face.

'Isn't the vi'lence a terrible t'ing?' he mimicked.

There is no telling how high the death toll would have been had the bus not, at that moment, with an embarrassed cough, run out of petrol. The engine died, the bus slowed and then stopped. The rending sound of metal that followed could be readily identified as a police car running onto our back bumper. Indeed one of the more perceptive passengers summed up the situation crisply: 'The bus has stopped,' he said 'and there's a bloody great police car run up the arse of us.'

From somewhere in the amorous embrace of the lady with whom he had been dallying McNally spoke for the first time.

'I have been working it out,' he said. 'And I don't see how we can get less than five years.'

The policeman who presently appeared, white faced and shaking, took a more pessimistic view of our future.

'By the time you lot get out,' he threatened, 'there will be steeple chasing on Mars. If I had my way I'd make you all swim back to Dublin with a Paki on your back.'

It was not original but it was effective. We knew he was angry and we also knew that he did not care how big any of us were because he was looking forward to a bit of violence himself.

'Right,' he said, and it was obvious control was becoming difficult, 'I am going back to my police car and then my colleague and I will follow you to the police station which is just two miles down the road. OK?'

'Excuse me, officer.' It was Howitt at his silkiest.

137

'I am afraid we will not be able to do that.'

The policeman looked down at him and threw an interrogative 'Oh?'

'First,' said Howitt, 'let me say how glad I am to see you. I have been endeavouring to remonstrate with these gentlemen. But one against so many....' He raised his hands.

'I see, sir,' the policeman said, 'but why can't you follow us?'

'No petrol,' explained Howitt. 'We ran out just before you ran into us. As these gentlemen will confirm, we were stationary at the time.' He paused. 'No suggestion of criticism of your driving, of course, but you were a little nearer than the Highway Code recommends. Thirty feet, I believe...'

'We were trying to overtake you,' protested the policeman defensively, but a bit of the cool had slipped from his manner and we all heard it drop. 'You were going like the clappers.'

'Us, officer?' said Howitt with dangerous innocence. 'How could we be? The tank is empty. We were just waiting here for a car to come along so we could get a lift to a garage. There are thirty men here who would swear to that in court.'

There was a wildness in the policeman's eyes. I have seen it before in the eyes of authority when it clashed with Howitt.

'I'll tell you what, officer, I will just nip out and see what damage has been done.'

He was back before the policeman had time to recover the advantage. 'It's OK, just your bumper is a bit bent and one of the Irishmen is straightening it. No harm done.'

He raised an arm to stem the policeman's answer.

'I have had a word with your colleague. I have suggested, and he has agreed, that we should siphon enough from your tank into ours so that we can precede you to the police station where we can straighten out this sorry affair. Indeed one of our party is doing that now. Your driver suggests you should sit with us. He'll follow in your car and we can sort everything out at the police station.'

'I'll look forward to that,' said the policeman settling in the nearest seat. Howitt signalled to Tommy to keep him occupied and positioned me and McNally where we would block his view through the back window. Moments later there was a lurch, the bus cleared its throat and we were in motion.

'What about my mate?' the policeman asked.

'It's all right, he's following on.'

I followed Howitt down to the back step. He was grinning evilly into a night which was unbroken by the sound of a police car engine. 'Where is he? What have you done?' I asked, and my voice was squeaky with panic for I truly believed Howitt had murdered the other policeman.

'What do you think I have done? I got the Mick to drain his petrol tank. Can't you hear him shouting?'

'Five years? Life,' opined McNally, who had joined us. 'What about my alimony? I can't pay that if I'm not working.'

'You don't have to in the nick,' said Howitt. 'Don't worry, I have not finished yet and they will never identify us. Our number plate fell off in the crash and I have hidden it under the stairs.'

'Not finished?' I was beyond control. 'Not finished? We've wrecked a police car, stolen police petrol and kidnapped a constable. They are not going to like that,' I warned him, 'they are not going to like that one little bit.'

'Likely,' said Howitt. 'These two buggers are never going to mention tonight's little fracas till their dying day. I know what I am doing.'

'So do I.' Now I was screaming. 'You are going barking mad.'

I was about to strangle Howitt but was prevented by Tommy's arrival.

'You will have to do something,' he said. 'That bobby upstairs is worried because he cannot see the lights of his car.'

I had saved a little moan for just such an occasion and I let it out.

'Don't panic,' Howitt said, then he called up the stairs, 'Officer, can you come down for a moment, I think there is something wrong.'

A frightening thought struck me. 'Don't push him off,' I begged, 'we are doing at least sixty.'

'Don't be daft,' said Howitt as the policeman clattered down the stairs to join us.

'I cannot see your colleague,' said Howitt.

'Stop the bus,' ordered the policeman.

'But officer...' said Howitt.

'Stop the bleeding bus,' shouted the policeman, 'or I'll have you for kidnapping.'

'Told you,' I muttered, but Howitt was ringing the bell.

'Don't anyone get off,' commanded the policeman.

'Now look here, officer...' Howitt started.

'No,' shouted the policeman, 'you look here. You're the worst of the lot. What the hell do you think you are playing at?'

'Playing at?' echoed Howitt, the picture of outraged innocence. 'What do you mean? You come roaring up out of the dark, crash into our back when we are stationary and frighten us to death. Then my friend almost poisons himself siphoning off petrol so you can take us into custody and finally your mate gets lost on a perfectly straight road. What are *we* playing at?'

The policeman shook his head slowly. 'Just take me back to the patrol car,' he said.

'Certainly,' said Howitt, 'at once.'

It did not take us long to get back to the police car where an interesting sight met us. The other policeman was outlined in his headlights. He was waving his arms and he appeared to be dancing on the spot.

'I think he is upset about something,' remarked Tommy.

'Wait here,' said the first policeman. He climbed down from the bus and started to walk towards his colleague but as he did the other policeman lunged at him and caught our policeman a resounding buffet to the side of his head. It had been an unhappy evening for our policeman and this was plainly the last straw. His left to his partner's jaw was a peach.

'They are scrapping,' said Tommy.

They were. We could hear them shouting at each other as they swapped blows.

'You bastard,' the other policeman said, 'you never did like me.'

'What could I do?' demanded our policeman hotly. 'Ring up the desk sergeant and tell him that some big Mick had siphoned off your petrol while you were sitting in the car?'

'This is no place for us,' said Howitt, ringing the bell, 'let's piss off.'

And we did.

I was so glad to get off that bus that I did not even worry that I was almost certainly for the sack when Cudlipp heard of our exploits, as he was bound to before the day was over.

I have never been at ease with the internal combustion engine since my days as a national serviceman when the army decided to teach me how to drive. I loved the army. There was a silver thread of silliness running through it that I found wholly endearing. The trick was not to take it seriously; to realise that one was taking part in an endless comic strip. Sadly my love of the army was not returned. The army was constantly court martialling me. In mitigation, I should say that I hold what is probably a military record for accelerated promotion.

Five minutes from bemused private to startled sergeant, though admittedly in a PR unit which doesn't count as real army. I didn't expect to be a sergeant very long and I wasn't. I also hold an army record for demotion. Three stripes lost in six weeks for separate offences. Mostly it was the discipline that brought me down with a low tackle.

I started well. As the most short-sighted soldier since Mr Magoo, I was told to take twenty-four other myopic militarians from our camp in Knutsford to the Medical Centre at Saighton camp, Chester, to be fitted with spectacles, metal framed, pairs one. I still don't understand why the army picked up the Arab habit of reading from right to left but that is another story.

So is the reason I lost them. Suffice it to say that while my attention was temporarily diverted they deserted to a man. When I returned to camp, alone save for twenty-four partly used travel warrants, the Duty Officer was greatly impressed.

'Good heavens,' he said, 'we didn't lose that many on D Day and they were firing on us then. You lost yours in Chester where not a single shot has been fired. In my view that deserves extra points.'

I offered to explain but he said, no thanks; he would prefer to think of the incident as a sort of military Marie Celeste. Though he said the Colonel might take a different view, the army having gone to such trouble to collect the chaps in the first place.

The Colonel did. But even as he castigated me I saw his point. The army had been to a lot of expense summoning the nation's gilded youth to the Colours. As he said, very fairly in my view, they just couldn't have chaps like me losing them the moment the army's back was turned. I have to say looking back, I do not think this incident did a lot to help me realise my ambition, which was to become a general and in consequence excused boots.

Then there was the business of the electric light fitting at the pre-OCTU to which I was unaccountably sent.

In those distant days prospective leaders of men had to pass an aptitude test that included assembling a domestic light fitting. I have subsequently read a fair drop of military history, even written two volumes myself. Nowhere did I find a single example where the ability to assemble a domestic light fitting has materially altered the course of a battle.

Picture the scene.

You leap from your horse onto the parapet of a front line trench.

'Men,' you say, 'the enemy artillery is posted on a commanding position on our left flank; over on the right we have the Republican Guard preparing to charge. In front of us the enemy air force is assembled for take off. There is only one course of action open to us. Assemble me a domestic light fitting.'

Say what you like, it doesn't have a ring to it.

You have to give it to the army. Having spectacularly failed to make me an officer and subsequently an infantryman in the Black Watch (RHR), it was plucky of it to bite on the bullet and attempt to turn me into a truck driver at its RASC drivers' training battalion in Yeovil.

I eventually got the hang of starting the things and driving in a straight line. Even so, I fear I was not ready for my first test that was in Yeovil on market day. The driving instructor had barely unscrewed the top of his fountain pen before the truck turned of its own volition into the market square, massacred a hen and brought the stall crashing down round the ears of its occupant.

I think he was trying to say something to me but I could not hear him for the noise the instructor was making, and I noticed he made the same noise when a fortnight later I went for my second test. I will never forget that instructor's face when he found me waiting for him. I expect that is why I drove the truck into the gatepost of Montacute House.

'I don't suppose you are going to pass me?' I said.

'No,' he replied, 'but if you want to transfer from the Black Watch to the Royal Engineers I will endorse your demolition certificate.'

It was just bad luck I got the same instructor for my third attempt though he seemed to think it was because his boss didn't like him.

'Move over,' he said, and climbed into the driver's seat.

Eventually we reached a stretch of straight road.

'If you can get to the other end without hitting anything or anyone, you have passed,' he said. 'Just promise me that if ever the urge to drive comes over you, you will transfer to the Tank Corps in Germany. Then I can look on it as war reparations.'

The least military of men, I nevertheless became in time provost sergeant of HQ 7th Armoured Division in Germany, though I had to go to prison first and I only got the job because the RSM was illiterate and had never heard of my job in Public Relations. He thought PR was short for provost.

It came about this way. The RASC battalion in which I became a driver was posted to Palestine at the time of the Troubles there, but I never did get to join it. On our last night at Thetford Embarkation Camp I was buttoning my greatcoat as I left the Green Dragon Inn. An army policeman pounced and started to charge me with being improperly dressed. It was a mistake. As a Black Watch soldier I was an icon for all the Glaswegians in the RASC, of whom there were many. Glaswegians are tiny parcels of aggression. Tiny because they all seem to be 5ft 5inches tall and I have heard it said that if you are 5ft 6 inches in Glasgow you have to move to Aberdeen. Several of these dynamic dwarves took violent exception to the policeman, reinforcements were summoned by both sides, and the upshot was that I was charged with assaulting six military policemen. I was taken off the draft to Palestine and sent instead to Germany, closely followed by the charge.

My new CO was a nice man and he looked surprised when I was marched in.

'I am a very bewildered officer,' he said. 'I was expecting Wyatt Earp and you do not look at all aggressive.'

'I am not, sir,' I said, and told him the story. He heard me out sympathetically and then said there was nothing he could do. A charge of that gravity was a court martial offence and he could only remand me for one.

'But,' he said, 'I can give you a piece of advice. Plead guilty.'

'I haven't done anything,' I said.

'That is obvious to me and it will be obvious to the court. But if you plead not guilty they will have to bring witnesses from the UK and it will count against you. They will have to convict because of the expense. You plead guilty and when they ask, your counsel – the Soldier's Friend as he is known – will tell them what happened and you will get off with a reprimand.'

I did as he advised. The so-called soldier's friend did not say a word and I got 56 days in the 3rd Military Corrective Establishment in Bielefeld.

I came out determined to desert the moment I got back to Rhine Army Headquarters at Bad Oeynhausen. I was on my way to the railway station when I heard what I thought was the Voice of God. It was much worse. It was the Garrison Regimental Sergeant Major, 'Jock' Grahame of the Scots Guards. A man so tall he was said to have replaced his cap badge with a warning light for low flying aircraft.

For 56 days I had been berated by experts but compared with Grahame they were selling platers. From his opening remark: 'You 'orrible little man' to his closing threat to take the red hackle out of my tam-o'-shanter and 'stick it up your arse so you'll hop around like a bleeding barn fowl', he proved himself the master of wounding rhetoric. When he marched off I was a limp rag and crept into a side street to hide my humiliation. Only to see him apparently following me. In a panic, I dived through the first door I came to and found myself confronting an office sign that read PR Army Newspapers. Without thinking I rushed in. A warrant officer looked up and asked in a kindly way what I wanted.

Goodness knows why I asked him if there were any jobs going in the unit. He said there was one but did I have any experience? As it happens I had been a printer's apprentice at Kemsley Newspapers in Manchester. 'I was on the *Evening Chronicle...*' I started to say.

'It's our lucky day,' he said. 'We've never had a real evening paper reporter before. Come and meet Kenneth.'

I was about to point out I wasn't a reporter but the use of Christian names to private soldiers was so unusual I said, 'Who is Kenneth?'

'The commanding officer,' he said, and vanished through an inner door.

For 56 days I had been saluting everything that moved and now I had been translated to a world where officers were called by their Christian names. I resolved to keep quiet about the printing job and followed him.

Kenneth was still a bit of a surprise. I learned later he had transferred to the Tank Corps solely to swap his brown beret for a black one, which he believed brought out the blue in his eyes.

'Paddy tells me you want to join us and of course we would love to have you. Just give me the name of your CO so I can put the transfer into immediate effect, then cut along to Stores and draw your sergeant's stripes.'

'A SERGEANT?' I yelped, and he looked quite hurt.

'Well you cannot expect to be an officer straight away,' he said.

So I became in a flash a sergeant, a bogus reporter, and two hours later was sent off on my own to cover my first story, and incidentally the biggest I have ever done – the Berlin Airlift.

Even on the Airlift trouble dogged my every step.

I had put my driver on a charge for biting a war dog. He had done it to demonstrate to me, as we were passing the compound where the war dogs were kept, that he had been in the past a dog handler. Since he had also at one time or another claimed he was Monty's driver, a guerrilla fighter and a Canadian lumberjack, I doubted him.

To prove his words, he crawled into the compound and bit a Doberman pinscher, a breed of dog that usually does the biting. This change in the arrangements surprised the dog into an outraged yelp that brought the corporal dog handler out of his tree. He was very cross to find a private soldier gnawing at the knee of his Doberman and insisted I put the gnawer on a charge. He said if people thought they could creep into his kennels and bite his Doberman pinschers there was no telling what chaos might ensue.

Lord Langford of Bodrhyddan Hall, Rhuddlan, in north Wales, was the commanding officer before whom I brought one Private Anderson. The charge was 'Damaging War Department property, in that he did bite a war dog'.

Forty years may have passed, and the Lord and I are still good friends, but I still find that reminding him of the occasion produces a startling response.

I never had much luck with my drivers. The only award I ever got was a weekend in Brussels covering a motorcycle race. I was at the time writing stories about what fun the army was. I wrote one about a retreat centre, which was praised by Cardinal Griffin, the Archbishop of Westminster, and my reward was the trip.

The unit driver by now was a Gordon Highlander of impenetrable thickness. He couldn't understand why he wasn't allowed to go with me. He said if he had not driven me to the retreat I would not have been able to write about it. The argument had a certain uneasy logic but it failed to convince our commanding officer, never a lateral thinker at the best of times.

So I went to Brussels with a photographer, and my driver went absent without leave with the unit jeep. Had he gone on his own I doubt if anyone would have noticed but we were a small unit and the jeep was our entire transport fleet. When the driver eventually brought the jeep back the commanding officer insisted I put him on a charge.

I didn't want to put my driver on a charge for an offence that, compared with biting a Doberman pinscher, was trivial. But you know how officers are when they have their minds made up. The driver's defence was brilliant. He said he had wanted to mark the occasion of his sergeant's achievement and he had a brilliant idea. While the sergeant was away he would have his jeep painted as a surprise. Alas, said my driver, army workshops could not do the job at such short notice. The solution came to this honest soldier in a flash. He would have the vehicle painted *at his own expense* in a civilian garage. He had driven it back in time for the sergeant's return. How was he being repaid, this kindly old soldier? By being out on a charge.

I could see he had got to the commanding officer. The old fool was trumpeting into his hanky and minutes passed before he was sufficiently master of himself to administer a rebuke for my insensitivity. Many more passed before I could persuade him to inspect the vehicle park where all the headquarters transport was kept. Lovely they looked, uniform in drab olive. It was easy to pick out mine. It was the only pea green jeep in the British army.

Military Observers, as we were called, were given a warrant card, signed by a field marshal, which ordered that no one whatever their rank was to interfere with the holder in the performance of his duties. I thought to take it a step further.

My original intention when I came out of the glasshouse was to desert. The warrant card gave me the opportunity to desert without leaving the army. Before I arrived at Wunsdorf to take up a presence on the Airlift I paid a Fraulein ten cigarettes to sew on two shoulder straps which read 'Official Army Observer', exchanged my tam-o'-shanter for a beret on which I did not display a badge and told the RSM that I was 'civilian attached' and the sergeant's stripes were to afford me entry to the sergeants' mess for messing and accommodation. It was nearly a year before I was found out.

During that happy time I found the warrant card invaluable in many ways. I used to fly to Berlin on Airlift Skymaster transport planes most weekends, even after I was returned to regimental duties.

When the Russians blocked the road to Berlin many of the soldiers stationed there were flown back to the Western Zone. If they were married to German girls they were allowed to bring them but the ladies were not allowed luggage. For a fiver a time I would fly into Berlin, pick up two suitcases of clothes from their homes and bring them to the West.

A rather smelly CSM in the Catering Corps had a more serious problem. His very beautiful German wife had a small son, from an earlier marriage, whom she was forced to leave in Berlin. The CSM said he would give me a tenner if I could bring the child into the Western Zone. This was highly illegal, of course, but a tenner is a tenner so I agreed.

Using my warrant card to get a flight and then in Berlin to commandeer a jeep and a driver, I went to the child's home, collected him, and flew back with him. I told officers who questioned me about him that I was doing a story on German orphans and needed him for photographs.

In general I found that officers were a pretty gullible lot. And not only officers. Many years later my friend Father Brian Jones took a party of parishioners to Cardiff, which the Pope was visiting for the first time. So that they could be distinguished in crowds, priests were issued with handsome umbrellas in the Papal colours. Brian thought his would make a wonderful souvenir so when the visit ended he tried to sneak one from the grounds. He was stopped by his Bishop who said, 'Brian, I am surprised at you.'

Covered in confusion, Brian spluttered an excuse but the Bishop went on, 'Don't steal one, steal a dozen and they will think you are collecting them.'

When I was appointed provost sergeant I was responsible for discipline in the HQ consisting of well over a thousand soldiers. They were no trouble. It was my regimental policemen who were out of control, even though I ran the guardroom as a soviet.

Prisoners were allowed out on day trips to the nearest town, but only if they took a regimental policeman as a chaperone and were back by guard mounting at 6pm. None let me down but that may be because I warned them that if they were late I would send my RPs looking for them with pick staves. My RPs were a terrifying bunch, they even frightened me. They were all undesirables from Highland Regiments who themselves had spent more time in prison than anyone in the HQ.

One of my prisoners, a Leeds boy called Hardisty, later made the splash in the *Daily Express*. He went AWOL in Berlin and wandered over to the Russian Zone. At that time pretty Russian girls lured British soldiers to go over to the Russian army with promises of sex. Then they were used as black propaganda. Hardisty went willingly and when a Russian female colonel interrogated him and promised him girlfriends he responded quickly.

'Right, get yer knickers off,' he said.

The colonel fled. After a week of increasingly disruptive behaviour the Russians handed him back to the British army.

When I was made provost sergeant I ordered my RPs to send to their regiments for kilts and they looked terribly smart when I turned them out every morning to greet the general. He always spoiled it as he returned our salute by saying to me in a loud voice, 'Good morning, sonny.'

In the event, the kilt idea was an unwise gesture on my part. Within three days they had, to a man, sold their kilts on the black market and I had to charge them all with theft. There was an irony that they would have appreciated. When it was my turn to be demobbed, I kept the kilt the regiment had issued and handed in a worn kilt my mother had bought from an advert in the *Manchester Evening News*. The RSM, never a fan of mine, was suspicious and brought a Black Watch officer to identify it.

Good as gold, he confirmed it was an army issue kilt but when asked *when* it was issued had to say, 'Judging by the regimental number, about 1917.'

That cost me one stripe. Subsequent insubordination to the RSM cost the other two. My discharge book read: 'Sgt Skidmore is a very reliable NCO.' The 'sergeant' had then been crossed out and 'corporal' substituted. Alas, there was yet another crossing out so that the book eventually read, 'Private Skidmore is a very reliable NCO.'

Truly the army moved in mysterious ways its wonders to perform.

Take Five

Of all the entertainers in the world Josef Locke was my favourite. A boozy, unpredictable Irishman, he had the voice of an angel. Which may be why he was a sensational success in his theatre show on the Pier and yet barred from several pubs along Blackpool's Rolled Gold Mile.

In contrast, *Mirror* editor Jack Nener was reputed to have the foulest mouth in Britain.

Once in the Midland Hotel in Manchester his language was so foul that another customer complained. Nener was livid.

'Do you know who I f...ing am, you stupid c..t?' he roared, 'I am the f...ing editor of the f...ing *Daily Mirror*.'

'That does not surprise me in the least,' the customer said.

Nener was no scholar. Subs have literary catchphrases with which they paper over the cracks of life's madness. A popular one came from *Tom Brown's Schooldays*. 'Flashman,' they would tell each other, 'you are a bully and a liar and there is no place for you in the school.'

In a lift Nener turned to his deputy Dicky Dinsdale. 'Who's this Flashman then, Dick?'

'Flashman? Flashman? I don't think we have got anyone of that name on the paper. Is he a reporter or a sub?'

'I don't give a fuck where he works. Get rid of him fucking quick. He is a bully and a liar.'

Nener was married to Audrey Whiting, a talented writer and a woman of towering height but no great beauty. He was heard over the phone breaking the good news of the engagement to a friend.

'I'm marrying Audrey Whiting,' he said. There was a long silence broken eventually by a barked, 'Of course I'm not pissed.'

Her opinion of him was not high either. She told colleagues, 'He was an absolutely awful man to work for, dreadful beyond belief. He swore like a trooper. The language was awful but it was deliberate. It wasn't until I married him and got to know him terribly well that he would laugh.'

Audrey subsequently told of a touching domestic scene involving a new Spanish maid with little English. She was trying to explain what a way Nener had with vacuum cleaners. 'This morning it no go,' she said. 'Signor Nener come in, 'e say "fucking thing" and kicks it and it go all day.'

Howitt, who, like the vacuum cleaner, had felt the force of Nener's anger resolved on retribution. He offered to get Josef into the party if he in return would do Howitt a favour.

'Name it,' said the generous Josef.

'Deck Jack Nener.'

Josef said he would be delighted to give the editor a slap but the problem was he had never met him.

'No problem,' said Howitt, 'he will be the only one in evening dress.'

So in a way it was Howitt's fault, and an understandable mistake on Josef's part, when later in the evening and after several bottles of champagne... he floored the headwaiter.

Reporters are great players of cruel practical jokes and Howitt had learnt from a master, Michael Gabbert, at that time news editor of the *People*.

Gabbert's greatest prank concerned a very hard-nosed *People* reporter Ken Graham, who looked in the news desk diary one morning and found that he was down to make a parachute jump.

'A joke?' he said.

'No joke,' said Gabbert. 'Not chicken, are you?'

'Course I'm not,' said Graham, though he had paled visibly.

Gabbert's pranks always had a cast of thousands. This one included an RAF PRO who rang a few moments later and asked Graham if he was insured because Air Ministry regulations demanded that civilians travelling by military aircraft and jumping out of them while they were moving be insured for £500,000.

What really started Graham pondering was the next call. It came from Neville Stack, the news editor of the *People's* sister paper the *Daily Herald*. Stack said that he had heard Graham was going to do a jump for charity and wondered if he would mind doing a piece for the *Herald*, too. Possibly taking a few pictures as he came down.

By this time Graham was giving little yelps and smoking heavily.

'How can I do that?' he wanted to know. 'I'll need my hands to pull the parachute strings.'

Stack said he had thought of that. They were going to strap a camera to his chest and fit a remote control, which would reach his mouth. All he had to do was press it with his tongue as he left the aircraft.

When Gabbert heard of the plan he said if the *Herald* was to have photographs so must the *People*. He didn't suppose Graham would go for the idea of two cameras on the chest and two remote controls.

'How about,' he said, 'if we had a cameraman on the ground? He could photograph you as you came out of the plane.'

'But there are other parachutists in the stick,' protested Graham. 'How will he know which one is me?'

'That's easy,' said Gabbert. 'As you jump out of the aircraft just shout, "It's me, it's me".'

'He'll never hear me.'

'He will if you have a megaphone round your neck,' said Gabbert slyly. Graham said was it all right if he went out for a drink?

To this day I do not know if it was by accident or design that when Graham got to our local, the Chicken Inn, the only other customer at the bar was a sub-editor who had been a corporal in the 6th Airborne.

'Eh,' said Graham, 'is parachute jumping dangerous?'

'Parachute jumping?' said the man. 'Easy as falling off a log. Jumping isn't dangerous.'

Graham looked relieved.

'Jumping's fine. It's landing that is dangerous. That's when the leg breaks. Snaps like a match if you land wrong.'

'How do you land properly?' Graham asked.

'It's sort of twisting and kind of bending really.'

'Like this?' said Graham, and tried.

'No,' said the sub-editor, 'not like that. Like that a busted pelvis is about five to one on.'

'The trouble is,' he said, 'you couldn't really learn how to do it, not from a standing position.'

In the Airborne, the sub-editor explained, they had learnt by falling off the back of moving trucks. Would Graham like him to get his car out?

'You could practise falling out of the passenger seat but you would have to be careful not to be hit by the door.'

Graham said wasn't there some other way and the sub-editor said, 'Well...'

151

Which explains why when we came over to the pub Graham was standing on a table, jumping off it, bending his knees gracefully on impact. And rolling along the carpet until brought to a halt by the foot rail at the bar.

Take Six

Many gallons of beer have flowed under the bridge of my nose; beer on which I have floated, sodden and occasionally disappearing beneath the waves, like an ill-made paper boat. My first wife, in the ways wives have, insisted that even by a modest compilation I put away about five thousand pints per annum, not counting wines and spirits.

I pointed out that I spilled much of it down my duffel coat, especially as the evening wore on, but she refused to allow any reduction.

In those days we expressed our individuality by all wearing identical duffel coats.

It seems so far away, that Golden Age before singers like Locke were displaced by the adenoid; before the dreadful dawn of denim enabled the young to demonstrate their individuality by dressing in identical drab garments, the livery of the itinerate American sod buster.

To us the duffel coat was all. My bookmaker wisely said that he who marries twice did not deserve the good fortune of getting rid of the first one. My own experience would incline me to disagree. Although I came very near to voting for the resolution when my second wife put down the footfall in the matter of my ancient duffel coat.

'It has got to go,' she said.

Wives have no wardrobe loyalty.

We are told we must recognise the world's poor and I will have no difficulty with complying. They will all be wearing my wife's cast-off frocks. Most women use carrier bags to take their unwanted clothes to Oxfam. My wife pioneered the use of the container truck. So fast is the wardrobe turnover at Skidmore Parva we could save time by buying the stuff and having it delivered direct to War On Want.

Easy come, easy go. Except for my duffel coat, which still rankles. The moment I put it on, my arms crept round my back and my hands gripped each other, just like the Duke of Edinburgh, though better tempered. Tugboats saluted me with blasts of their sirens.

I know of no more consoling garment. Hooded and toggled to the neck, duffelled almost from top to toe, you are bug-snugged against anything the world can hurl at you.

There was a time when I doubt if you would have been admitted to a symphony concert unless wearing one. Duffel coats give authority. Without them the early promenade concerts would have been a mere jetty.

Why, do you suppose, they always include a Fantasy of Sea Shanties?

It was a tribute to devotees of the duffel, the only garment known to man that is improved by chip fat or the cunningly placed oil stain.

I will go further. Duffel coats are grateful for any drop of beer the wearer consents to spill down them. If you listen very carefully you will hear the fabric lapping it up, absorbing it with many a smack of toggle against rope.

My good friend the distinguished composer Wil Mathias, or Wil Sol Fa as we of the cognoscenti knew him, frequently invited that duffel and me to concerts at his St Asaph music festival.

In a duffel coat one is armoured even against Wagner at his most militant. Brahms is never more seductive than when one is diapered in duffel. Only when swathed in duffel is the mind nimble enough to unravel Ravel.

Before that dreadful dawn of denim there was a time when cinema queues were composed of long, cosy quadrilles of duffel coats. They had the romantic air of patient Esquimaux. I often felt a brisk trade might have been done if, during the interval, usherettes could have passed amongst us with cartons of whale blubber.

And that was another thing. The duffel coat could be pushed under the seat and retrieved un-ruffled at the end of a performance. Whoever heard of a ruffled duffel? The noble garment does not so much keep out storm and tempest as deny their very existence.

How to recognise the genuine article? Easy. It was RN issue and always had the name of its first naval owner printed on the inside back. In ink. The duffel reigned over a world unburdened by biro. Only the first owner, mark you. Subsequent owners retrieved lost duffels not by their own name but with that of the man who wrote it when first it was launched. Probably in the Western Approaches or the defence of Scapa Flow.

Without his duffel the late Jack Hawkins might never have made it to the Hall of Fame. His duffel in *The Cruel Sea* gave some of the most remarkable performances of the stiff upper hood known to man.

I am told there are still high priced garments purporting to be duffels that are apparently wrought from fur scraped from the tongues of dead bookmakers. They crease.

The duffel coats to which I refer were Royal Navy issue and obtainable only in second-hand shops. Mine, like most of my wardrobe, was ex-Oxfam. Sleeping in it for a week the most I got was the appearance of having been lightly ploughed.

My first wife was even less forgiving of my eccentricities than the second. She took me to the marriage guidance.

We went in together and the counsellor said, 'What is the matter?'

To which my wife replied, 'He is never sober and he keeps being sick on the roses.'

Then we went out and my wife returned to the room on her own.

When she came out she said, 'Come on home.'

'But I haven't had my turn,' I protested.

'Never mind your turn, we are going home,' she said.

She was silent on the bus and still remained shtum when I left her to clock in at the Red Lion. So it was not until some time later that I was able to ask her what the matter was.

'Matter?' she said. 'Matter? I will tell you what the matter is. How did you manage to corrupt the girl at the Marriage Guidance?'

'I never laid a finger on her,' I said. 'You were there the whole time.'

'I don't mean that,' she said. 'She was on your side.'

'How do you mean?' I said.

'You know very well what I mean. I told her how you always peed on the roses when you came home from work and when I said that was very rude, you said all night workers pee on the roses. That is why they have such good roses. And do you know what she said?'

'No.'

'She said I was very lucky. She said her husband came home last Saturday night, opened the wardrobe door, went in and peed all over her shoes. Then he came out and said, "It's time we got a light in that bloody bathroom".'

No news editor in those happy days ever complained about two hour luncheons. Intoxication was almost a job requirement and the newspaper trade was illuminated by the oddest people. None more odd, more witty and more thoroughly unscrupulous in his fight to survive

155

than the picture editor, George Harrop, who could drink more whisky and remain coherent than anyone I have ever met.

Harrop, never a man to miss a party, died the day *after* his 80th birthday. The cause I do not know but it certainly was not a hangover. Like Richard Burton he was a stranger to that curse although in his prime he drank two bottles of whisky a day without visible effect. The doctor treating him said, 'George, by the state of your liver I take it that you're a whisky drinker, a bottle a week perhaps?'

George replied indignantly, 'I spill more than that!'

Nor did drink loosen his tongue. He was born with the loosest tongue in the West.

Once as he was talking on the phone the sports editor Peter Thomas tweaked his line out of its socket. Thomas said wonderingly afterwards: 'He not only didn't notice; he went on talking for a full five minutes.'

His house hid behind an unkempt privet hedge. One night, drink taken, he couldn't find the gate, so he hurled himself at the hedge until he had made a hole big enough to walk through. The gap stayed for years.

He was a master gunner of the Christmas card artillery barrage. If you met him once you got a card, usually in November. He liked a full mantelpiece and a card sent guarantees a return. Less amiable gunners send on Christmas Eve when it is too late to reply.

Nowadays you need a degree to get into this trade. George was a cinema manager. His only journalistic qualification was wit. It was his press club conversation that persuaded *Express* editor 'Strangler' Lewis to give him a job on the picture desk.

George did not fear the Strangler, a formidable former Commando major who lost his temper in 1943 and never regained it. Once in the office he roared, 'George, get off the bloody phone.'

'Have to go,' said George in a voice everybody in the room heard, 'the editor wants permission to change a crosshead.'

Geoff Mather, an old *Express* chum, recalled George's description of an *Express* foremen's Christmas lunch at the Midland Hotel: 'They went pouring through the swing doors in their suede clogs and cloth caps shouting, "Where's the foremen's lavatory?"...'

He was appreciative of wit in others. When I claimed that, come Twelfth Night, the Press Club's inadequate cotton wool decorations would be back in the ears of the poor he joyfully adopted it as his own.

Paul Roche, the *Mirror* manager, and Mike Terry, our one-eyed editor, arrived from lunch showing signs of having enjoyed the outing.

'Here they come,' said Harrop, 'Roche and ricochet.'

News desk assistant Les Stringer was a hypochondriac and the deputy news editor Ken Tossell was forever yawning. He called them Sick and Tired.

Watching a rather tired male reporter cross the editorial floor with a new female reporter, who was smartly dressed but vaguely showing the outline of her underwear, he observed, 'Knickered and knackered.'

When I wrote George's obituary in my newspaper column, another reporter, Brian Stringer, recalled:

'In the 1960s George and I had been good chums – that is, we met often in the old Manchester Press Club. I joined him there after escaping from the *Daily Express* night newsdesk. This arrangement came to an end one Christmas when, having met George as usual and then bade him farewell with seasonal greetings, I left the Press Club around 3am to go to a party in Altrincham. I used the then traditional mode of transport – an Autax on the account of the *Daily Express*, the chitty signed by either Bert Howes or Claude Lescure.

'Only as we neared Altrincham did I realise that George was also in my cab, fast asleep on the back seat. He followed me into the party. Suffice to say he was in truculent mood, his capacity for making new friends much impaired by his earlier festive merrymaking in the Press Club.

'It was not long before our host, Mr William (Billy) Wilkinson, who was in plaster from hip to ankle having broken his leg and other bones in an accident the previous day, wanted a quiet word with me. He required that I should remove George at once and he gave me his car keys so that I could take him home.

'And so it was that I found myself, George at my side, in the driving seat of an unfamiliar car at 5am making my way along the main Chester road heading back to Manchester.

'Distracted by my companion who thought he was still at the party, I drove over the bumpy flowerbeds of a roundabout at Stretford. This startled George, who demanded to know where he was and how he could open the steamed-up passenger window. Concentrating on trying to avoid any further flowerbeds, I told him I had no idea – it was something he would have to work out for himself.

'A few moments later I felt a breeze and assumed George had opened the window. But his seat was empty and when I looked in my rear mirror I was horrified to see a bundle of rags rolling down the road following the car. It was George – he had opened the door and fallen

157

out. There was no doubt in my mind that he was a goner. I stopped the car and ran back to the motionless rags that had once been my friend in an overcoat. Half a dozen Pakistanis at a bus stop – obviously some factory's dawn shift – watched quite bemused by the horror of the scene as George came to a stop in front of them. None came to help, presumably fearing they would lose their place in the bus queue.

'Numb with fright, I knelt in the road beside the rags and their contents and wondered what one was supposed to do in a pickle like this. All my prayers were answered when George's head emerged from the tattered overcoat – scratched, but very much alive. He got to his feet, dusted himself down and in the ripest language insisted I should take him to the pub 500 yards down the road.

'The Old Cock was in darkness, but George hammered on the door until the bedroom lights went on and the landlady appeared in her dressing gown and curlers. "Madam," she was told, "I am sorry to have awakened you, but there has been a terrible accident."

'The good woman asked how she could help. "A victim is in shock – a large medicinal brandy would help."

'Still half asleep, she seemed about to oblige and only began screaming for the police when George explained that he was the victim and that he preferred his brandy without ice or soda.

'At this new setback, George and I made off to Manchester where we abandoned the borrowed car and found a *Mirror* drinking den. There George licked his wounds, showing off the remains of the thick overcoat that he swore had protected him, perhaps even saved his life. The rest is unclear.

'I eventually got home on Boxing Day to find my wife had left me – she had run off to my mother. Also party host Billy was quite unreasonable, attacking me with his crutch when I told him I could not remember where I had left his car.

'That was the last time I saw George. Although remaining telephone friends, we mutually agreed that we were a bad influence on each other and it was best for the world if we kept apart. It is an odd coincidence that I attended Billy's funeral just a few days before George died. His widow Kath said he often spoke of that Christmas – she reminded me that, apart from the car trouble, the party had led to them being given notice to quit their rented flat.'

Peter Thomas, our sometime sports editor, was another ebullient character, the most affable of men and a great raconteur. He was a *Mirror* man and he was a very sad man when he left the paper in 1966 to join the *Express*. He could not bear the idea of a party and a new recruit photographer Eddie Rawlinson drove him home.

Eddie recalled: 'I had bought him a couple of bottles of scotch as a farewell gift as there was no big farewell party. We went through the two bottles, two thirds to Peter and a third to me, as I had to drive home. He was a broken man as the *Mirror* was one of his two loves, the other was Middlesbrough FC where his father was chairman. It was through Peter who had moved on to be night editor from the sports desk that I was taken on the *Mirror* staff.'

Geoff Mather, who was features editor, recalled his arrival for me:

'Peter Thomas arrived at the *Daily Express* to (in John McDonald's, the then editor's, words) "ride herd". This meant that he could flit from department to department and bring his talents to bear on any one of them. His title was associate editor. His arriving party in top Yates's Wine Lodge was, for him, largely a Gordon's Gin affair. It did not slow him down much but it brought most others to a crawl. He associated quite a lot with everybody – convivial, full of outrageous anecdotes, and with a presence. He had gone to school in York. His family was influential in Middlesbrough Football Club. And his passion was cricket. This combination gave him a degree of assurance. Jeff McGowan, who was to become news editor of the *Star* and who subsequently moved onwards and upwards, called him Puffing Billy. Peter always had to have his pipe in action. As he moved from desk to pub, he would be patting his pockets, his head in wisps of smoke. A pat here – Swan Vestas matches. A pat there – tobacco pouch. A pat here – spectacles. A pat there – wallet. He wrote a book on great Yorkshire players – not your chapter by chapter thing, but each player in turn. He was knowledgeable about times, places, scores. So he was able to point out to Neville Cardus that he could not possibly have been at a match he had described. Cardus said it felt as though he had been there.

'We shared an office and I used to accuse him of going home to a tapestry of W G Grace, which (I said) filled one wall. I inferred that he sat on the floor and tugged on the tapestry corner occasionally to make it look as though Grace was batting. It was not the truth. But in an allegorical sense, it was. His strength lay in being a central figure, goading, encouraging. He did a lot of both. His encouragements went beyond the *Daily Express*. If he liked a writer, he pursued him for earnest conversation. Patrick Barclay of the *Guardian* was one of his "outside" interests.

'He was also a member of a club in the centre of Manchester that was full of large, unread books and cheese on toast. The club enabled him to disappear from view. He loved fun. The more outrageous the better. At a management-editorial affair in a Manchester club, he got on hands and knees in front of the then *Express* general manager and began to feel in his turn-ups. "What are you doing, Peter?" said your man sharply. "Looking for all the names you keep dropping," said Thomas. When an editor arrived at the Land o' Cakes late one lunchtime he showed unaccustomed effects of drink. By careful questioning, Peter Thomas reached a judgment that the freebie the editor had just left had a huge punch bowl in the centre of the table and that the editor – considering that the biggest must be his – had drunk it. If another editor was missing a pub outing for any reason, Thomas would put his spectacles over the plastic pineapple used for keeping chunks of ice, and address it as if it were the man himself. His drinking was monumental – although in the latter stages of life it stopped altogether – and Mike Dempsey, sports editor, one of those Thomas admired and whom he called Spring-Heeled Jack because of the noticeable lilt in his walk, complained that he had been given a page make-up which consisted of a couple of squiggles on the back of a cigarette packet. The editor of the time was perturbed, but Peter carried on.

'He started the Monday morning sports supplement, a great success, and the idea was followed elsewhere. He took to writing columns, which was, perhaps, a mistake. It got him out of the office (which he liked), but equally, it kept him from the primary purpose for which he had been recruited in the first place.

'He was a great man for music of all kinds. Joan Armatrading was one of his favourites. But he liked classical stuff, too. Shortly before he died, various people visited him at his home. They knew it was the end. He suspected it. One male visitor encouraged in his work by Peter to his great advantage kissed him on the forehead. It was like a Mafia farewell. It was 1984. A day of angry weather in Britain and not a few floods. A few people went back to his home after the funeral. I was one. The visitors tended to mill about in or around the kitchen. I looked into the room where his gramophone lay. There was no one in that room. The turntable was revolving. I have no idea to this day why that should be so. He was a great loss. Few matched him in wit. Many would like to have matched him in his enthusiasm for, and part in, journalism. He could have been up there in London with the top men. But, apart from one mild foray, he remained in Manchester.'

The final member of the Three Star Club, Bob Johnstone, worked a

16-hour day masterminding the paper and, as I have written, was only caught sleeping while standing at a corner of the bar in the Press Club.

A fastidious man, he had such a loathing for the hotel the *Mirror* had booked him that whenever his linen became a talking point he would send a messenger to Marks & Spencer for replacements and throw the old ones away.

Although I was still a reporter on the *Daily*, on Saturdays I worked as a casual on the *Sunday Mirror* where I was night news editor.

One Saturday I had been puzzled through the evening when, one after another, local correspondents all over Yorkshire phoned in paragraphs about sightings in their town of the great Charlie Chaplin. When in the last one Chaplin was reported to have booked in at the Danum Hotel in Doncaster, Bob Johnstone, who was also chief sub on the *Sunday*, walked over.

He said, 'It looks as though he has been touring the theatres in Yorkshire where he worked as a young comedian. When the shift ends why don't we grab a taxi and drive over to Doncaster? That way we can interview him in the morning before he goes on his walkabout.'

I agreed. He thoughtfully ordered a taxi and two bottles of scotch, and at 1am we set off for one in the Press Club before leaving for Doncaster. One drink led to another and it was 5am before we arrived at the Danum. To our consternation, an American from Associated Press had beaten us to it. He told us that he had fixed to have breakfast and an exclusive interview with Chaplin who was leaving after the meal for London.

'No time for you guys, I am afraid,' he said.

Bob told me to go away and get some sleep while he had a wee drink with the American before we returned bootless home. The American's eyes lit up when Bob produced a bottle of scotch because in those days even hotel bars closed at 10.30pm.

There were no beds to be had, but a fiver to the night porter brought a mattress and a bath in which to sleep.

I was awakened the next morning by Bob who said, 'It's OK, he has passed out. Away to your breakfast with Chaplin.'

If Charlie Chaplin was surprised at the substitution he was far too good mannered to mention it and we chatted amicably. He told me that during a visit to London he had suddenly felt nostalgic for the Yorkshire towns where he had played as a boy comedian. I said the management in London were worried about him because he had left all of his luggage in his room and apparently disappeared.

With a smile he brought out a well-filled wallet. 'My boy,' he said, 'this is the only luggage a man needs.'

None of the members of the Three Star Club was a university graduate. In those days journalism was the only profession that did not require entrants to have degrees so most of us were working class boys with brains and an urge to write. Graduates had higher ambitions in politics, the law and science that were closed to us. I only knew three newspapermen who were graduates. One was Harry Whewell, a great eccentric, the son of a dustman, who was news editor of the *Manchester Guardian*. He was the only news editor I knew who had a canary in its cage in his office, or indeed who ran a newsroom so quiet that it could be heard singing all over the building.

But then the *Guardian* was an unusual newspaper. In the days when I first knew it the only telephone was in the sub-editors' room because the news editor insisted the ringing would disturb the creative processes of his reporters. When there was a message for one of them it would be announced by a messenger boy and the reporter would reluctantly take the call. A friend who subbed there swore he had heard a reporter tell a caller indignantly: 'Madam, the *Manchester Guardian* does not take details of murders over the telephone.'

But to return to Harry Whewell and his canary. When the paper closed down for a Christmas break, Harry took the bird home over the holiday. Once as he was passing through the loading bay, a driver called, 'What you doin' wi' that then?' Harry said, 'I'm taking it home for Christmas.'

'Are you?' replied the driver scornfully, 'we are having turkey.'

I had a nasty experience with a turkey once, which involved one of the other graduates I met, Bob Ashton, with whom I worked before I was sacked from the *Manchester City News*.

The third was Gordon Sigsworth, a tall, cadaverous man who was so mistrustful of the elements that he carried an umbrella indoors and out, though he hardly ever went out. He went from office, to bar, to bed. We once took him to a Game Fair at Chatsworth where the exposure to fresh air in bulk so upset him we had to take him back to the car, close the windows and blow cigarette smoke at him until he revived.

Bob Ashton was an ex-naval officer who had gone to Oxford on an ex-serviceman's scheme. We met on the *Manchester City News* and together devised a joke routine where we imitated two Old Contemptibles from the Manchester Pals. It amused our mates but surprisingly it also amused a BBC producer who was drinking nearby.

He offered us an audition that would lead to a weekly show. Alas, we could not accept because we would have to go to Broadcasting House to record it at 6pm, which clashed with our drinking arrangements. When we told the producer he said he quite understood. He said not to worry because he had just heard a company director of a sausage factory talking at its annual dinner. If we couldn't do it he would sign him up for the spot. The director's name was Al Read.

There was more humour about then. In Liverpool the last tram from the press club in Lime Street was full. Losing her temper with the crowd, the conductress swore lustily.

A passenger protested, 'Madam, I am a rabbi.'

'I don't care if you are f....ing Popeye, the tram is still full.'

On another crowded tram a small boy was quietly kicking the ankles of an elderly pensioner. His mother warned him, 'If you don't stop that I'll tell your dad.' The child fixed her with a malevolent glare that you only see on the faces in the playgrounds of Liverpool schools or the paintings of Hieronymus Bosch. 'You do and I'll tell him you peed in our new plastic bucket.'

Inevitably I was eventually sacked by the *City News* by its owner, Harold Geldeard. When I was appointed he asked me to spell 'accommodate'. I spelt it and got the job. I commented to his secretary that the interview had been very unusual. She said, 'More unusual than you think. He cannot spell it. I had to write it down for him.'

Sacked and by this time married with a daughter Gay, things were pretty hard. Walking through the city one day just before Christmas after failing to get yet another job as a clerk, I met Bob Ashton. When he heard how things were he said, 'I suppose you are in for a pretty bleak Christmas?'

He told me that at least I could get a Christmas dinner cheap. 'On Christmas Eve at Shudehill market they sell off turkeys and other birds really cheaply so they can get home to their families. And I can fix the drink too. They are having a press party that night at the Continental Cinema on Market Street. We'll fix a time to meet and I will get you into the party.'

Worked like a charm. On Christmas Eve with a tiny chicken that I had bought for sixpence tucked under my arm, I met Bob, gate-crashed the party and, not having eaten for two days, soon set up a course and distance record for eating chicken vol-au-vents.

Unfortunately the party got a bit boisterous. An assistant manager grabbed the chicken from under my arm and using it as a rugger ball made a pass to another hireling who threw it to a third who missed it. I watched as my family's pitiful Christmas dinner flew gracefully out of the foyer into the street, where it was crushed under the wheels of a 42 bus.

The manager, sensing my dismay, said, 'That wasn't your Christmas dinner was it?'

'Oh no, just a chicken I picked up for Boxing Day,' I lied.

Half an hour later, as the party was breaking up, he appeared and gave me a 12lb turkey.

Unfortunately in the flat where we lived we had only a tiny cooker. To cook the turkey we had to cut it in pieces and roast it over the fire. I think we had Christmas dinner that year at 4pm.

That marriage to a childhood sweetheart started badly and got worse. Two days before our very smart wedding in a top Manchester hotel I lost my job on a trade news agency.

When my wife wanted to know where we were going for our honeymoon I insisted it was a surprise. It certainly was. We weren't going anywhere. When we walked down the aisle at St Paul's Church, Withington, I was completely broke. Happily, during the reception new rich relatives kept pressing money on me. So we were able to enjoy a luxurious weekend at the Blossoms in Chester.

Things got a little better when I landed a Saturday shift on the *News of the World*. There were two snags. The NoW offices were on the other side of the city. I could afford an all night bus home after I had been paid but I had to walk ten miles from our home to the office every week. I was paid £4.10s a shift and the rent for the flat was £2.10s. Out of the remaining £2 I had to pay for our linen to be washed because my wife from a rich Jewish family refused to do laundry in our cold-water kitchen sink.

I did not know from week to week whether I was going to be employed. I had to go to a city pub – a five-mile walk – to join the editor and his assistant for drinks. At some period the editor John Milligan would say, 'OK for Saturday, Skid?' I would pause as though riffling through a mental engagement diary before saying casually, 'Yes, I think that will be OK, John.'

I had to save half a crown out of the housekeeping to buy my way into the drinking school. Yet another problem. I had only one white shirt. It would go out with the washing, which we left out on the front doorstep. Until it came back on Wednesday I walked around in a tatty pullover.

One day after I had put out the washing there was a knock on the door. On the step stood a tramp.

'Can you give us the price of a cup of tea,' he said. 'I have just come out of prison and I haven't a penny.'

'Mate, I'd love to help but I am borasic myself,' I replied.

With a look of piteous disbelief he turned round and shuffled down the drive. Watching him, I remembered the half crown I had set aside for getting into the drinking school. I could always pretend I had forgotten my money, just for one day.

I ran after him and gave him the coin. I thought he looked embarrassed. Later in the morning I discovered he had stolen the washing, including my only shirt.

Take Seven

My last Scottish incursion had been to report the visit by the prime minister to the Queen at Balmoral; my next was to cover the visit of the US president to Turnberry in Ayrshire. President Eisenhower, an obsessive golfer, had been loaned a grace and favour apartment in Culzean Castle, which was within motoring distance of the links.

Whenever the president flies abroad a second airliner carries the White House press corps who made up, on that occasion anyway, what they lacked in reporting skills with deep conversations about politics and the significance of what the president had for breakfast. To aid them, there was a press conference every day when they were told the president's timetable in minute detail. An impressive follow-up was the posting on a blackboard of a verbatim note of the conference within minutes of it ending. From that notice the correspondents took their stories, filed them and then were free for the rest of the day to talk about politics. Much money might have been saved if the details of Ike's day had been cabled to their offices. As it was, they were, as a group, the men – and one woman – with the easiest jobs in journalism.

The president's press officer was a very likeable man called Jimmy Hagerty. Like the correspondents, he had a great deal of spare time and after one conference he asked the assembled reporters if they knew where he could get a decent glass of whisky.

'My hotel has forty varieties,' I informed him.

'I'll meet you there in an hour,' he said.

I had been saddled with a manic reporter from the *Daily Record* as my leg man. He was a Glaswegian, bearded and minute, further supporting my theory that anyone over 5ft 7 inches was barred from being born in Glasgow. He was, like all Scottish reporters, desperately competitive.

When he heard Hagerty's agreement to come to my hotel, he

whispered, 'What a bliddy masterstroke. We'll get him pissed and then ask him a' aboot Korea.'

I have to say that the idea of getting Hagerty – who, as well as being a top aide, looked like a two bottle man – drunk and garrulous seemed a bit fanciful. And so it turned out Haggerty seemed to drink by osmosis. Tumblers of whisky emptied as soon as they touched the bar. It was not long before the *Record* man passed out. Hagerty took his feet, I his head, and we carried him out of the bar. As we poured him into a cab he whispered urgently: 'Don't forget. Ask him a' aboot Korea.'

Hagerty and I returned to the bar and he said that part of his job was to tell the president, who did not enjoy freedom of movement, interesting things about countries they visited.

I said in that case he must tell him about Albert Turtle. I thought of Albert because it was common knowledge that Eisenhower was severely hen-pecked by a voluble wife.

Albert was a drinking friend of my fathers at their nightly haunt, the Red Lion in Withington. They drank in the vault where no woman except the barmaid Elsie was allowed. I cannot blame them. That vault was the nearest place to a drinker's heaven I have ever enjoyed. The floor was flagged, there was a huge kitchen range with a blazing fire that was regulated by opening the oven door and swinging it over the fireplace. Comfortable red benches went round walls that had been stained a homely yellow by generations of nicotine.

Albert fell into disfavour in the vault because, alone among his friends, he brought his wife Amy for a drink every Thursday.

Hagerty said the president would be amazed that any man could exercise control over a wife and I told him he hadn't heard the best bit. Albert brought his wife but he did not sit with her. He put her in the 'best room' and settled her with a milk stout before returning to the vault. What upset my father was that every twenty minutes he sent her another bottle and at the end of the evening collected her and they walked home in amiable conversation.

My father spoke for everyone in the vault when he told Albert, 'You are spoiling that bliddy woman.'

Hagerty said the president would love that story and as we parted asked, 'By the way, what was it your friend wanted to know about Korea?'

'No idea,' I said.

The next day before the press conference began he pulled me on one side.

'Your story has made the president's day,' he said. 'He asked me to tell you he is sorry he hasn't any plans to visit Manchester otherwise he would have insisted on meeting Albert Turtle.'

Though the president never visited Manchester the city did once have a Royal Command Performance at the Palace Theatre. It starred Liberace, a very camp pianist who had recently and successfully sued the *Mirror* and our columnist Cassandra for a typically vituperative column which, to put it mildly, questioned his sexuality.

When he sent me to cover the rehearsals, Roly Watkins, the news editor, warned me not to go near Liberace. 'We don't want to pay out any more money,' he said.

At the theatre I ran into an old pal, the comic Ted Lune, who was also on the bill. When I asked him how things were, he said, 'Dreadful. I've got a dressing room on the top floor up a bloody spiral staircase. We are not allowed to leave the theatre and I am gasping for a pint.'

It was a hot day and I was wearing a short-sleeved shirt and thin trousers. So when I volunteered to smuggle a couple of pint bottles in I was puzzled to know where to hide them. At the death I just shoved them into my trouser pockets and started to climb the stairs. Liberace was on the staircase in front of me and two embarrassing things happened. The bottles fell forward in my pocket like a double erection and I rammed into the rear of Liberace.

He turned with a winning smile and said, 'Oh my! How nice,' and continued on his way.

That night I joined the stars for a buffet supper at the Midland Hotel where I shared a table with Vivien Leigh and had a very nice time with the actress Dorothy Tutin. We both laughed when Liberace arrived and made a beeline for a boy ballet dancer.

In the early hours of the morning my phone rang. It was a waiter from the Midland who thought the *Mirror* might like to know that he had just seen Liberace slip into the ballet dancer's bedroom. I thought the *Mirror* would too, but when I woke the news editor he said he didn't think he would bother; Liberace had caused the paper enough trouble. So I didn't tell him about the incident with the bottle.

That was the time when the theatrical unions lifted their ban on American stars coming to Britain. After their appearances there was usually a party in their hotel suites to which Harrop and I invited ourselves every week. In that way I met all the greats, people like Armstrong, Basie, Kenton and best of all a lovely drunk called Guy Mitchell, who was a great singer.

Over the years I met most of the stars of the day but the one that gave me the happiest memory was Hoagy Carmichael.

I was working on the *Daily Dispatch* in Liverpool, and because I was sending most of my wages back to my family in Doncaster, the only real meals I had were the free lunches we had on the great trans-Atlantic liners when they docked in the city. Some weeks I had so little money I not only worked in the *Dispatch* office. I slept in it.

It was pretty good too. Every morning the cleaner would bring me a cup of tea to bed. I was just enjoying it this morning when the phone rang. It was *Mirror* man Bill Marshall. He said that Hoagy Carmichael was staying in the Adelphi Hotel before a rare British appearance at the Empire Theatre and we should go over and pay our respects.

We were very warmly welcomed by Hoagy and quickly on the right side of a glass of whisky. A second one emboldened Bill to ask Hoagy if he would play Stardust, his greatest hit, for us.

'Bill,' he said, 'I have heard and played that damned tune so often I cannot stand it but if you care to hang on I have to do my daily practice and I will play you some of the tunes I really liked but could never get published.'

So for two hours, with the whisky bottle within easy reach, Marshall and I had a private concert by one of the greatest entertainers of the twentieth century. Around noon, Marshall suddenly jumped up. 'Christ,' he said, 'I should have been in court at 10am. The news desk will have my guts for garters.'

'Is there anything I can do?' asked Hoagy.

Bill thought a little and then said, 'Well, my news editor Roly Watkins is a great fan of yours. If you could ring the news desk and play a snatch of Stardust and then say, "Hello Roly" and explain that I am with you...'

'For you Bill, even that,' agreed Hoagy.

Marshall rang the paper and was put through to the desk. Then he held the receiver over the piano while Hoagy played Stardust. Right on cue he said, 'Hello Roly, this is Hoagy Carmichael and I am with Bill....'

There was a pause and then he repeated, 'This *is* Hoagy Carmichael. No, I am not Bill Marshall and I am not pissed at twelve o'clock in the morning.'

After Hoagy played his concert that evening we invited him over the road to the Press Club. He not only came, he played for another hour before he said, 'That's it.'

By this time Bill had become very proprietorial.

'Play, Hoagland,' he growled.

Hoagy said, 'Bill, I have been playing an hour, I got twelve hundred quid from the theatre for not much longer than that.'

'Oh, so money's your god,' said Bill, and bringing out his cheque book made out a cheque for twelve hundred quid, flung it at Hoagy and said, 'Now will you play?'

Hoagy was amused and played another half hour before he finally put the piano lid down, bid us a courteous goodnight and went back to the Adelphi accompanied by half his audience apologising for Bill.

The next morning Bill rang me again.

'What the hell did I spend twelve hundred quid on? The bank manager has told me not to sign any more cheques.'

I told him, and he insisted we go to the Adelphi to get his cheque back.

Hoagy was very apologetic. 'Bill, I didn't know you were joking,' he said, 'I have already put it in the bank with my cheque from the theatre.'

He let Bill sweat for a few minutes, then he said, 'OK, I was joking. But you cannot have the cheque back. I am going to have it framed for my den in memory of a great night.'

So Hoagy Carmichael's name is up there with Josef Locke on my list of stars.

Shortly after that the *Mirror* bought out the *Daily Dispatch* and I was not on the list of reporters they wished to buy as part of the deal. In fact I did not know it had gone down.

In dock at that time in Liverpool there was a minesweeper the Admiralty had apparently forgotten. It lay at its moorings for years. In common with all other naval officers who put in at Liverpool, the skipper and first lieutenant had been made members of the Press Club and with great generosity they made us members of their ward room. It was a very small ward room and I was there most afternoons after the pubs closed, waiting for them to open again and filling the gap with some excellent G and T.

On one such day a messenger came from the office to tell me I need not put any copy over because the paper had been sold to the *Mirror* who had promptly closed it down. With three children and a huge overdraft, I was out of work.

The captain saw my ashen face. 'Anything wrong, Skiddy?' he asked, and I told him. He was furious. 'If their Lordships at the Admiralty had taken my ship out of commission without a prior signal I should send them a pretty snotty signal to complain.'

I said that if I knew Lord Kemsley, our proprietor's, telephone number I would give him a piece of my mind.

Another reporter we called Harry Slime or the Turd Man gave me Lord Kemsley's number. I had to ring him or lose face. Bolstered by several more G and Ts, I picked up the skipper's phone.

'Lord Kemsley is not at home,' a voice said. 'I am his butler. May I take a message?'

Made much bolder by the news, I dictated a fiery denunciation, which the butler took down with obvious pleasure.

When I had finished the skipper took the phone out of my hand. 'And that goes for Her Majesty's Royal Navy,' he barked down the receiver.

The story went the rounds and reached Cudlipp, who was much amused and told the Manchester editor to hire me.

Ian Skidmore

Take Eight

I covered forty-eight annual International Eisteddfods at Llangollen. This magnificent festival began immediately after the war when a reporter on the *Liverpool Daily Post* called Harold Tudor, at that time working for the British Council, heard a milkman in the town singing in perfect pitch as he delivered his bottles. Tudor thought what a wonderful idea it would be to hold a concert where all the nations in Europe could come to sing and dance and end their difficulties.

It was a bold concept. Tudor invited to the first Eisteddfod a German choir from Lubeck, against violent opposition. There was much head shaking over the reception this former enemy would get in competitions against their former victims from all over Europe.

Their arrival was a disaster. The conductor was robbed of his wallet in which he was carrying all the funds for the choir's stay. Bravely they decided to sing anyway but as they assembled on the stage the compere announced their loss and told the audience that ushers bearing buckets would pass among them and would accept any contributions. Within ten minutes, the buckets had been filled by an audience that included performers from France, Holland and Belgium whose countries had only recently been occupied by the German army.

It was not all goodwill. During the cold war the performers from the Eastern bloc were accompanied by grim-faced minders, party members who forbade them to have any contact with the other performers.

I first came to Llangollen by train from Manchester. Change at Wrexham. My children were babies then; now they are middle-aged and my grandchildren are at university or working in newspapers. The only trains from the town are privately owned and you can travel to the terminus and back in the time it takes to eat a gourmet dinner.

The marquee that held the stage and was as hot as a gypsy's oven has long ago been folded away. In its place there is a three and a half million pound surrealist pavilion, opened in 1976 by the Queen, her second visit in only forty-three years.

I used to think fondly of the International as two tenors singing under an umbrella. I began my first broadcast from the field likening it to those Mickey Rooney musicals where someone says, 'Why don't we put the show on right here in our own backyard?' Now who remembers Mickey Rooney, let alone the musicals?

In those early days every national newspaper ran special Eisteddfod editions and sent at least four staff men to cover every cough. We were not well received. To the young committee we were as strange and exotic as Andalusian clog dancers, but nowhere near as welcome. The first musical director WS Williams loathed us; he couldn't understand why we wrote about the competitors in bigger type than we wrote about the competitions. There were some marvellous stories, though. A choir of German children arrived with a song that had been written for them. It was an instant hit. Indeed 'The Happy Wanderer' went on to break records all over the world.

There was shock at the news that a team of nubile Zulu maidens would dance bare-breasted. When it emerged they were all married to the lead dancer, the non-conformist committee was appalled. The lucky husband was puzzled at the fuss. 'In my country we have many wives and no girlfriends. You British have one wife and twenty girlfriends. Who is most dishonourable?'

A young Italian singer making his first wide-eyed visit abroad competed with his father's choir in one of the first Eisteddfods I covered. He became a vice-president: his name was Luciano Pavarotti. Other international stars are honoured to appear at celebrity concerts and the standard of the competitions is awesome.

In the early days the choirs and dance troupes partied all night. You could see the fires of their barbecues dotting the hills that surround this little goose pie of a town.

This greatest advertisement for Welsh hospitality is more formal now. There are notices in the pubs during the world's biggest *Gesangfest* banning singing. The impromptu street concerts have disappeared. The police presence is heavier. I remember diving out of the back door of a pub and hiding in the shrubbery when a team of policemen arrived at a riverside pub after closing time. I thought it was a raid but when they emerged wiping their mouths after a brief period, one stopped by the shrubbery and said,

'You can go back in now, Skiddy. We only called in for a pint.'

During one all night party I crept out into the street in the early morning with a hunting horn. I intended to wake the town but no sound came. A policeman loomed out of the shadows, grabbed the horn, blew a triumphant 'Gone home' and handed it back. 'Trouble with you bloody English,' he said, 'no sense of music at all.'

I met Celia, my future widow, at Llangollen. She was a *Daily Mail* reporter, newly arrived from London, and had been sent to cover a visit by the eccentric explorer Tony Blashford Snell. He was about to mount an expedition to discover the source of the Blue Nile. He had brought his team to Llangollen to train in white water rafting in the Horseshoe Falls on the River Dee. Part of the training was to shoot handguns in the water to deter the fearsome Nile crocodiles without holing their canoes.

Below the falls there is a chain bridge and at its side a pub, which was then run by Charlie Charlotte, a friend of mine. Every morning he considerately laid a table in the centre of the bridge with a bottle of champagne in an ice bucket so that I could watch the training in comfort. Celia arrived just as a waiter uncorked my champagne so of course I sent the waiter for an extra glass. As I poured our drink Blashford Snell and his team swept into view round a bend in the river, firing into the current. At the same time a holidaymaker was crossing the bridge. She was terrified. 'What they doin'?' she screamed.

'It's perfectly all right madam,' I assured her, 'they are only shooting crocodiles.'

Her husband had rushed to join her. 'Bloody heck, our Bella, what they doin' for God's sake?'

'He says they're shooting flamin' alligators,' his wife told him.

'Crocodiles,' Celia corrected her, 'there are no alligators in the River Dee at Llangollen.' Celia and I have been married for thirty-two years now and I still have not managed to have the last word.

I have always married above myself. Indeed my first mother-in-law, the ex-chorus girl wife of a very nice Jewish inventor and successful businessman, told me I was council house scum. This did not worry me since she always pronounced cognac with a hard G.

Celia is a middle class girl who went to an upper class convent and read history at St Hilda's, Oxford. Her relations were formidable. Her father, whom I loved much more than my own father, was a doctor and a brilliant scholar with a photographic memory; her cousin was second master at Winchester; one of her uncles a diplomat and the other a well-to-do company director. Her stepfather Angus Menzies, a Highland GP who served as MO with the RHA in the desert campaign at Tobruk and El Alamein, was legendarily bad tempered. On our first meeting, anxious to make a good impression, I took him fly fishing on a stretch of water owned by my friend Lord Langford and rented to a man Jack Tyrrel, who as Lt Colonel had also served in the desert with the RHA.

When they met on the river Jack said, 'I do not recall the name. Our MO was a sandy haired Scot who was a brilliant surgeon and doctor but was the worse tempered man I have ever met.'

Driving home, Angus wondered whom Jack could possibly have meant and got very bad tempered with me when I said, 'It was you, you daft bugger.'

He was proud of the fact that he chased a man out of his surgery in the Fens and down the long drive because when asked what was the matter with him the man replied, 'I have a sexual problem I would like to discuss with you.' I asked him how he dealt with troublesome patients. 'First sign of ill discipline I have them posted out,' he said.

My mother-in-law Joan was reserved when we first met but that did not prevent me from registering that she was the most glamorous woman I have ever met. And that includes Dietrich, Roc, Kent and Lockwood, the great stars of their day. When I took her for dinner in Chester on our first meeting while Celia was working, we bumped into some friends who assumed I was two timing. I totally failed to convince them that she was Celia's mother.

The most formidable relations were Sir Sidney and Lady Barratt who lived in great style surrounded by fabulous antiques at Crowe Hall in Bath. Sir Sidney had been chairman of Albright and Wilson and although we were to become the best of friends I was very nervous when Celia took me on a tour of her family, like a matrimonial trooping of the colour.

We went for lunch at Crowe and although I wield a pretty stylish fork I was awed by the Georgian silver on the table, which made it look like a showcase at Mappin & Webb.

'Sauce', as Lady B was known in the family, had a pet pigeon Mr Pooter who was allowed to fly free in a house furnished with renaissance bronzes and hung with a Canaletto, Gainsboroughs, Ramseys and other great painters. It walked the length of the dining table and then flew to perch on a Giambologna bronze before flying over to alight on my head. I am not sure what the etiquette is for conducting a conversation faced by an armoury of silver with a pigeon on your head but I stopped trying when it crapped down my neck.

And I was very relieved when it flew off and Uncle Sidney said, 'You must be all right, the pigeon likes you.'

Thirty-two years later I am still uneasy when I recall that my entry into this loving family was secured by a pigeon with loose bowels.

In addition to being second master, the Barratts' son-in-law Martin was housemaster to the most brilliant, and frequently most mentally disturbed, scholars at Winchester. As deputy head of the school, he lived in a grace and favour house that was haunted by a pair of gaitered legs. They belonged to a bishop who for centuries had haunted an upper room. The ceiling of the dining room had at some time been raised but the bishop was clearly unaware of the change and continued to pace what had once been the floor of his bedroom.

Martin also told of one scholar who had taken a dislike to a college porter. Once when the porter was taking visitors on a tour of the college the boy hid in the rafters of the Great Hall with a fire extinguisher. When the porter posed under it for a short talk the boy squirted the extinguisher over him. The porter disappeared in a triangle of foam from which he emerged, wiping his mouth, to tell his bemused audience, 'That will be the organ, it's always doing that.'

After meeting these distinguished relatives I thought I ought to do something to polish my own image so I decided to write a book. By this time my old CO Lord Langford had become my closest friend. Often when I visited him he would reminisce about his war in the Far East. One story he told was of his escape from Singapore after it fell, which ended in his sailing a battered dhow across the Bay of Bengal to India. It took a month and included some amazing adventures.

I was night news editor of the *People* at the time and suggested I should write a feature about it. The features editor, himself an author, saw what I had written and suggested I turn it into a book, which I am delighted to say became a bestseller.

For my second book *Owain Glyndwr* I spent so much time researching it in Wales that eventually we decided to live there.

Working in Wales in the days before being Welsh became a profession was pure delight. Maggie Williams of Conwy's Smallest House sang *penillion* to us in remote mountain inns; I won a bet with Derek Taylor, who went on to be PRO for the Beatles, that Welsh hotel staffs were the most obliging in the world. In proof, at the Bridge End Hotel in Llangollen, I asked a chambermaid if she would stand on a chair for me and fix my electric razor into the light socket. I said I could not stand on chairs because I was afraid of heights. Not only did she arrive every morning for four days: on the fifth morning a different girl knocked on my door and said, 'The lady who usually stands on your chair is off today. I have come in her place.'

The 78-year-old chambermaid at the Lion Royal in Bala used to bring you the morning paper she thought your status entitled you to, regardless of the paper you had ordered. She also awarded an orange to customers she liked at the end of their stay. It was like getting a knighthood.

When I was a child in the 1930s you could still travel by train from Manchester to Pwllheli, changing at Caernarfon. At that time, though it was still spelt with a V, it bustled with more vigorous Welsh life than it does now it is spelt with an F and largely given over to the offices of local government. Once my father asked the station master from the window of our Pwllheli train the times of return trains. The station master handed him the station copy of *Bradshaw's Railway Guide* and said, 'Leave it on the seat. I will get it on the return journey.'

I stayed in Llangollen recently at the Bryn Howell, one of the best hotels in Wales, and remembered when the landlord of the Bridge End, Albert Lloyd, invited me to visit a derelict mansion he thought of buying. Bryn Howell looked like a Hammer film set.

'What do you think?' asked Albert. 'Wouldn't touch it with a barge pole,' I said. Just as well I chose writing for a career and not property speculation.

One good thing about new Wales has been the growth of festivals. I occasionally put on the suit of lights – or, more accurately, the illuminated waistcoat – to entertain at the festivals at Hay-on-Wye and Beaumaris.

At Hay I met the Booker Prize winning novelist Bernice Rubens, who left Cardiff when she was twenty and was puzzled on her return by the bilingualisation. She called it 'Street signs with sub-titles'. Another writer, puzzled by the Welsh on the drawers of a chest in a school used as a Green Room during the festivals, was told that it was where they kept the vowels.

Ian Skidmore

Take Nine

There were few media awards in those days. No drunken dinners followed by insincere speeches, trophy lassoing and subsequent brawling such as we see since graduates were allowed into the profession.

The only one I recall was Journalist of the Year. One year it was won by a *Daily Mail* reporter who was away on a cure for his alcoholism. The *Mail* executives wanted to celebrate so he was dragged from a meeting of Alcoholics Anonymous to share a champagne dinner at which he drank orange juice. After what must have been a night of agony, they insisted he should accompany them back to the office for more drink and a look at the 'foreigners' (competing newspapers). The *Express* had a crime story that the *Mail* had missed. The executives decided it was the fault of their Journalist of the Year who had missed a call from a contact because he was at the champagne feast. He was sacked.

My own attempts to cure alcoholism were doomed to failure. I went to see a psychiatrist called Madden. He began his examination by asking me how much I drank and I asked him how much he had got. He asked if I had difficulty remembering what I did the night before and I said, no, the trouble was forgetting some of the things I got up to. He asked finally if in moments of stress I gave myself a drink but I said no to that one too because I usually had one in my hand.

He said, 'I have just described to you the classic pattern of the alcoholic.'

I told him he had just described everyone I knew.

My second attempt was more serious. Celia was unhappy about my drinking so I booked myself into a drunks unit at the Mostyn Hospital in Chester. We were protected from the female ward by a sitting room where we all met in the morning to decide what we were going to do that day. It was very depressing. One woman suggested dancing lessons, another a visit to Chester Zoo. I was ejected when I suggested going for a drink.

I got out after a second psychiatrist asked me what I was doing there.

'Dr Madden says I am an alcoholic,' I said.

'Rubbish,' he said, because he knew me rather better than Madden did. 'You just drink too much.'

In my defence I must say I was part of a drinking culture. You were bound to buy drinks all round in the pub if you got a by-line, a rare event though not necessarily a recognition of merit. In a single edition I more than once had by-lines on the front page, the back page and the middle page spread.

A dour sub-editor warned me, 'Don't get big headed. You just have the amount of letters in your name to provide a satisfactory break between headline and copy.'

A nasty breed, sub-editors. My two best intros were stolen and used as headlines. In the first, a pair of cranes escaped from Chester Zoo and settled near the RAF station at Hodnet in Shropshire where their droppings fell on nice, clean aeroplanes. The commander created a furore by having them shot. My stolen intro was 'The stains from cranes fell mainly on the planes'.

In the second incident a mini race riot broke out in Moss Side at a Sikh wedding. I arrived to find the entire wedding party fighting in the middle of the street. On the kerb stood a single, very large policeman, rocking from toe to heel in the time honoured peeler manner.

'What you gonna do?' I asked.

'Well, I did think of sending for a gunboat but in the end I decided to wait till they wear themselves out and then nick one of the buggers.'

'You've identified the ringleader then?'

'Doesn't matter, they are all called bloody Singh.'

Again the subs stole my intro which was 'It was just one of those Singhs'.

I fear I was never politically correct in matters of race. I think that is

179

because my best friend at school was a negro we all called Blackie and who called me Speccy Four-Eyes. In the army another friend was a West Indian who was delighted when we begged him to sing 'Mammy'.

But a friend Don Smith, who became my deputy when I was silly enough to allow myself to be made night news editor, still recalls the night we were sent to report on the road deaths in their car of two pimps and their girls. He says he was shocked when I mused, 'They were driving a Jaguar? Just think, ten years ago they would have been chased by one.'

Beaverbrook at that time was always rewarding his stars with Jaguars. When he gave one to Manchester sports writer Henry Rose, an envious colleague told about it said he hoped it would claw him to death. When Henry was killed in the Munich air crash his funeral cortege paused as a mark of respect at Liston's Music Hall, a disreputable pub in Market Street, one of Henry's haunts.

When Harrop heard it had also paused at the Black Lubianka, the all glass *Daily Express* building on the site of a corset factory, he said, 'Just like Henry to go to the office on his day off.'

Henry Rose had a nice turn of phrase. One night he won £2,000 playing poker in the Cromford Club and when he got home he put it under his pillow. The next morning it had gone. When his sister Becky with whom he lived brought him morning tea she asked how he was.

'Becky,' he said, 'I don't feel two grand.'

No doubt he felt better when she told him, 'I've put it in the drawer under your shirts.'

I had a nasty experience with morning tea after my first marriage broke up. I bought an alarm clock that heated a kettle which, when it boiled, sent water up a pipe to infuse a pot of tea.

In those days, when not otherwise engaged, I took to bed an apple and a book. I set the Teasmade, put the apple beside it on the chest and my false teeth on my Vatican dome of a belly for handy mouth-assembly in case I felt the need for the apple in the night. Unfortunately on one occasion I forgot to put the pipe into the teapot and when I slumbered it hung over me like the sword of Damocles. The next morning I was awakened by a stream of scalding water on my chest. When I leaped in the air, my false teeth fell from my stomach and came to rest under me and, when I landed on them, bit me in the arse.

I regret to say that my daughter Lynn won the first of several journalistic prizes by stealing the story and writing it up for her school magazine.

I do not know what possessed me to accept a promotion to night news editor. It must be the most boring job in the world. Worse, I lost any opportunities to write that most rewarding of all fiction, the expense sheet. On the news desk I sat doing nothing for hour upon hour, broken on rare nights by half an hour of intense excitement when a story broke.

I remember only one occasion when the job was rewarding. An Oxford undergraduate, Brian Lapping, had done a thesis on tabloid journalism for his degree. He took it to Jack Nener who told him when he graduated to come to him for a job. Naturally he did not mean it so he was nonplussed when a newly graduated Lapping arrived at the office. As always he got out of an unhappy situation by sending him to Maurice Wigglesworth, the absurd news editor in Manchester. Wigglesworth also adopted the traditional get-out by unloading him on me as my 6pm to 1am man.

By this time Harrop and I had evolved a procedure to make the evenings less boring. We put our deputies in charge and spent most of the evening in the pub. It was Lapping's bad luck that my deputy was off that night so I put him on the desk and told him to recall me at the slightest sign of activity.

Alas, that night we were still in the pub well after midnight when it was raided by the Vice Squad, whose head Louis Harper later apologised but said he had no alternative. 'I didn't mind people staying after hours,' he said. 'It was the buggers who woke the neighbours hammering on the door at midnight demanding to be let in.'

In view of recent stories of police corruption it is perhaps worth recalling that when Louis' will was published he had left more than he had earned in his entire service. The first I knew of the raid was when a man in a peaked cap, who I took to be a bus driver, sidled next to me at the bar and the landlord threw my pint of beer over my shoes. Since there seemed no point in returning to the office, once we were released Harrop and I went to the Press Club. First I rang the office and told the luckless Lapping he would have to write the overnight memo that recorded the events of the evening. Since the only event that evening was the raid on the pub it needed only to be a short memo.

When I went into the office the next evening Wigglesworth, not the most scholarly of men, threw the overnight memo at me saying, 'Were you pissed last night? I cannot make head nor tail of your memo. All the bloody letters have run together.'

It had been written in Latin. 'It seemed a good idea at the time,' said Lapping when I later questioned him.

'Don't do it again,' I said. 'It has taken me twenty years to teach Mr Wigglesworth English.'

I do believe one award I should have received during the years I worked as a freelance was the Booker for fiction, so creative were some of the stories that earned me a living.

It had been my intention to retire at thirty while I was still young enough to enjoy it, financed by some leisurely freelancing, and then go back to work for the rest of my life. I could not have chosen a better place. In Chester nothing ever happened, apart from racing. Inevitably I became part of a small group of bookmakers and professional gamblers who spent most of the day drinking in pleasant surroundings at sundry racecourses.

Death was treated lightly among the gamblers. Tony Vye, the landlord of the Bowling Green Inn, enjoyed three things above all others. They were the long-haired bandits (as women were known), backing favourites and drinking Tia Maria.

We were in the bottom bar of the Grosvenor. Tony had just backed a winner and emptied a glass of Tia Maria when he collapsed. A blonde he had fancied for many weeks bent over him and tried to give him the kiss of life. It was no use. He was dead. Lol the Horse looked down sadly at the corpse and said, 'Poor Tony, he will never know that he just got the Treble up.'

At his Court of Common Sense Mr Harry 'Justice' Daniels purveyed draught Bass of a quality that, in the words of an Elizabethan dramatist, 'would make a cat speak'. On us the effect was quite other. The Bass of the day was a muscular brew that frequently robbed us of the power to utter. Bolder friends told me of another famous Bass house across the City on the Rows in Watergate Street but I was never much of a traveller. I was content with the Eagle, with its oaken bar and frosted fittings that came down to cap level, the nicotine tanned walls and the rexine settle that girded them. Had the brewery not ruined both the drink and the decor, forcing Harry into retirement, I would be there yet.

Take Ten

I am a pagan. I believe with Hermes the Thrice Great, an Ionian philosopher, that God is a circle, the centre of which is everywhere and the circumference nowhere. Despite the fact that I count a bishop and several clergymen among my friends, I believe that religion is nothing more than the politics of belief, in which the members of every party believe that only their party will get its Reward. I believe fervently in God, but not in Heaven as a sort of eternal Eisteddfod with the endless strumming of harps and people looking ridiculous in long white gowns, with a bearded benevolent God as Arch Druid. I know I have an eternal soul which is permanently young and which will one day leave me like a driver leaves an old banger, to join whatever God is.

As we approach the biggest pagan festival of all, I am just waiting to read a call for a ban on Christmas. After all, we are about to celebrate the Feast of Mithras. Christ was really born in September and the killjoys who rule our lives have no sense of fun.

For the first time since the 17th century the witch finders are on the streets. And Christmas was banned then, don't forget. Common sense isn't fashionable any more.

Instead everyone goes to university and acquires silly theories. Universities are increasingly places where it is possible to become an adult without all the bother of growing up.

We have social diseases no one ever thought seriously about in more rational days. The latest is Satanic possession. Satanism and witchcraft are different religions. Satanism is devil worship; witchcraft is straight paganism. But you don't expect experts to know anything about the ills they invent. So they make the same mistake that bigoted men made in the 17th century.

Recently the Evangelical Alliance warned that children who dressed up as witches on All Hallows Eve could get dragged into Satanism. Two hundred years ago a book was written saying much the same thing. It was called *Malleus Maleficarum* (The Hammer of Witches) and because of it a great number of innocent old women suffered horrible deaths.

In Rochdale in Lancashire a small boy told social workers about witches' Sabbaths and devil worship in which he claimed to have been involved. As a result, children have been taken out of their parents' care and there were headlines about a 'Rochdale Devil Cult'. The boy was an addict of horror videos and is pretty sure to have been making the story up.

Again the parallels with the 17th century witch-hunt are chillingly clear. Not far away from Rochdale is Pendle Hill where they burned witches.

Devil worship has been defined as a social evil in America and what American social workers don't think about deeply enough today, our social workers take as gospel tomorrow.

The trouble is that the new Archbishop of Canterbury, unlike many in high church office, actually believes in God. On the whole it is a good thing to have bishops who believe in God. But it is a mixed blessing, if you will pardon the phrase.

All manner of weird fundamentalists have suddenly become fashionable. In Wales, we had churchmen trying to get schools to ban Hallowe'en parties and trick or treat jokes in the playground. Another group of Christian fundamentalists wants to ban all witches, goblins and magic spells from children's books. No more Snow White, Cinderella, Aladdin or any of the stories that make childhood magic.

Oddly enough, I have not seen any criticism from any quarters about some pretty basic departures from the script line in Star Trek. The Enterprise, as ever, is staffed by a crew with faces made of plastic and who wear their underpants on top of their tights. They go from one galactic civilisation to another – destroying them. Social workers in nylon body-stockings. The writers discovered a new star system. It's called sex. Captain Kirk's successor, we were told, was going to boldly go where no Star Trek man had gone before – and the lady crew members were going to let him. The new batch of scripts included a female crew member being stripped by aliens, drug abusers and an IRA victory in Ireland. Goodness knows what our social workers would have made of them but perhaps fortunately they were never asked.

I liked all the clergy I have written about earlier but the Dean,

Addleshaw, was a poisonous man eternally at war with the Bishop. In Chester we had a thalidomide baby whose mother tirelessly, and it must be said tiresomely, fought for the rights of such children. On one occasion she organised a sale of work in the vestry of the cathedral. It made £100 and the dean charged them £90 rent. The mothers were naturally upset but when I taxed the Dean he told me loftily, 'You must never think of the church as a charitable institution.'

When the Archbishop of Canterbury, Dr Rowan Williams, was Bishop of Monmouth he appeared on a panel I chaired at the Hay Festival to discuss the disestablishment of the Church. I had no idea what disestablishment was so I buttonholed a great chum, Dr Barry Morgan, now Archbishop of Wales but then Bishop of Bangor. He was a handsome man whose flock dubbed him Barry Bish the Dish. He was also, despite a relaxed and friendly manner, as godly a man as I have met. I told him I knew nothing about the subject for discussion and he said, rather unkindly, 'That has never worried you in the past.'

'Rowan Williams is on the panel,' I said, 'and he was Chichele Professor of Divinity at Oxford, a university chair.'

'He's a pal of mine,' said Barry. 'Tell him if he gives you a hard time it will be Croziers at Dawn when we meet on Saturday.'

Barry was an unassuming man but capable of firm leadership which sometimes mired him in controversy. He confessed to me he had a sovereign cure for stress. 'I make a massive cream gateau,' he said.

I subsequently tasted one and it was delicious.

At first I went to Wales only to work, usually to the Assizes on the Isle of Anglesey at Beaumaris, with its tiny Jacobean courtroom, its castle and its rows of colour-washed Georgian houses.

What brought me to live there for thirty years? Partly it was to research my *Owain Glyndwr* but mostly it was draught Bass. The late managing director of Bass Charrington told me that the bass at Ye Olde Bull's Head in Beaumaris was the best in Britain. It was.

There was so much to do on the Isle of Anglesey: fly-fishing and shooting, more leisure centres per head of population than anywhere else in Britain and a vivid cultural life.

Sir Kyffin Williams, the painter, and his brother Richard who was an erudite ornament of the Chester Bar, became in turn close friends. Other good friends from the arts world included the two professors, Wil Mathias, the composer, and David Crystal who edited the Cambridge Encyclopaedia from his spare room in Holyhead, the mystery writer B M Gill and the author of animal stories Joyce Stranger.

In Beaumaris there was an annual Arts Festival in May and I was asked to interview the stars before an audience at the Henllys Hall Hotel. I talked to Victoria de los Angeles, Moura Lympany, Sir Geraint Evans, the famous musical family Lethiec from Nice and Michala Petri from Denmark, unquestionably the finest recorder player in the world.

There were painting and sculpture exhibitions, a straits regatta, a brass band concert, a tea dance, a cookery demonstration, poetry readings, lots of jazz and a fringe with street theatre.

Craig Raine the poet, Acker Bilk, Alan Price and George Melly were among other celebrities appearing. When I interviewed Moura Lympany I confessed I had been in love with her since childhood when I attended her wartime concerts at Belle Vue in Manchester, she was always so beautifully dressed in flowing gowns.

She was much amused because, she told me, they were all made from curtains. Sad that my first love was for a few yards of soft furnishing. The love did not last, alas. Moura invited me to her home in Rasiguerres in the south of France where she had launched yet another arts festival. She wanted me to write her biography but when she saw the first draft, which contained a good deal of her very active sex life, she decided it was not at all the sort of biography she wanted.

My happiest professional commitment was the Grand National, which I covered every year for the *Sunday Mirror*. I took modest pride that in the decade I covered it, I hardly saw a horse, always got in without a ticket and never once put pen to paper.

I did try in the early days but whatever story I found I was told I had better leave it to the racing man or the gossip man or the feature writer, all specialists who also attended. When I asked what I was doing there they said, 'You are there in case.'

The year Oxo won the Grand National I was taken to witness its triumph by Mike Gabbert who owned a vintage Citroen, late the property of the Paris police.

Oxo was owned by a hospitable butcher called Mr Big. He kindly invited our party to the Adelphi Hotel for the post-race celebrations and an impromptu tasting of black velvet, an inspired co-habitation of Guinness and champagne. He also wanted us to see the chocolate horse, which in the days before it became a hamburger bar, the Adelphi dressed in the marzipan colours of the winning owner. I cannot remember the horse causing much comment amongst our party but the Black Velvet won several votes of confidence.

For all that, the most enduring memory of that day and the best jump was the one the Citroen did on the way home, easily clearing – and with much in hand – a traffic island on the East Lancs Road. I think it would have been a contender for a mention in the *Sporting Life* but for hitting the bumper of a police car on the far side of the island.

The policeman in that car trapped well. He was out of the wreck like Mick the Miller, notebook at the high port. He opened our door very courteously all the same and invited the front seat occupant to step outside and tell him how much he had drunk that day. It took a quarter of an hour and filled four pages of his notebook. In fairness, I will say that every time the narrator fell over the policeman very civilly picked him up.

But he was a bit brusque at the death when he asked, 'After all that alcohol do you think you are fit to drive?'

My friend was deeply offended. 'Certainly not,' he said, 'I am the passenger. This is a left hand drive.'

Chester gave me a taste for the high life, which, I thank God, has never deserted me. I was sitting in the champagne bar of a Manchester hotel with Lord Langford, an earlier Marquess of Milford Haven and Louis Edwards, at that time the Lord Mayor.

The baron requested Mumm, the marquess murmured Moet, and Edwards, predictably, Louis Roderer.

It had been a long, moist evening. Hesitantly I said, 'Could I have a chip butty?'

It came on a silver salver. Chips tall as guardsmen swam in a sea of farm butter on a bed of bread.

'By God,' said Langford, 'that looks good, can you make me one?'

'And another one for me,' said Milford Haven.

'Make that three,' ordered His Worship.

I have achieved little in life but I did introduce the chip butty to Debrett's. The chip butty, which was for years my favourite food, embraces all the principles of classic Chinese cuisine with its contrasts of texture, temperature and colour. I might also couple its praise with the sausage butty but there may be family reasons for that.

There is a Skidmore Sausage, obtainable in the Cotswold village of Sherston, made from a recipe unchanged since 1660. Not always by the hand of a Skidmore born but always by a Skidmore named. Whoever takes over the shop has to change his name to Skidmore. I cannot find it in my heart to blame them.

My life has been a constant pursuit of the nineteenth century. I think of myself as being attached to the twenty-first century solely for the purpose of rations and accommodation. Real life is billeted elsewhere and, as like as not, reading a page of that promising young writer, Charles Dickens.

It was in his company that I found my way into that best of all times. We met, Dickens and I, on a bookstall in the Hen Market in Shudehill, Manchester, where it was the nineteenth century right through to 1959 and the dreadful dawn of denim.

Manchester contained as many Dickensian characters as Nicholas Nickleby itself. The original Cherybles were two Mancunian brothers whose warehouse was only a hundred yards away from the Hen Market.

But Dickens would have been just as proud to have created the publican in the Sugar Loaf who never gave florins in change; he hoarded them for their silver content, on which he planned to retire to Bispham, near Blackpool. Or the editor of *Two Worlds*, the spiritualist trade magazine that published my first column even before I became 'Chiel Amang Ye' in the *Hairdressers, Wigmakers and Parfumiers Gazette*.

The spiritualist editor was a closet Calvinist, a dour Ulsterman who invented illustrated conversation. The walls of his office were covered with framed photographs of the famous and his conversation was peppered with their names. As he spoke one, so he would scurry across to stand under the appropriate face on the wall, at which he pointed dramatically.

In time, the nineteenth century and I abandoned Manchester to the dissonant drum and the guitar. We bumped into each other again in Stockport, which in those days was the Florence of Cheshire. Both were built on precipitous hills and in Stockport, as in the Florence of the renaissance bankers, the population lived by borrowing from each other.

I only worked briefly there for a news agency before I was dismissed after catching a train for Wilmslow and being taken on to Crewe.

The same thing happened to a passenger in 'Oh, Mr Porter', a Victorian comic song, but my employer, Jimmy Lovelock, like that Queen, was not amused at the cost of repatriating me to my home in Whalley Range by Express Bus. I understood. He needed every scrap of philanthropy for the other reporter, Mickey, who had to be paid daily. Mickey's Pavlovian reaction to receiving money was to put it on the nearest horse. To give him a week's wages in a lump sum would have been disastrous.

I fancy Dickens would have appreciated Mickey, who always called Lovelock 'Master' and spent every leisure moment trying to discover the secret of limitless wealth. He read avidly, questingly, the memoirs of the newly rich, hoping that one of them would qualify the phrase they all used, 'With my first £500 I bought...'

Mickey was convinced if he could only find out how that first £500 was made the next ten million would be child's play and a real challenge to get rid of all in a day.

In the 1950s Cheshire was still a landscape Alken would have recognised, inhabited by people who had dropped from the nib of Dickens' great predecessor, Surtees. They were to be found in a hundred Cheshire inns, which were mostly run by retired officers of unparalleled rudeness, awesome pretension, and intelligence so limited that to empty ashtrays and simultaneously speak was a feat beyond their powers.

It was also the Mecca of foxhunting, an activity so firmly rooted in the nourishing soil of the 1800s that I would have gone to any lengths to take part. And did.

When subsequently I worked nights on the anti-hunting *Daily Mirror*, rather than miss even a Cubbing Meet, I would change into 'Ratcatcher' in the lavatory at the end of a shift and, too poor to buy a car, catch an all-night bus to Altrincham, bowlered, breeched and booted; deaf to the ribaldry of home-going printers.

From Altrincham to the Meet I was given a lift in a horsebox by one of the few paralysingly rude ex-officers who was not running a pub. So close did he sail into the financial wind it was said he would not eat an egg unless it were poached. He wore faded pink and the collar of an unregistered and obscure hunt, of which he claimed to have been master. Only I knew that it was a Scottish drag, which he founded, supported virtually single-handed, hunted the hounds, served as kennel man and closed just by moving south. So aggressive was he, so terrifying in his white rages, that once when the wheel of the horsebox caught fire as we left Altrincham, we had reached Dunham Hill before I found the courage to tell him. I used to hire his horses until I was given one of my own through the kind offices of that most princely of twentieth century Victorians, the late, bitterly lamented, permanent tenant of my heart, the champion show jumper 'Curly' Beard, of the Rookery, Tattenhall.

A veteran freelance, Tom Campbell, late news editor of the *Daily Express,* once said to me, 'Freelance reporting is easy. All you need is a fountain pen that works, the price of a phone call, the back of your cheque book to write on – and thirty years' experience.' It was, perhaps, the most effective lesson in creative writing I have ever heard, save for Hemingway's gem, 'Stop when you know what you are going to say next.'

My own advice? The one unfailing mark of the professional writer is the placing of his desk. Views are out. The man who does it for a living writes facing a blank wall.

By the courtesy of another good friend, the Marquess of Anglesey, and at the intemperate urging of the Midland Bank, I moved into a tiny lodge owned by him on the River Braint in Llanfairpwllgwyngyll on Ynys Mon.

My new study was a stone building in the centre of a garden and I was surprised to find myself arranging it so that my desk was under the window. It would have been the first time since I began writing for a living forty years earlier I had ever looked out from my desk at anything. Clearly the subconscious was telling me it would soon be time to put away my Thesaurus and the Fowler, whose precepts I can never master, and potter among the roses.

I do not share the Johnsonian view that no one but a blockhead ever wrote except for money. But I never have. The day I get out of debt is the day I will sell the VDU, which effectively means that I will still be scribbling away until the moment they lay the pennies on my eyes.

Until I was forty, I made a handsome living writing lightly disguised fiction for the news columns of the tabloids. Then I married above myself. It was more to give my new wife a flag to fly in family conversations than for any other reason that I decided to write a book. We were far from being an intellectual family. My father was a street-fighting motorcycle cop. He loved to fight so much that when he was fifteen he was already serving with the 1st Battalion The Royal Scots in the trenches in World War 1.

On his first day in the police he was being paraded when a dentist asked to see the bobby who patrolled his street. It was my father. The dentist said he was troubled with mice and it would be worth half a crown if my father could find a stray cat and put it down his coal hole. Foolishly my father told the other bobbies and that night most of them put cats down the coal hole.

The next night a very battered dentist arrived and said, 'Here's ten bob to buy your mates a drink. But if you find the one that put the dog in with them I'll make it a quid.'

In 1921 my father fought IRA terrorists in the Erskine Street siege where he was shot in the head. Years later when I came out of the army he traced his assailant, Shaughnessy, to the Phoenix Park in Dublin, of which he had been made a manager because of his 'martyrdom' in an English prison. We went to see him and the IRA man apologised. He said there was nothing personal in the shooting and my father said, 'That's all right, I never blamed you, I always thought it was my inspector who did it. He never liked me.'

Father had no respect for authority. Every year the police had a huge parade with the chief constable leading it on a white horse. As they stood in the ranks the police band was playing. In a break my father shouted, 'Can you play the refrain from *Smoking*?'

Like many another cop, he was a crook. He was the last of the international budgie smugglers and he loved gifts. You could have given him leprosy just so long as it was free.

During the psittacosis epidemic in the early thirties people were giving away parrots on every street corner. My father was the only man to accept one. He brought it home, but when he went back on duty, the cat ate it. We were living with my granny at the time and she could have given Machiavelli five blacks and still beat him. She said to my mother, 'Leave it to me!'

When the old man came back she told him the parrot had dropped dead and she had buried it. 'Good God,' he said, 'Psittacosis!' and proceeded to burn every stick of furniture we possessed. I was in my 'cradle', a drawer, watching this. When he had finished I spoke for the first time. 'Naughty pussy ate the parrot,' I said. The subsequent row went on for twenty years but at least I knew where my future lay. I had seen the power of the spoken word. I was going to be a broadcaster.

For some reason, his little section of motorcycle cops always took their holidays in Llangwnadl on the Llyn peninsula. God knows how they discovered this remote village on the westernmost tip of Wales. It was a time when those few members of the working class who had holidays went to Blackpool, or if they had ideas above their station, Southport.

Twenty years ago I went back to Llangwnnadl and got into conversation with a Welsh farmer who said, 'You won't believe it, but fifty years ago a Scotch policeman from Manchester used to steal my apples.' I said, 'You won't believe it, but it was my father.' During the war my father drove the detectives who were supposed to break up the black market. They joined it. There was so much black-market food in our house I thought my father was a uniformed grocer.

My ancestors were nobler. They were hod-carrying knights. Edward the Confessor brought the first of them from Normandy to build castles along the border to keep the Welsh out.

My first recorded ancestor was Ralph the Knight, who was ordered after the Conquest to build a motte and bailey at Dewchurch in Herefordshire. He chose a meadow that was suitably slippery (an early defence tactic) on a stretch of land that is still called Skidmore (or Scudmor). He had no surname and thought it would be a good thing to call himself after his stretch of land, without inquiring why it was slippery. In fact it was the village privy and a correct rendition of our surname is de Shittybog.

Since then, our American led Skidmore Society has discovered that my ancestors have included the original of Sir Amoret in Spenser's *Faery Queen*. He was an Elizabethan courtier who was thought the soul of gallantry until it was discovered that when he left his home, Kentchurch Court in the Golden Valley, he manacled his wife and chained her to the wall. Another ancestor had a very busy job. He was a gentleman of the bedchamber to Henry VII. A later ancestor, Sir John Skidmore, married Owain Glyndwr's daughter in the hope of getting his hands on her lands (Glyndwr was the richest Welshman in Wales). Unfortunately Henry had already promised them to his illegitimate brother, the Duke of Beaufort. To get Sir John out of the way, and because he was thought to have funded Glyndwr when he was constable of Beaumaris Castle and Glyndwr stormed it, he was sent to France where his son died at Agincourt.

Other ancestors included one who was involved in the most scandalous divorce of the 18th century, another who lost Hereford to Cromwell, and Charles II's Ambassador to France who came home with the first Herefordshire cattle and the red streak apple, which founded the cider industry and Bulmer's. Someone wrote a poem about the apple: 'Of no regard till Skidmore's courtly hand/ Taught it its savage nature to subdue.' It was said of his cider that you could see the footprints of rats going towards the barrel but never coming away. The cider ate them.

My great uncle Bill was Al Capone's legal adviser and ward man.

I am very proud of my ancient name. I recently took a DNA test which established that on the female side my ancestry can be traced back 150,000 years to a tribe that came from Spain via the Pyrenees to Norway, Normandy, then Britain.

I'm also deeply proud of my contemporary relations like Auntie Jeannie. She was the widow of my Uncle Tommy, a Scottish Nationalist, so incandescent that ten years after his death his wife was still afraid to visit England.

Jeannie's son-in-law Jackie, who looked after the boats of an emir in the Middle East, invited her to visit. 'It's no in England, is it?' she inquired fearfully.

In the event, she had a great time, including supper with the emir in his palace. She was not impressed.

'Does he aye get his dinner on tin plates?' she asked Jackie.

'They're no tin,' whispered Jackie, 'they're real gold.'

'Maks nae difference,' said my Auntie Jeannie. 'Puir man, ye cannae keep food hot on tin plates.'

The day she got home she went to an Edinburgh market and bought the emir a six-piece china dinner service. Alas, we have lost the charming letter of thanks the emir sent.

My Auntie Jeannie was the Great Imperturbable. The nearest thing we had in our family to a tradition was the Hogmanay Fight. My father emigrated to Manchester but always returned home to Edinburgh on 30th December. He went a day early to get in training for the whisky-drinking marathon that was the family New Year.

By teatime on Old Year's Night, whisky had washed away any seasonal goodwill. By 9pm, naked hostility had replaced it. My father invariably ignited it by taking out a provocative cigar.

'Bloody Englishman,' growled Uncle Tommy, socialist principles enflamed at the sight of such a capitalist accessory.

'That makes bliddy two of us,' my father would reply every year.

Uncle Tommy's darkest secret was that he, the most passionately Scottish of the family, had been born in Lancashire. It is curious: the more passionate the patriot, the more likely he is to have been a foreigner. Hitler was an Austrian, Napoleon was a Corsican, Catherine the Great was a German, as was that most English of kings 'Farmer' George III. Blows were exchanged. Three step-brothers, Jimmy, Matty and Alec, who tried to join the row, were rebuffed by Uncle Tommy on the grounds they weren't family.

This made Jimmy, Matty and Alec madder than anyone. While five brothers fought in the middle of the room, the wives moved their chairs to the wall and continued their conversation. Auntie Jeannie served tea.

193

At 11.45pm she would say, 'Tommy, have you seen the time?'

The fight ended at once and quarter of an hour later the brothers had their arms round each other and were singing Auld Lang Syne.

They don't make Hogmanays like that any more. Or Auntie Jeannies. Nor, for that matter, Uncle Tommys.

Uncle Tommy was a road digger in Edinburgh who discovered grand opera late in life when my father played him a recording of Bjorling singing *None Shall Sleep*, at which, incidentally, he could give Pavarotti three blacks and still beat him out of sight. That same day Uncle Tommy blew his life savings, amassed over the previous week because he was sadly improvident, on a radiogram and all the arias he could cram into a carrier bag.

The family has a loose association with opera. The Victorian impresario Carl Rosa invited my great aunt Bella to join his opera company but my great grandfather withheld permission. He did not believe it was a suitable occupation for a lady.

It was a view I shared when forty years later I saw that once great company performing *Aida*. Non-operatic readers may wish to know that the opera concerns a war between Egypt and Ethiopia and marks the only occasion in military history when the Egyptian army won a battle.

By the fifties Carl Rosa was in decline and so short of cash that the Egyptian army in the production was down to platoon strength and the tomb in which hero and heroine are immured collapsed under the weight of a soprano. The scenery in most of the company's productions at that time displayed the bravura of an excitable tenor. So impermanent was it that it made the cardboard walls in *Prisoner of Cell Block H* granite-like in comparison. I saw a production of *The Flying Dutchman* in which the eponymous tenor was instantly grounded when the flies fell on him. So pinched were the productions that in *La Boheme* it was the audience's imagination and not Mimi's tiny hand that was frozen.

I was not for many years a fan of opera; indeed it acted on me like musical mogadon. I attribute this largely to Carl Rosa productions although it would be churlish not to acknowledge the part played by various provincial opera companies in Germany in the immediate post war years.

Take Eleven

Newspapermen don't come much better than Vincent Mulchrone, a friend since weekly paper days. The last time we met before his too early death, I had been hired by the Brewers' Society to argue the case for Sunday opening of pubs in Wales. A cause close to my heart.

The most graphic way to illustrate the anomalies, it seemed to me, was to hire a coach and get my friend Robin Wills, the manager of the Grosvenor Hotel in Chester, to make a massive, extravagant picnic because Robin did extravagance better than anyone I knew, as befitted a tobacco company heir.

I would invite Fleet Street's finest to join me in a tour of the Welsh border, visiting pubs. Pubs where you could get a drink in the snug, but not the lounge, the bar but not the dining room, and in one case where the boundary between England and Wales ran through the centre of the pub, on the left hand side of the bar but not the right.

Mulchrone was first on my list.

Late in the afternoon we left the main party and settled down to have a comfortable drink in the Crown in Denbigh, which had never closed in living memory. It was there that Vince told me the story of the time he hired a man to wear a Flook suit at a seaside promotion by the *Daily Mail*.

Flook was a very popular furry bear, star of the paper's cartoons page. Vince said he found a reluctant candidate at the town's labour exchange.

'A fiver,' Vince wheedled, 'just for a morning's walk on the sands.'

'Deck chairs?' the man asked suspiciously. 'I couldn't give out deck chairs. It's me back and I can't stand heat.'

'It's not the bloody Sahara,' Vince said. 'And we'll throw in a water bottle. All you've got to do is be nice to a few kids.'

The man's eyes blazed with panic. 'It's not Father Christmas, is it? I couldn't do Father Christmas; not again. I 'ad to do it three years ago. Horrible it was. I give out the wrong parcels and a little girl hit me wiv a bleeding train.'

'It's mid-summer,' Vince told him. 'You don't have Father Christmas in summer.'

'They had me in September that year,' the man countered. 'I wouldn't have to give anything out, would I?'

'Lollipops. In a tray,' Vince told him quickly. 'Round your neck. When you've given the last one out you've finished.'

'They wouldn't have to sit on my knee, would they? I couldn't have kids sitting on my knee. They all have wet drawers, you know. It's the excitement.'

But he was weakening. 'How many lollipops?'

'Fifty.'

He made up his mind. 'OK!' he said. 'But not a word to this lot. I don't want to lose me amchoor status. And no sitting on bleeding knees,' he warned. 'I ain't 'aving a conviction for that. Definite.'

'Flook has no knees.'

When they got to the Entertainments Shed on the prom and he saw the Flook outfit, the little man changed his mind. 'I'm not getting into that bleedin' thing,' he said. 'It's horrible.'

He agreed when Vince doubled the fee but not even the lure of a third fiver, which Vince had to give him to put on the plastic head, would induce him to remove his cap.

The incessant electronic barking of Flook obviously unnerved him, Vince told me. With a sudden, desperate jerk, the little man tore himself away from the grips of a circulation man and, banging and dipping his plastic head, shot through the hut door and out into the Great World.

Colliding almost at once with a group of holiday makers, he tumbled and rolled down the promenade steps to the beach where the weight of his head sent his feet shooting into the air. In a moment he was up and running, little gauntleted hands waving wildly as he struggled to unfasten the head. Zig-zagging across the beach, terrifying holiday makers.

'Look at him!' A circulation man fumed. 'He's ruining the whole bloody thing, leaping about like that. He should be walking slowly, chatting up the children.'

From that day many readers of the *Daily Mail* were able to get instant obedience from their young by threatening them that Flook was coming. He emptied that beach faster than rain, or even a deck chair attendant. At first the children had been delighted. You could hear a concerted shout of

'OOOOOH' all over the front as a horde of children threw away the spades with which they had been burying their fathers and made for Flook. No doubt it was the lollipops that attracted them, for the trail of red toffee that charted his progress down the beach soon became a line of struggling, laughing children. But the mood changed dramatically when, brought to bay at last, the little man turned on his pursuers and started throwing lollipops at their heads.

'It's all wrong,' said the man from the circulation department pettishly. 'There should only be one lollipop to each child. That little girl has been hit twice.'

Vince said he admired the man's aim: he could not see and was directed solely by sound. Under the circumstances Vince thought he put up a creditable performance. Even when the last lollipop was discharged the man in the Flook suit fought on, hurling pebbles and even rocks of a respectable size. When he finally put the children to flight and sent parents scuttling for the protection of the promenade wall, the little man stood for a moment whimpering, a lonely figure on a deserted beach.

He threw himself down on the sand, kicking at the air as he struggled to pull off his head, which by now was dented badly. Finally, he scrambled to his feet, skidding in the wet sand at the sea's edge. Soon he was paddling, if you could so describe his nervous leaps and surges, as the water washed first round his ankles, then his knees, his little furry thighs and finally his middle as he floated further out to sea.

The circulation man must have had a sticky few moments on the phone calling out a lifeboat to a man in a bearskin. When he came back he wore the air of a man who has known suffering. 'They wanted to know, if they tow it in, do they get salvage money?' he said.

Take Twelve

I had this friend who fished twenty years for salmon. Never had a bite. When at last he did gaffe one, I congratulated him. He was less than pleased. He said, 'Yesterday I was unique. No one else fished for twenty years without success. Today I am just another fisherman who has caught a salmon.'

I knew how he felt. My daughter Lynn May became Journalist of the Year; my son Nick Regional Feature Writer of the Year, both while working for the *Daily Post*. My wife Celia can scarcely sign a cheque without getting a literary award – Tír na nÓg, Irma Chilton, they festoon her walls.

Me? Fifty years in the front line and not so much as mentioned in despatches. Until I was rewarded for half a century slaving over a hot microphone with a gold-plated microphone for services rendered to broadcasting. Now I am just another award winner. As with everything else in what I laughingly call a life, the award came dripping with ironies.

Shakespeare tipped me off and I should have listened to his warning in *King Lear*: 'As flies to wanton boys are we to gods; They kill us for their sport'. In my case they just took the piss.

Just once it would have been nice to get a job as a result of an interview but I never managed it. If you have stayed with me so far you will have noted that when I did get a job it was the result of an event that must have brought the house down in Valhalla.

I expect those Gods are still playing re-runs of my debut as a broadcaster.

I had a pal called Pete Evans, a cameraman with BBC Wales and probably the only one who took his pet goat in his car for company on jobs. It was never lonely because he also took several dogs to keep the goat company. Pete's was not a car you got into lightly if you had a decently developed sense of smell.

By the time I was thirty I had come to the conclusion that being a reporter was not a job for a grown up and was looking for a way out. Pete said if that was how I felt, why not come and be his presenter. In those days all freelance cameramen had a reporter to tell the story because the truth is every picture doesn't.

He fixed an interview with his boss Twdr, who said, 'Great to 'ave you, boy. Just one thing. Keep the stories light. Nothing heavy.'

So I did. And I was dropped. Some time later I shared a lift with Twdr in Broadcasting House. I had become a radio star by this time so I was able to ask him, 'Why did you drop me?'

'Had to,' he said. 'You did nothing but light pieces. Nothing heavy.'

I had managed to get one or two pieces taken up by Tonight, a flagship programme on BBC1. One of them took the fancy of a man called Dewi Smith, who was then head of light entertainment on the BBC in Wales. It was he who offered me a chance to work on Radio Wales and I now say, in the deepest gratitude, made sure I had regular work for the next thirty years.

He is more elegant now but when I first met him he was heavily bearded and arrayed in a curious fur-collared anorak. It was difficult to work out when Dewi ended and the anorak began.

He came from Rhosllanerchrugog in north Wales, a small village that has produced, among others, the founder of an African university who invented crispbread, a marshal of the Royal Air Force and so many teachers that eight buses left the village every morning to take them to their various schools. It had a view of itself, which I found commendable. The man who founded the university was the son of a miner who, early in his career, held a chair at Kings College, London. When he was appointed, he invited his mum, the miner's widow, down from Rhos. At a sherry party someone asked her what she thought of London. 'Very nice,' she said, 'but it's so far from everywhere.'

Had the Mappa Mundi been drawn in Rhos, that village not Jerusalem would have been the centre of the world. Like most of my friends and all the people I love, Dewi was a bit odd.

He was a child prodigy, but so was everyone else in the village. Dewi just got better as a pianist as he grew older. When he went to the Royal Northern College in Manchester he was so good that even as a student he gave recitals at various halls in the city. Unfortunately he was at the College with John Ogden and when Dewi heard him play he decided he was not going to be the best pianist in the world and gave up the piano to become a sound engineer in the BBC. We worked happily together for thirty years and remain friends to this day but I have never been able to persuade him to play the piano.

Thanks to Dewi, I became a promising broadcaster and was brought to the attention of the big boss, Teleri Bevan.

She came to visit us in Brynsiencyn to decide whether I could front a major programme. Naturally we gave her lunch and I was supposed to sparkle. In fact I had pressed her to so much wine I fell asleep. I have a vague memory of her getting up from the table, whispering her thanks to Celia and saying, 'No, don't wake him up, he looks so peaceful.'

Bless her, she decided I had a future in broadcasting.

The gold-plated award was made not a month since the BBC had dispensed with most of the services I was rendering and I only heard about the award by accident because the BBC neglected to tell me I had won one. I learned about the honour when the organisers, *Ffowcs*, a media magazine, rang to ask what time I was arriving in Aberystwyth that day and I said I wasn't and they said, well how are you going to get your award?

The other irony is that for thirty years BBC Wales thought it cheaper to give me an engineer rather than a microphone after I wrecked six tape recorders in a month. That was when Dewi recruited me as a Good Morning Wales reporter. He gave me the first of the tape recorders I smashed which, even in those days, cost £250. He also gave me fifty quids' worth of tapes and three boxes of batteries. But he wouldn't give me a key to the Wrexham studios because I wasn't staff.

It was my first taste of BBC logic. I was loaded down with £350 worth of portable property I could have sold in the first pub I went in. Yet he wouldn't give me the key to an office from which I could derive no illicit profit.

Some years later I started *Radio Brynsiencyn*, which had listeners in Boston (USA) and an appreciation society at Oxford University. My junior reporter on the programme was the singing star Aled Jones, my foreign editor the late Angus MacDairmid, the distinguished BBC foreign correspondent who had covered Watergate and the Congo wars. His great preoccupation was visiting towns all round the world named after his hometown, Bangor. Although it was a programme, a lot of the BBC top brass thought it was an actual station. It certainly had a large catchment area. A neighbour once got the winter glooms that visit

Anglesey islanders. He jumped in his car and drove across France. He stopped to picnic on the banks of the Loire, switched on the car radio and heard Radio Brynsiencyn broadcasting from outside his house.

Later, I took over Archives on Radio 4, where I also did an interview series. One of the subjects was Lady Williams, a Russian aristocrat who married a British diplomat. After the Revolution they fled penniless to Britain.

She told a wonderful story about her father, a Prince, going for a job as a butler. The maid mistook him for a luncheon guest. His host thought his wife had invited him. When he discovered his mistake he asked why the prince had come.

'For a job as a butler?' he exclaimed. 'I couldn't possibly employ anyone as grand as you!'

When he heard the prince's story he gave him an allowance for the rest of his life, educated his daughters and sent them to Oxford.

Unfortunately I had a hangover when Masha Williams told this story in her Hampstead drawing room at twilight with a fire crackling. She spoke in a magical mixture of Russian and Oxford, which put me to sleep instantly. I only woke up as she came to the end of the story.

My producer hadn't noticed, Masha hadn't noticed, so I kept shtum. The programme consequently was a virtual monologue, which was against all broadcasting rules. I thought I was for the high jump but was pleasantly surprised when the BBC was inundated with mail from listeners saying: 'Thank God for an interviewer who doesn't interrupt.'

I do not go much on cars but I once made a TV series in which I drove and fell in love with an Austin Seven tourer. It is the one car that everyone of my generation has owned at some time or another. Wynford Vaughan Thomas was very envious. He said that changing gear in it was like milking a mouse.

My wife owes her TV debut to that car. I was supposed to drive round Wales in it, but it was in the days before the diet and there wasn't room in the front for me and the steering wheel. She was hired on the spot to do the driving.

That gave me the opportunity to spot something unusual. Wherever we went you could see the expressions of passers-by softening when they saw the car. The pre-war Austin Seven tourer, it seems, conjures happy memories for everyone. I have noticed similar expressions on visitors to the Llangollen Motor Museum, which was run as a costly hobby by two friends of mine, the Ted Broadhursts, father and son.

Son Ted used to be an editor but found draining sump oil more intellectually rewarding. Ted father was an engineer so senior that his firm gave him a Rolls Royce. He is happier now with smaller and older cars. He once ran a garage but gave it up. He told me it is the only job where the customer knows better than the expert he employs. They always told him what was wrong with their cars and were rarely right. In self-defence he opened an electrical business because no one knows anything about electricity and they take your word for it, on the rare occasions electricians can be persuaded to keep appointments, that is.

I wish I could have been the Broadhursts who opened a barn door in Herefordshire and found six pre-war Austin Sevens and three tons of spares, all in their original wrapping.

They had been bought thirty years before by a businessman who planned to build Austin Sevens when he retired. That sort of eccentricity the two Teds would have completely understood.

They were on the same wavelength as the Warwickshire man who invented an insect killer that consisted of a vacuum gun and a bottle of whisky. He built the gun out of transparent tubing, a broken hedge trimmer, a garden chair and the melted down parts of a battleship's telescope. Insects were sucked into a tube fitted with a valve so they could not escape. In the manual version, a cord operated the piston that created the suction but there was an electric version that worked like a small vacuum cleaner. You can kill wasps, flies, moths, anything of that kind. It is more efficient than corks round your hat, swifter than flypaper and if you don't like killing insects you can take them out of the tube, carry them out into the countryside and release them.

If you wanted to kill them humanely you had to take the insect carefully between the finger and thumb, remove it from the tube and hold it over a glass of whisky. The fumes kill 'em. I am not making this up. The inventor was Alan Freeman, he was 78 and he lived in Rugby in Warwickshire.

I had been teetotal at the time he invented his killer and after two years, six months, three weeks, two days and an hour and a half of unwilling teetotalism I could find it in my heart to envy those insects.

Take Thirteen

My interview series *Conversations with Ian Skidmore* lasted for fifteen years. The year I was awarded the Golden Microphone for services to radio, it and my other two radio programmes were dropped and my income fell by nearly £30,000 a year. As the broadcaster Robert Robinson wrote to me when he learned of it, 'Beware of executives bearing gifts.'

But the Brave Don't Cry…

I learned from another broadcaster, Lionel Kelleway, that we had both been dropped because of our English accents. I decided to join him in taking the BBC to a race relations tribunal.

The BBC wanted me to say that my belief that I was dropped because of my English accent was a misunderstanding. Worse, the Commission for Racial Equality wanted Kelleway and me to take the £1,500 the BBC offered.

After I refused, the CRE dropped me on the day I was due to go before the tribunal. The tribunal was sympathetic and I won the right to represent myself. I said I would sell everything I had to finance the fight. It would not have taken very long.

Kelleway's tribunal went ahead and it was a strange affair. The BBC lawyer mounted the curious defence that Wales does not exist as a country. One felt quite sorry for Henry VIII wasting all that money on an Act of Union when there was nothing to unionise. Particularly upsetting to hear this in Shrewsbury where in 1410 my ancestor Philpot was beheaded for helping Glyndwr make that very point. Shrewsbury was not a lucky place in which to be a Skidmore. Another ancestor Barnabas was court-martialled for losing the city to the Roundheads.

Pointedly the chairman drew counsel's attention to an identical case, which BBC Scotland lost, which enshrined in law Wales's nationhood.

Quite a relief to Max Boyce.

The hearing was adjourned but the fight went on. The BBC claimed I was dropped because of my age. I pointed out that Alastair Cooke, at 92, was 20 years older than me, Humphrey Lyttelton was 80, Anthony Howard 73. I listed five other presenters who were as old as me. I offered a press report reporting that Social Secretary Alastair Darling had called in the Director General Greg Dyke for an assurance that the BBC was not ageist. Dyke insists it is not.

I should have known I would be dropped by the CRE when the chairman of the CRE in Wales denied the BBC was racist; though CRE counsel's opinion had been that there was a case to answer. As one of my witnesses said after the court appearance, 'The Taffia moves in mysterious ways its wonders to perform.'

My complaint was not really against the BBC, which I have always loved dearly. It was directed at a man who was briefly commissioning editor.

I had a great deal of support from listeners. One, Cliff Pritchard who worked at Wylfa Nuclear Power Station, told me the workers there agreed that only three things could stop them working: a nuclear accident, a strike and my programme *Radio Brynsiencyn*.

I conducted a very successful press campaign which brought to light heart-rending cases, not only of racial discrimination against Englishmen, but against Welshmen who were denied jobs because they did not speak Welsh. A Bangor policeman, for example, who was posted to Barmouth ran into a storm of abuse from councillors because he was not a Welsh speaker.

My efforts were rewarded when a Welsh extremist website honoured me with the title of Traitor of the Week. I shared it rather puzzlingly with Ryan Giggs, S4C, Radio Cymru, the Welsh Language Society, the Welsh Language Board and a very nice man called Jonesy, who is a Radio Cymru presenter.

I had abusive emails, death threats, the whole bag. But they were always anonymous.

Shortly after I lost my programmes and was no longer a celebrity, I lost my column on the *Daily Post* that had suddenly, in the face of falling circulation, discovered a Welsh identity. I was replaced by an all-in wrestler. In Welsh.

I had been growing crops of words on strips of blank newsprint called a column, man and boy, for fifty years. I have been the sole proprietor of so many columns I am known in the trade as the Parthenon Kid.

I eventually got my name over the door but when I started it was the High Noon of the flamboyant pseudonym. In the trade magazines, I was at the same time Bookworm, Hod Carrier and Pro Bono Publico. In the *Hairdressers, Wigmakers and Parfumiers Gazette* I was, as mentioned before, A Chiel Amang Ye, which any parfumier worth his ambergris knew was a subtle allusion to the *Chiel* in the poem by Burns who gathered notes. In those days a reader had to keep his wits about him. The *Manchester City News* changed me into a Greek lady called Thea Page (Theatre Page to the wide awake). I was Townsman in the *Yorkshire Evening News*; in the *Yorkshire Evening Post,* which was renowned for its perversity, I was Countryman. I was even Streetwalker – I still think I could sue – in the *Sunday Pictorial*.

Odd name for a column, but are there worse? Not really. 'Random Jottings' is a cliché, 'Writer's Notes' is pretentious. No professional newspaperman of my generation would have known what to do with a notebook. The other favoured label for this sort of column is 'Through My Study Window', which is nonsense. The one unfailing mark of the professional writer, as I've said before, is the placing of his desk. Views are out. The man who does it for a living writes facing a blank wall.

I cannot say I am sorry the future is nearly over. It has been a long, hard struggle trying to make a living from my pen; feeling like the only employee of the Midland Bank who qualifies for neither holiday nor pension.

When I interviewed the Danish recorder player Michala Petri before an audience at the Beaumaris Festival, my wife and my producer at Radio Wales, who both believe they have established squatters' rights in my head, were furious with me. Michala had told me how she needed an audience to bring out her best work and I said that when I was writing I never thought of the reader. I wrote for the word processor and the Midland Bank. They accused me of demeaning my talent and yet it was no more than the sad truth.

To my surprise, my first book was a best seller, so I went on to write twenty-eight more, including a second best seller about the lifeboat cox, and one of the finest men it has been my privilege to meet, Dick Evans of Moelfre on Anglesey. That took a decade and at the end of that time I did my sums and discovered that I would have earned more money if instead of writing books I had spent the ten years on Social Security.

I decided to go on Social Security and the lady in Llangefni said that would be fine. I explained I would only need the money to tide me over while I wrote another book. She said that wouldn't do at all. She said I could have the money every week just so long as I promised not to do any work. I realised I was not the right sort of writer to handle that. Who I needed to be was Dean Swift, than whom no one could better handle a crazy world.

Looking back, I realise I was outrageously cheated by a number of publishers I ought never to have trusted in the first place. But I have written two novels and three other books I am proud of, and only one I am thoroughly ashamed of, and that isn't a bad record surely? Not when you are writing with your nose pressed against a red column in a bank statement.

I wish I had picked up the trick of attracting arts council subsidies and creative writing contracts. But I never had the time, what with having to write all the time and sometimes even speak the writing on radio.

And there is always this. It does put me in distinguished company. Shakespeare was a working writer and so was Sam Johnson. I revere them both and am as mad as I expect they are that industries have built up explaining them and poking about in their private lives. All I need to know when I read those essays in the Rambler is that Johnson wrote them, often in a crowded room and I bet never anywhere near a window, while the printer's boy shuffled his feet in the hall. Or that, more often than not, the reason Shakespeare wrote passages of lyrical beauty was that there wasn't any scenery. It was like writing for radio, which is maybe why I enjoy listening to him better than watching the plays.

Or that Johnson wrote *Rasselas* to pay for his mother's funeral; or that Shakespeare didn't really want to be a playwright. What he wanted to be was a landowner in Stratford. And I will bet you anything the bank will let me borrow, that when he moved back home and pawned his quill he put his desk firmly under a window. You only have to look at his garden to know that.

Take Fourteen

When Tom Firbank bought a mountain in Snowdonia, he knew where his home was. A farm called Dyffryn on the slopes of the Glyders, which he immortalised in his unforgettable book *I Bought a Mountain*.

'Bought it the day I saw it, in fact,' he said. 'Felt like home.'

I met him when he took a plane to Wales from his home in Japan. He did not know what to call his destination. 'Home? How can it be? I have lived in Japan for forty years. I prefer to bow in greeting rather than shake hands.'

Being bowed at by an 85-year-old, ramrod stiff, former Coldstream Guards colonel, author of a best-selling book that has gone through 29 editions and is still in print, would be too much. So when we met in Ruthin we nodded and smiled.

Home or not, Tom was very excited by what was happening in Wales. One of the reasons for his return was to observe the Welsh Assembly on the ground.

'It could be a wonderful thing,' he said. 'The last time I was over I had a talk with Dafydd Wigley and I was very impressed. I think it a mistake to put the Assembly in Cardiff. It should be in the centre of Wales, both culturally and geographically, and that is Aberystwyth.

'I want to get the feel of Wales again. My mother was Welsh and a cousin was high sheriff of Monmouth.'

More unlikely was another Welsh cousin, the effete author Ronald Firbank whom Betjeman called a 'jewelled, clockwork nightingale'. Who, according to a recent biography of Lord Berners who found his body, 'could be identified only by his mother's address in Monmouthshire'.

The infinitely tougher and resilient Tom Firbank had a second reason for returning to Wales. Another book was to be republished. *A Country of Memorable Honour* is an account of a walk Firbank took in the fifties from Llangollen to Cardiff. It is among my favourite books about the Principality. Quite the equal to H V Morton's *In Search of Wales*.

'It is not a guidebook to the country,' Firbank insisted, 'as much as to its inhabitants. I met most of the people who were working to remould Wales into what it is now. There are sad moments. I arrived to see Clough Williams-Ellis on the morning after his house burned down and found him standing in the rubble. In Aberystwyth, Gwynfor Evans and I had a great time planning the invasion of England. An army staff college course taught me how to invade.'

In fact he had first hand experience. During the war he was recalled from a new job at SHAEF to join the team planning Arnhem, where he subsequently fought with the Paras.

That story of how he joined the Coldstream Guards as a ranker and rose to command a troop of the airborne cavalry fighting in the Italian campaign and finally, as a colonel, fought at Arnhem, is told in another book *I Bought a Star*. It is one of the best books by a fighting soldier in World War II.

Firbank had fond memoirs of the Italian campaign.

'The main thrust of the invasion was up on the Apennine side. I was seconded to a Para brigade that fought a separate war along the Adriatic coast. We joined Roy Farran's SAS and a private army run by a man called Popski. It was very exciting and great fun. A decent mobile war, not like that dreadful trench warfare. I must say I enjoyed the army right from the start. Never get the camaraderie ever again.'

Incredibly for a man of his age, his third reason for returning to Wales was to write yet another book. He might have called it *I Bought a Country* because it tells how, after the war, he conquered the East as a super salesman for Perkins Diesels, selling their engines wherever he could find a buyer.

He said, 'I was born under Gemini which means I am a traveller and restless after a little while in a place. My life has been a series of reincarnations. Sheep farmer, soldier, salesman. This job suited me because I was never out of a plane.'

His territory covered twenty-two countries and included China, Burma, Malaya and Japan. He was one of the first British businessmen in Japan and he loved it from the day he arrived. But it was someone else – not Firbank – who told me in what respect he was held among the Japanese industrial giants and statesmen whom he first met when they were struggling young businessmen. He married a Japanese girl and settled in Japan because, in the fifties, it was at the centre of things.

'It is a romantic sort of place and the countryside is like Gwynedd. Seven-tenths of it is mountain but it is a country that, apart from a little brown coal, has no raw materials. Until the end of the 19th century it was still living in the Middle Ages. Now it is the most literate country in the world. Alas, this has its drawbacks. They accept everything they are told and never question anything at all.'

Escape from the Rising Sun, the story of Geoffrey Langford's amazing escape in World War II from Singapore, via Sumatra to Ceylon, to which I referred earlier, was my first book. The second was *Wildlife in Custody* and it was a worldwide success.

'PC' Ken Williams loved life more than any man I have ever met and lived each minute with an intensity that gave off heat. His life was a 71-year magical childhood. Sadly he died at that comparatively early age in 2000 after contracting a liver disease caught on safari in Kenya. He was taken ill on holiday there and flown home in an air ambulance. He died in his private wonderland, Pandy Cymunod, near Holyhead on the Isle of Anglesey.

Ken was the only police constable who was a TV star on his day off. His HTV country programme *Over the Gate* was the most popular of the day. He had been both very poor and very rich. At one stage he was the only serving police constable in Wales with a holiday home, staffed with servants, in Mombasa.

International fame came when he persuaded the board of Anglesey Aluminium to lease him part of the Penrhos sporting estate at Holyhead, on which they planned a massive smelter. Aided by an army of schoolchildren, he turned the headland of the inland sea there into one of the most successful nature reserves in Britain, which he ran between shifts as a police constable in Holyhead. He performed miniature miracles most days. Feeding orphan seals had been impossible until Ken approached one in black waders he had rubbed with fish oil. The orphan assumed their fishy, slippery surface was another seal and happily ate the fish that Ken hand-fed it.

Wildlife in Custody was the book I helped him write about his life and the reserve and it was one of the most enjoyable and entertaining experiences of my life. Ken was awarded the MBE and made a Fellow of the Royal Zoological Society. He became a close friend of the Prince of Wales and was wildlife advisor at Highgrove.

He could have gone far in the police force. I was present when one chief constable begged him to take promotion. He refused. He told me, 'I had enough of responsibility as a Guards sergeant. I will leave the police as I joined it. As a constable.'

He did, but not quite in the way he imagined.

In 1971, Ken met and married his third wife Chris. It was love at first sight. They were made for each other though they came from vastly different backgrounds. Chris was the daughter of one of Kenya's richest men. Hers was a very different world from the one Ken knew but he was soon at its epicentre. He organised safaris and mixed as an equal with some of the richest people in the world. This ex-sergeant's friends included generals and members of the aristocracy. The couple crossed the world together but not always in state. They crossed America by Greyhound bus.

Ken was at his happiest at Pandy. He dug a network of lakes, which he stocked with eagerly suicidal trout, built a small zoo for his collection of birds of prey, and a heated swimming pool. He made a study in an outhouse where he was surrounded by the mementos of his incredible life. Pride of place went to his policeman's bike and the uniform he enhanced by wearing it.

I write this as an appreciation of his life rather than an obituary. Ken deserves better than the mournful sound of the last post. He was a reveille man.

His grandfather and three of his uncles were policemen. He was born in Abergynolwyn in the Dysynni valley in Merioneth, where his remarkable father was the local bobby, the subject of a best-selling book and a better poacher than most of those he arrested. Ken went to school fitfully, preferring to spend his life roaming the countryside learning about the creatures and the flora. He was fascinated by the cormorants that nest on Bird Rock, miles from the sea, and kept secret the peregrines that also flew there. Had there been A-levels in country knowledge he would have been an A* before he was ten. He had a remarkable rapport with animals. He trained a pair of kestrels to dive for food in his pockets and fish queued up to be caught by him.

It was unthinkable that he would be anything other than a village bobby, which in those days meant first serving in the Welsh Guards. He learned discipline when he was posted to the Brigade Battle School at Pirbright. His brother Leslie, who was a sergeant instructor there, greeted him by putting him on a charge for not shaving.

'But he is my brother, sir,' Ken told the platoon commander when he was marched before him.

'I have reason to believe that is substantially correct, sir,' his brother admitted.

Ken was a quick learner. When he was demobbed after adventurous service in Palestine where he went on desert patrol with Glubb Pasha's legendary Legion, Ken was sergeant of the Prince of Wales platoon, the elite of the elite.

We met when he was village constable in Bala. I was constantly writing stories about his bravery rescuing farm animals but I kept very quiet about his poaching expeditions. He wasn't just the constable: in his world he was the 'chief constable'. When a farmer's wife complained her husband was drinking too much and was in danger of injuring himself, Ken called him to the police station and confiscated his gun licence for six months.

'Will there be a fine?' asked the farmer.

'Not this time,' said Ken. 'First offence.'

The only consolation for Ken's untimely death is that people like Ken do not know about dying. He will still be at Pandy a hundred years from now.

Another unforgettable character I wrote about was Captain Richard Matthew Evans BEM SGM (Silver Gallantry Medal), who died at the age of 95 and was one of only two lifeboat men in the history of the RNLI to be awarded two gold medals, the recognised equivalent of the Victoria Cross, for outstanding bravery at sea.

He came from a line of lifeboat men from the closely knit fishing village of Moelfre on the Isle of Anglesey. Before the RNLI was formed, one of his ancestors had helped save survivors from the *Royal Charter* that was wrecked off Moelfre in the great storm of 25 October 1859. By supreme coincidence, it was a hundred years to the day when Dick, as coxswain of the Moelfre lifeboat, launched in another great storm on the first of the two spectacular rescues that have made him revered by lifeboat men the world over.

He was born in a cottage near the lifeboat station of which his uncle was coxswain and his father, a master mariner, a member of the crew. One grandfather had been second cox of the same boat, the other a member of the crew. When in time Dick became cox, his three sons, David, Derek and William, were members of the crew.

The village did not welcome outsiders and there were mutterings when he married Nansi, a farmer's handsome daughter who was born not a dozen miles away.

Dick went to sea at the age of 14 as a cabin boy on a coaster the *Daisy* bound from Moelfre to Preston with a cargo of hay. At 23, he became a master mariner and took command of the 320-ton MV *Colin*. He was outraged when after a family counsel he was ordered to swallow the anchor and run the family butcher's shop. His uncle Matthew Evans was leaving the shop to become full time lifeboat cox. Dick's only consolation was that he could become bowman of the boat, still in those days powered by oar and sail.

During the war he was promoted to second cox and made signals sergeant of the Moelfre Home Guard Platoon, which was made up of retired sea captains. The Moelfre boat made many daring rescues, for one of which Cox'n Matthews was awarded a silver medal and Dick won his first of many medals, a bronze.

In 1954 Dick, who had served in the lifeboat since he was 16, became cox'n, a position he held for seventeen and a half years. The rescue of the crew of the *Hindley* on 26 October 1959 was to bring him his first 'VC'.

In a 23-year-old relief boat *The Edna and Mary Robinson*, about the handling of which he knew nothing, Dick and his crew put to sea in a 90-mile-an-hour gale. The MV *Hindley*, a 506-tonner, was reported dragging her cable in Moelfre Bay. She had been sheltering overnight from a sou'wester but when the wind veered rapidly to the north she was caught and driven on to rocks when the *Royal Charter* had struck. When an hour and a half later the lifeboat reached her, she was 200 yards from the rocks and pitching on the point of capsize. Her 9ft propellers were only 10ft above the lifeboat. Pitching wildly, the *Robinson* went alongside in huge seas, which eventually pitched her clear onto the deck of the *Hindley*. Miraculously, a second wave, which should have capsized them, lifted them clear as two of the crewmen plucked off the last mariner. All ten of the crew were saved and the only injury was a broken ankle.

Dick fought his way back through 30ft waves to his mooring – and forty-five minutes later launched her again on another rescue.

Dick won his second gold medal at the age of 61 when he rescued the crew of nineteen on a 1,287-ton Greek freighter the *Nafsiporous* on 29 November 1966. She was struck by a cyclone in Liverpool Bay with little ballast and driven ever nearer to the jagged rocks of the Skerries off the northern coast of Anglesey. The Moelfre lifeboat had been out on a service since 7.45am. She launched for the second time at 1.55pm. Eight miles out, Dick felt the lifeboat plunging sometimes up to the mast. The sea had ripped away two deck ventilators leaving gaping holes. Dick sent his own son David, with second cox Murley Francis, to make temporary repairs.

He explained later, 'I could not have stopped Murley but I had to send my son with him. If I had sent someone else and they had been washed overboard, I'd have had to live with the reputation of a man who saved his son at the expense of his crew.'

In the event, he rescued ten crew members and brought back the lifeboat with a wrecked compass, no electric power and holes in the bow. When they finally moored they had been twenty-three hours without food and Dick had been at the wheel for twelve and a half hours.

When he retired in 1970, the RNLI had the brilliant idea of sending him round the country telling the story of his rescues at fund raising gatherings. A senior official confessed, 'He was a star. You cannot total the number of legacies we received as a result of his appearances and he collected many thousands of pounds.'

When he spoke at the RNLI's 150th anniversary at the London Guildhall he was given a standing ovation.

From the time he had joined it in 1921 until his retirement, the Moelfre lifeboat was launched 179 times and saved 281 lives. Dick's first award was 'Thanks on Vellum' in 1940; in 1943 he won the bronze medal; in 1960 the Queen's silver medal for gallantry and his first gold medal; in 1967 he won his second gold medal and was voted 'Man of the Year'; and in 1969 he was awarded the BEM. He was a fellow of Manchester Polytechnic and a Bard of the National Eisteddfod.

At his funeral in the chapel at Moelfre where he had worshipped all his life, a tribute was paid by Mike Valasto, the RNLI chief operations officer. Then the coffin, draped in the flag of the RNLI and carrying Dick's cap, his medals and a floral anchor, was carried out on the shoulders of the Moelfre crew, followed by lifeboat men from all over Britain to whom he was a revered figure.

The coffin was lowered into the grave to the sound of exploding maroons. It was the first time that the maroons had gone off for Dick when he did not answer them.

I had more or less retired when I had a telephone call from a man who wanted me to ghost his memoirs. At first I refused but he sounded so much fun I changed my mind and thus met yet another remarkable man.

Captain William Higgin, who sadly died a year later on the day the book was published, was one of the finest game shots of his generation. His game diaries, which he had kept meticulously since the age of eleven, show a total of 357,000 birds and vermin. Not recorded was the Dornier bomber he shot down on his family estate at Puddington, Cheshire, or the two sacred peacocks that almost got him lynched by angry villagers in India.

He shot the Dornier bomber while on leave as a ranker in the Cheshire Regiment as it came in very low on its run to the iron works at Queensferry.

'It was quite an easy shot,' he recalled, 'and the next day Western Command in Chester confirmed it had come down.'

The peacocks he shot in India, on safari, and was saved from angry tribesmen by the head man, 'a Cambridge graduate, who smuggled us out at night.'

His shooting career almost ended when as a 19-year-old company commander in the 5th Baluch (Jacob's Rifles) Regiment, King George V's Own, a bullet whistled past his ear on morning parade. It had been fired by a deranged sepoy. Bill's dilemma was that if he reported him to the CO, the sepoy would have been shot. He noticed the man was wearing a marksman's badge and he ordered another sepoy to rip it off.

'If you missed me at that range,' he said, 'you are clearly wearing it under false pretences.'

He felt justified when six months later the sepoy won the Military Medal.

Fighting on the North West Frontier was conducted in a gentlemanly way. If a sepoy was shot or a village became obstreperous, it was given a warning that on an appointed day the Indian Air Force would bomb it. On that day, the villagers would scatter into the mountains and the Air Force would come over and drop a few bombs. 'Not many casualties and very little blood letting,' Bill remembered.

Posted to the Burmese jungle in World War II, he was struck down with polio and it took ten days to get him out of the jungle to hospital.

'I had warned my soldiers I would shoot anyone I found drinking water from a pond,' he said, 'then twenty-four hours later, like a bloody fool, I drank from one.'

After a year in hospital, disguising his polio limp he was back on duty in India as ADC to army commander Sir Henry Finnis.

Subsequently he was Pandit Nehru's warder when Nehru was imprisoned in a cage by the British. He remembered, 'I looked after Nehru for six months and he didn't address a single word to me. Can't blame him. He was kept in appalling conditions, literally in a cage built onto a shed like a dog kennel where he slept.'

Invalided home at the end of the war, he commanded a POW camp at Ledsham, Cheshire, a mile from his home at Puddington. He was delighted he could live at home and soon got his prisoners working for his father and his friends.

After the war, he ran three farms in Cheshire, north Wales and Shropshire, but still managed to shoot five days a week. He was incensed when a shooting friend said, 'You have spent a fortune shooting.'

'I have spent three,' Higgin corrected him.

He bought Peplow Hall, the second finest house in Shropshire with 3,000 acres of shooting. It had a church in the grounds with a congregation of six and a very fine choir of twelve. The head chorister, who was 92, used to beat for shoots. One of Higgin's guests missed a partridge and shot the chorister in the forehead. Higgin thought it would be the end of the choir but a couple of weeks later the man was back singing.

In 2000 his shoulder collapsed and he was unable to lift a gun. Then in December 2002 the polio returned and he was rushed to hospital where his leg was amputated. He seemed to be making a recovery but had a stroke and died.

His hilarious biography *Koi Hai* was published the day he went into hospital.

Higgin's ancestors included the Restoration rakehell the 2nd duke of Buckingham, who killed the Earl of Shrewsbury in a duel while the Countess looked on... and a Pendle Witch.

Ian Skidmore

Take Fifteen

Nowadays I am completely retired, though I am writing four books as a way of passing time. I am an alcoholic only in the evenings. Not a drop passes my lips until 6pm when a modest half bottle of vodka suffices.

For five years I was a teetotaller worldwide till I went to the Loire on a bus and managed to fall off the wagon at a wine tasting. Then for a while I was teetotal only in areas covered by the National Health Service, because I didn't want to be disqualified from going into hospital on the grounds that I was not healthy. But I fear I occasionally declared our dining room French territory and I kept a tricolour in the drawer under my shirts for lightning nationality changes.

Thanks to the pension I was awarded by the Royal Literary Fund, the days have gone when I cashed so many cheques in my Anglesey local the bank manager thought I was being blackmailed by the landlord.

But I am no longer an occasional prey to a hangover. On such occasions I did not put in my teeth because I could not bear the deafening click, and I tried to teach the dog to mew because the bark forced the roots of my hair through the scalp and I was shattered by the sound of hair crashing onto the carpet.

There was a time when hangovers were delivered every morning to our house with the papers. Those were the days when I was so keen on retirement as an art form I worried that by the time I retired I would be too old to enjoy it. So I retired when I was thirty and had fifteen glorious years in a mist of perpetual revelry. Then I went back to work.

Alas, there is very little money in perpetual revelry. Champagne being the price it is, there was no money left to buy a weekly Health Stamp. When I went back to work it was fine. I wrote a few books, did a couple of TV series and hired the voice out for money. In no time I had enough to put back the stamps, even before the DOS realised they weren't

216

there. They could still have docked a fiver a week off my pension because I paid late. I suppose if I hadn't paid at all they would have shot me. In fairness, you can appeal and, when I did, a Portia among women came from the Contributions Agency in Colwyn Bay and took pity on me.

But the sixty quid was well below the fare for the long journey to my anecdotage and the RLF pension has been a boon.

My wife's youth was golden. She was a privileged child, educated at the University of Oxford in surroundings that recall *Brideshead Revisited*. My youth wasn't, and I have always looked forward to a time when people do not invariably interrupt when I am speaking, policemen call me 'Sir' and I no longer have any interest in writing a best-selling novel or even in being rich. Being seventy-plus is fine. The sixties are fine.

I suspect my wife and I do not differ from other people. We have realised that our chosen space in time has nothing to do with the body's ageing. The body is a vehicle you buy at the current registration letter; it becomes first veteran and then vintage but the driver remains the same age.

Most of my over-sixties friends are like my wife. Their age has little to do with the length of time they have occupied their bodies. This is not new. The angelic dead in medieval paintings have the faces of children. When we all climb out of our graves at the day of judgment it will be, God help us, a youthful jamboree and not a pensioners' outing. And parenthetically, isn't it odd that as you get older you meet fewer atheists?

I do not see the seventies as the beginning of the end but rather the end of an overlong beginning, a time for which my earlier life has been a wearisome preparation. I realise I have been lucky. I have had, by any standards, a good career in congenial circumstances. Journalism introduced me to a way of life to which birth had not entitled me.

Alas, if the road to hell is paved with good intentions, it is roofed with lost opportunities. I spent forty years in that mist of perpetual revelry, and looking back from the sad shores of near temperance, I see how much more I could have achieved in material terms.

But they are right about burning the candle at both ends – it does give a lovely light.

I console myself with the view that it does not matter, there is still time ahead, and in life you get everything you want, if you want it badly enough; though you never get it when you want it.

I like old saws. They represent the distilled wisdom of centuries and I try to follow their advice. Especially the one that says you should study as though you were going to live forever and live as though you were going to die tomorrow.

The over-seventies I enjoy principally because I can study only those subjects that give me pleasure. I can read all of Trollope and Balzac; I have time to take Voltaire's advice and cultivate my garden and to fish with friends.

Career prospects? I am the last person to ask. I earned my living as a broadcaster. If I had not been paid for it I would have paid to do it.

Retirement? Don't be silly. Age has a final consolation. I do not mind giving my wife the last word, which is usually about my weight. She had much ammunition when Luciano Pavarotti announced he was dieting on a fierce regime in which he restricted himself to 1,800 calories a day. Dieters will know that 1,500 calories is the absolute maximum one should eat, 1,800 represents a pile of food that Red Rum couldn't have jumped over.

If I sound a trifle bitter it is because Pavarotti sold the pass. He was the white hope of all us tubby hubbies. When those of us who are an ounce or two over the accepted norm were dragged by our wives, struggling, to the muesli breakfast, we had a defence. We could say we were worried about the effect a diet would have on our voice.

Life is tough for us. I am five feet, eight inches, and I weigh eighteen and a half stone. You can see immediately what is amiss. The weight is fine. I'm the wrong height. Yet when I go to the doctor's, it's always the weight he goes on about. Would it be so hard, just once when I go into his surgery, for him to look up and say, 'You could do with putting on an inch or two?'

Everything conspires against us tubby hubbies. I started going for long walks round the lanes every day. Put on three pounds in a week. My wife said it was all new muscle. I said, 'If muscle weighs more than fat, I'm better off with the fat. I don't want to be dragging heavy muscle round with me.'

It is true being fat affects one's life. I got up to speak at a dinner and the toastmaster asked me to stand fourteen inches from the microphone. 'Fourteen inches is the nearest I can get to anything,' I told him. Fat is contraceptive.

I used to console myself by saying, I may be a bulk buy but I'm British through and through. Now if I have a transfusion I might have an armful of French blood. The European Commission made blood a commodity that could be traded freely among member states. Good news for the French who, as you would expect, have more blood in their plasma banks than anyone else. Stands to reason. They didn't shed all that much in the last war.

I am by no means anti-French but I do think it a little odd that a nation that in the past five hundred years has produced the finest painters, the most original thinkers and so many towering novelists, has not in that period – to judge by the state of the public lavatories in Paris the last time I was there – managed to train a single plumber.

Visits to the doctor are not the happiest moments of my life. More in wonder than in anger, the doctor once looked at my latest health tests and said, 'I don't know how with your lifestyle you are so well.' And the nurse said, 'That's easy, he bribes the lab staff.'

The doctor says that at my weight and with my way of living the best odds are of being carried off by a heart attack. A nice respectable way to go but worrying that some interfering jackanape might try and bring me back.

'Should I,' I mused, 'have "Do Not Resuscitate" tattooed on my chest, provided I can find a tattooist who can spell resuscitate?'

The doctor said, 'I am never sure whether that is your stomach or a hernia.'

And the nurse added, 'Have it tattooed on your stomach then you can have it in really big letters.'

'If you are at my deathbed,' I said acidly, 'I will have no chance of getting a last word in.'

Anyway, they told me about this scheme called a Living Will where in certain cases no one strives officiously to keep you alive. Now I have got this card telling people to lay off me if I collapse. The doctor warned the only snag was that I might collapse in the street and be leaped upon by someone who had just done a first aid course and was too polite to look in my wallet.

That really hit me where it hurt. I have this recurring nightmare that I find this diary and am just taking it to a police station when I am knocked over. A super-efficient paramedic looks in the diary and pumps me full of Rhesus negative because that is what it says under personal memoranda.

'That would be terrible,' the doctor agreed. 'They would have killed the wrong man.' I sometimes wonder if the doctor has Irish blood.

'You just have to hope you get taken to a hospital where they will let you die in peace,' he said. He had a cruel tongue.

'Don't sit down,' he once said, 'I don't want you dying in the surgery. Bad for the image. Diabetic and eight stone overweight? I couldn't get better than evens on you getting home upright...'

If you do come across me in the street, let me lay where I fall, though you are permitted to smell my breath in case it is a mild attack of drunkenness.

As a wise man said, we are keeping people alive now in states that if we did it to an animal we would be arrested.

Talking of animals, there was a time when a dog was a man's best friend. How come that all of a sudden he is his worst enemy? In the days when I used pubs I always took Kip, my old long dog with me. Now there is hardly a pub where dogs are still welcome.

Why? Miss Kip was the best mannered, most kindly and loyal friend. She was fastidious to a degree I wish human beings would emulate. Yet if I took her equally ladylike successors, the only bloodhounds in Gwynedd, on those island beaches I would face a heavy fine. Or their successor Taz, another long dog, who I hope does not die before I do. Why limit it to dogs? Children on a beach can translate hamburgers and ice cream into body waste faster than the speed of light. There is a line in Max Boyce's poem, *Barry Island*: 'When I see the sea I want to pee/If I couldn't I would cry.'

I suppose there might be a case for banning dogs from food shops – although surely if the shopkeepers expose the food they sell they are breaking the law? But bookshops, newsagents, travel agents and dry cleaners? Where is the sense in that?

Celia's cousin has an estate in Bath. He opens his gardens to the public and every year he adds to his entry in the National Gardens handbook the words 'Dogs Welcome'. Other garden owners are less inviting, yet he tells me that in all the years he has been welcoming dogs, he has never had a single case of bad behaviour. Children? That's different.

That is probably why when last I stayed there, the Maes y Neuadd Hotel at Talsarnau, near Harlech, welcomed dogs but banned children under the age of eight.

The anti-dog lobby constantly tells us about the terrible diseases you can get from dog waste. Have you ever heard of anyone who caught it? I doubt it. But I can provide you with a considerable list of people who have suffered everything from paralysis to the Black Vomit after bathing in the sea.

I would walk on any dog-crowded beach without a second thought.

But if any of my grandchildren wanted to paddle in the people-polluted sea I would insist they wear gumboots and waterproof trousers. It is not dogs that are a grave health risk. It's people.

The interesting thing about reading in retirement is that you pick up some delightful facts to muse over.

I was fascinated to learn that we have actually got two brains. There is the nice, civilised brain in the neat bed-sitting room behind the eyes. Then there is the other brain. The animal brain left over from our tree-swinging days, Cro Magnon, a survival like our coccyx, which is all we have left of our tails.

If you want to meet prehistoric man, the brontosaurus baser, the chest thumper with the dinosaur dangling from his belt, just go straight up the spine, turn left at the ears and you cannot miss him in his dark little nest.

The moment I read about him I recognised him at once. He is the one who has been getting me in trouble all these years.

I am a stout elderly gentleman of quiet pursuits and academic leanings. That is the influence of Better Behaved Brain. Nice little property he has up there in the head. 'First Floor Front,' the address runs, 'Forehead under the hair, Upper Nose on the Brow, ME.'

You will get him there most times, enjoying *Country Life* like as not and listening to music. He does all my thinking and worrying for me and as a tenant is very desirable. He is not a scrap of trouble. About once a year he will come out, give me a nudge and say, 'About time we were writing a book, isn't it?'

I say nervously, 'It won't hurt, will it?'

'Of course not,' he reassures me, and off we go arm in arm to the word processor. Never a cross word, but we are sometimes puzzled. Sometimes Better Behaved Brain and I have dozed off during our evening gin and wakened to find the glass empty and the bottle all but dry. Then we notice the sherry has gone too and the wine we were going to have with dinner. Some nights we have even had our suspicions about the washing-up liquid.

Now we know it is Animal Brain. The moment our eyes closed, there he was swinging down the spine looking for trouble; emptying every bottle in sight and playing havoc with my good name.

It's all clear now but I used to wonder why people who invited me to their dinner parties were always a touch frosty when we met the next day. It was the old story. You get invited twice. Once to apologise.

It got so bad that after the 100th birthday party of his mother, I had to write as follows to my host Lord Langford: 'It has come to my attention that your mother's party was disrupted by a person posing as me. Sadly this is not the first time this has happened. I can only assume that some impudent fellow lies in wait for the post and steals my invitation...'

Fortunately my old friend has a sense of humour and I was forgiven. Now I realise that no blame should have attached in the first place. It wasn't me who goosed his cousin, a governor of the BBC and the one who taught Mrs Thatcher to be a lady, emptied three decanters, sang *The Gallant Forty Twa* and marched up and down the Boudoir playing imaginary bagpipes. It was Animal Brain. He had locked the forehead so that Better Behaved Brain and I could not get out and taken over the piloting of the body.

It was he who started arguments in pubs, sent rude letters to editors and producers. He is the racehorse urger. It was his nose that twitched with desire all those years ago. He who when I won a pig in an army raffle insisted on riding back to the camp where I was provost sergeant on the orderly corporal's motor bike with the pig on the pillion.

I will bet it was Animal Brain, too, who was forever pushing me off bar stools.

With Better Behaved Brain you know where you are. Stuff some chocolate caramels into his dressing gown pocket, poke up the sitting room fire and give him a Ngaio Marsh to read and you can leave him for hours. He likes a glass of wine, of course, and I keep a small cellar of choice wine just for him.

Animal brain is jealous. Not only is he programmed to self-destruct; he wants to take Better Behaved Brain with him.

As you know, our Better Behaved Brains have a quadrillion of cells. That is a million with nine noughts. The trouble is every time you have a hangover you wipe out a million. Even worse, the ones that go first are the cells of memory with the result that, thanks to Animal Brain, I am heavily overdrawn at the memory bank. I think I am down to five.

Have to finish now. I have forgotten what I was going to write.